ACKNOWLEDGMENTS

I t is a pleasure to bring Jeanne de Jussie's chronicle to an English-speaking audience, and I am grateful to all who helped make this translation possible. I thank Yvette-M. Smith, who first mentioned Jussie to me and who offered insight and wise counsel as I began my research. I owe a great debt to Helmut Feld for his transcription of the two extant manuscripts of Jussie's text, on which this translation is based, and to the staff of the Bibliothèque Publique et Universitaire in Geneva for graciously giving me access to these manuscripts and to early editions of the text. I also thank the staff of the Bibliothèque Nationale de France in Paris. I thank the organizers of, and participants in, the "Attending to Early Modern Women" conference hosted by the Center for Renaissance and Baroque Studies at the University of Maryland in 2000 for giving me the opportunity to present and discuss my early work on Jussie. Above all, I am grateful to Albert Rabil, Jr., for his dedication, encouragement, careful editing, and good cheer. I thank the anonymous reviewer for the University of Chicago Press for many helpful lexical and bibliographical suggestions. Finally, I thank DePauw University for its support of this project.

Carrie F. Klaus

THE SHORT CHRONICLE

THE
OTHER VOICE
IN
EARLY MODERN
EUROPE

A Series Edited by Margaret L. King and Albert Rabil Jr.

RECENT BOOKS IN THE SERIES

Jeanne de Jussie

THE SHORT CHRONICLE

A Poor Clare's Account of the
Reformation of Geneva

ᔓ

Edited and Translated by Carrie F. Klaus

THE UNIVERSITY OF CHICAGO PRESS
Chicago & London

Jeanne de Jussie, 1503–1561

The University of Chicago Press, Chicago 60637
The University of Chicago Press, Ltd., London
© 2006 by The University of Chicago
All rights reserved. Published 2006
Printed in the United States of America

15 14 13 12 11 10 09 08 07   2 3 4 5

ISBN: 0-226-41705-0 (cloth)
ISBN: 0-226-41706-9 (paper)

Library of Congress Cataloging-in-Publication Data

Jussie, Jeanne de, 1503–1561.
[Petite chronique. English]
The short chronicle : a Poor Clare's account of the reformation of
Geneva / Jeanne de Jussie ; edited and translated by Carrie F. Klaus.
p. cm. — (The other voice in early modern Europe)
Includes bibliographical references and index.
ISBN 0-226-41705-0 (cloth : alk. paper)—ISBN 0-226-41706-9 (pbk. : alk. paper)
1. Reformation Switzerland—Geneva—Sources. 2. Geneva (Switzerland)—Church
history—16th century—Sources. I. Klaus, Carrie F. II. Title. III. Series.
BR410.J8713 2006
274.94′5106—dc22   2005022500

♾ The paper used in this publication meets the minimum requirements of
the American National Standard for Information Sciences—Permanence
of Paper for Printed Library Materials, ANSI Z39.48-1992.

CONTENTS

THE OTHER VOICE IN
EARLY MODERN EUROPE:
INTRODUCTION TO THE SERIES

Margaret L. King and Albert Rabil Jr.

THE OLD VOICE AND THE OTHER VOICE

In western Europe and the United States, women are nearing equality in the professions, in business, and in politics. Most enjoy access to education, reproductive rights, and autonomy in financial affairs. Issues vital to women are on the public agenda: equal pay, child care, domestic abuse, breast cancer research, and curricular revision with an eye to the inclusion of women.

These recent achievements have their origins in things women (and some male supporters) said for the first time about six hundred years ago. Theirs is the "other voice," in contradistinction to the "first voice," the voice of the educated men who created Western culture. Coincident with a general reshaping of European culture in the period 1300–1700 (called the Renaissance or early modern period), questions of female equality and opportunity were raised that still resound and are still unresolved.

The other voice emerged against the backdrop of a three-thousand-year history of the derogation of women rooted in the civilizations related to Western culture: Hebrew, Greek, Roman, and Christian. Negative attitudes toward women inherited from these traditions pervaded the intellectual, medical, legal, religious, and social systems that developed during the European Middle Ages.

The following pages describe the traditional, overwhelmingly male views of women's nature inherited by early modern Europeans and the new tradition that the "other voice" called into being to begin to challenge reigning assumptions. This review should serve as a framework for understanding the texts published in the series the Other Voice in Early Modern Europe. Introductions specific to each text and author follow this essay in all the volumes of the series.

TRADITIONAL VIEWS OF WOMEN, 500 B.C.E.–1500 C.E.

Embedded in the philosophical and medical theories of the ancient Greeks were perceptions of the female as inferior to the male in both mind and body. Similarly, the structure of civil legislation inherited from the ancient Romans was biased against women, and the views on women developed by Christian thinkers out of the Hebrew Bible and the Christian New Testament were negative and disabling. Literary works composed in the vernacular of ordinary people, and widely recited or read, conveyed these negative assumptions. The social networks within which most women lived—those of the family and the institutions of the Roman Catholic Church—were shaped by this negative tradition and sharply limited the areas in which women might act in and upon the world.

GREEK PHILOSOPHY AND FEMALE NATURE. Greek biology assumed that women were inferior to men and defined them as merely childbearers and housekeepers. This view was authoritatively expressed in the works of the philosopher Aristotle.

Aristotle thought in dualities. He considered action superior to inaction, form (the inner design or structure of any object) superior to matter, completion to incompletion, possession to deprivation. In each of these dualities, he associated the male principle with the superior quality and the female with the inferior. "The male principle in nature," he argued, "is associated with active, formative and perfected characteristics, while the female is passive, material and deprived, desiring the male in order to become complete."[1] Men are always identified with virile qualities, such as judgment, courage, and stamina, and women with their opposites—irrationality, cowardice, and weakness.

The masculine principle was considered superior even in the womb. The man's semen, Aristotle believed, created the form of a new human creature, while the female body contributed only matter. (The existence of the ovum, and with it the other facts of human embryology, was not established until the seventeenth century.) Although the later Greek physician Galen believed there was a female component in generation, contributed by "female semen," the followers of both Aristotle and Galen saw the male role in human generation as more active and more important.

In the Aristotelian view, the male principle sought always to reproduce

---

1. Aristotle, *Physics* 1.9.192a20–24, in *The Complete Works of Aristotle*, ed. Jonathan Barnes, rev. Oxford trans., 2 vols. (Princeton, 1984), 1:328.

itself. The creation of a female was always a mistake, therefore, resulting from an imperfect act of generation. Every female born was considered a "defective" or "mutilated" male (as Aristotle's terminology has variously been translated), a "monstrosity" of nature.[2]

For Greek theorists, the biology of males and females was the key to their psychology. The female was softer and more docile, more apt to be despondent, querulous, and deceitful. Being incomplete, moreover, she craved sexual fulfillment in intercourse with a male. The male was intellectual, active, and in control of his passions.

These psychological polarities derived from the theory that the universe consisted of four elements (earth, fire, air, and water), expressed in human bodies as four "humors" (black bile, yellow bile, blood, and phlegm) considered, respectively, dry, hot, damp, and cold and corresponding to mental states ("melancholic," "choleric," "sanguine," "phlegmatic"). In this scheme the male, sharing the principles of earth and fire, was dry and hot; the female, sharing the principles of air and water, was cold and damp.

Female psychology was further affected by her dominant organ, the uterus (womb), *hystera* in Greek. The passions generated by the womb made women lustful, deceitful, talkative, irrational, indeed—when these affects were in excess—"hysterical."

Aristotle's biology also had social and political consequences. If the male principle was superior and the female inferior, then in the household, as in the state, men should rule and women must be subordinate. That hierarchy did not rule out the companionship of husband and wife, whose cooperation was necessary for the welfare of children and the preservation of property. Such mutuality supported male preeminence.

Aristotle's teacher Plato suggested a different possibility: that men and women might possess the same virtues. The setting for this proposal is the imaginary and ideal Republic that Plato sketches in a dialogue of that name. Here, for a privileged elite capable of leading wisely, all distinctions of class and wealth dissolve, as, consequently, do those of gender. Without households or property, as Plato constructs his ideal society, there is no need for the subordination of women. Women may therefore be educated to the same level as men to assume leadership. Plato's Republic remained imaginary, however. In real societies, the subordination of women remained the norm and the prescription.

The views of women inherited from the Greek philosophical tradition became the basis for medieval thought. In the thirteenth century,

---

2. Aristotle, *Generation of Animals* 2.3.737a27–28, in *The Complete Works*, 1:1144.

the supreme Scholastic philosopher Thomas Aquinas, among others, still echoed Aristotle's views of human reproduction, of male and female personalities, and of the preeminent male role in the social hierarchy.

ROMAN LAW AND THE FEMALE CONDITION. Roman law, like Greek philosophy, underlay medieval thought and shaped medieval society. The ancient belief that adult property-owning men should administer households and make decisions affecting the community at large is the very fulcrum of Roman law.

About 450 B.C.E., during Rome's republican era, the community's customary law was recorded (legendarily) on twelve tablets erected in the city's central forum. It was later elaborated by professional jurists whose activity increased in the imperial era, when much new legislation was passed, especially on issues affecting family and inheritance. This growing, changing body of laws was eventually codified in the *Corpus of Civil Law* under the direction of the emperor Justinian, generations after the empire ceased to be ruled from Rome. That *Corpus*, read and commented on by medieval scholars from the eleventh century on, inspired the legal systems of most of the cities and kingdoms of Europe.

Laws regarding dowries, divorce, and inheritance pertain primarily to women. Since those laws aimed to maintain and preserve property, the women concerned were those from the property-owning minority. Their subordination to male family members points to the even greater subordination of lower-class and slave women, about whom the laws speak little.

In the early republic, the *paterfamilias*, or "father of the family," possessed *patria potestas*, "paternal power." The term *pater*, "father," in both these cases does not necessarily mean biological father but denotes the head of a household. The father was the person who owned the household's property and, indeed, its human members. The *paterfamilias* had absolute power—including the power, rarely exercised, of life or death—over his wife, his children, and his slaves, as much as his cattle.

Male children could be "emancipated," an act that granted legal autonomy and the right to own property. Those over fourteen could be emancipated by a special grant from the father or automatically by their father's death. But females could never be emancipated; instead, they passed from the authority of their father to that of a husband or, if widowed or orphaned while still unmarried, to a guardian or tutor.

Marriage in its traditional form placed the woman under her husband's authority, or *manus*. He could divorce her on grounds of adultery, drinking wine, or stealing from the household, but she could not divorce him. She could neither possess property in her own right nor bequeath any to her children upon her death. When her husband died, the household property passed not to her but to his male heirs. And when her father died, she had no claim to any family inheritance, which was directed to her brothers or more remote male relatives. The effect of these laws was to exclude women from civil society, itself based on property ownership.

In the later republican and imperial periods, these rules were significantly modified. Women rarely married according to the traditional form. The practice of "free" marriage allowed a woman to remain under her father's authority, to possess property given her by her father (most frequently the "dowry," recoverable from the husband's household on his death), and to inherit from her father. She could also bequeath property to her own children and divorce her husband, just as he could divorce her.

Despite this greater freedom, women still suffered enormous disability under Roman law. Heirs could belong only to the father's side, never the mother's. Moreover, although she could bequeath her property to her children, she could not establish a line of succession in doing so. A woman was "the beginning and end of her own family," said the jurist Ulpian. Moreover, women could play no public role. They could not hold public office, represent anyone in a legal case, or even witness a will. Women had only a private existence and no public personality.

The dowry system, the guardian, women's limited ability to transmit wealth, and total political disability are all features of Roman law adopted by the medieval communities of western Europe, although modified according to local customary laws..

CHRISTIAN DOCTRINE AND WOMEN'S PLACE. The Hebrew Bible and the Christian New Testament authorized later writers to limit women to the realm of the family and to burden them with the guilt of original sin. The passages most fruitful for this purpose were the creation narratives in Genesis and sentences from the Epistles defining women's role within the Christian family and community.

Each of the first two chapters of Genesis contains a creation narrative. In the first "God created man in his own image, in the image of God he created him; male and female he created them" (Gn 1:27). In the second, God created Eve from Adam's rib (2:21–23). Christian theologians relied principally on Genesis 2 for their understanding of the relation between man and woman, interpreting the creation of Eve from Adam as proof of her subordination to him.

The creation story in Genesis 2 leads to that of the temptations in Genesis 3: of Eve by the wily serpent and of Adam by Eve. As read by Christian theologians from Tertullian to Thomas Aquinas, the narrative made Eve responsible for the Fall and its consequences. She instigated the act; she deceived her husband; she suffered the greater punishment. Her disobedience made it necessary for Jesus to be incarnated and to die on the cross. From the pulpit, moralists and preachers for centuries conveyed to women the guilt that they bore for original sin.

The Epistles offered advice to early Christians on building communities of the faithful. Among the matters to be regulated was the place of women. Paul offered views favorable to women in Galatians 3:28: "There is neither Jew nor Greek, there is neither slave nor free, there is neither male nor female; for you are all one in Christ Jesus." Paul also referred to women as his coworkers and placed them on a par with himself and his male coworkers (Phlm 4:2–3; Rom 16:1–3; 1 Cor 16:19). Elsewhere, Paul limited women's possibilities: "But I want you to understand that the head of every man is Christ, the head of a woman is her husband, and the head of Christ is God" (1 Cor 11:3).

Biblical passages by later writers (although attributed to Paul) enjoined women to forgo jewels, expensive clothes, and elaborate coiffures; and they forbade women to "teach or have authority over men," telling them to "learn in silence with all submissiveness" as is proper for one responsible for sin, consoling them, however, with the thought that they will be saved through childbearing (1 Tm 2:9–15). Other texts among the later Epistles defined women as the weaker sex and emphasized their subordination to their husbands (1 Pt 3:7; Col 3:18; Eph 5:22–23).

These passages from the New Testament became the arsenal employed by theologians of the early church to transmit negative attitudes toward women to medieval Christian culture—above all, Tertullian (*On the Apparel of Women*), Jerome (*Against Jovinian*), and Augustine (*The Literal Meaning of Genesis*).

THE IMAGE OF WOMEN IN MEDIEVAL LITERATURE. The philosophical, legal, and religious traditions born in antiquity formed the basis of the medieval intellectual synthesis wrought by trained thinkers, mostly clerics, writing in Latin and based largely in universities. The vernacular literary tradition that developed alongside the learned tradition also spoke about female nature and women's roles. Medieval stories, poems, and epics also portrayed women negatively—as lustful and deceitful—while praising good housekeepers and loyal wives as replicas of the Virgin Mary or the female saints and martyrs.

There is an exception in the movement of "courtly love" that evolved in southern France from the twelfth century. Courtly love was the erotic love between a nobleman and noblewoman, the latter usually superior in social rank. It was always adulterous. From the conventions of courtly love derive modern Western notions of romantic love. The tradition has had an impact disproportionate to its size, for it affected only a tiny elite, and very few women. The exaltation of the female lover probably does not reflect a higher evaluation of women or a step toward their sexual liberation. More likely it gives expression to the social and sexual tensions besetting the knightly class at a specific historical juncture.

The literary fashion of courtly love was on the wane by the thirteenth century, when the widely read *Romance of the Rose* was composed in French by two authors of significantly different dispositions. Guillaume de Lorris composed the initial four thousand verses about 1235, and Jean de Meun added about seventeen thousand verses—more than four times the original—about 1265.

The fragment composed by Guillaume de Lorris stands squarely in the tradition of courtly love. Here the poet, in a dream, is admitted into a walled garden where he finds a magic fountain in which a rosebush is reflected. He longs to pick one rose, but the thorns prevent his doing so, even as he is wounded by arrows from the god of love, whose commands he agrees to obey. The rest of this part of the poem recounts the poet's unsuccessful efforts to pluck the rose.

The longer part of the *Romance* by Jean de Meun also describes a dream. But here allegorical characters give long didactic speeches, providing a social satire on a variety of themes, some pertaining to women. Love is an anxious and tormented state, the poem explains: women are greedy and manipulative, marriage is miserable, beautiful women are lustful, ugly ones cease to please, and a chaste woman is as rare as a black swan.

Shortly after Jean de Meun completed *The Romance of the Rose*, Mathéolus penned his *Lamentations*, a long Latin diatribe against marriage translated into French about a century later. The *Lamentations* sum up medieval attitudes toward women and provoked the important response by Christine de Pizan in her *Book of the City of Ladies*.

In 1355, Giovanni Boccaccio wrote *Il Corbaccio*, another antifeminist manifesto, although ironically by an author whose other works pioneered new directions in Renaissance thought. The former husband of his lover appears to Boccaccio, condemning his unmoderated lust and detailing the defects of women. Boccaccio concedes at the end "how much men naturally surpass women in nobility" and is cured of his desires.[3]

---

3. Giovanni Boccaccio, *The Corbaccio, or The Labyrinth of Love*, trans. and ed. Anthony K. Cassell, rev. ed. (Binghamton, NY, 1993), 71.

WOMEN'S ROLES: THE FAMILY. The negative perceptions of women expressed in the intellectual tradition are also implicit in the actual roles that women played in European society. Assigned to subordinate positions in the household and the church, they were barred from significant participation in public life.

Medieval European households, like those in antiquity and in non-Western civilizations, were headed by males. It was the male serf (or peasant), feudal lord, town merchant, or citizen who was polled or taxed or succeeded to an inheritance or had any acknowledged public role, although his wife or widow could stand as a temporary surrogate. From about 1100, the position of property-holding males was further enhanced: inheritance was confined to the male, or agnate, line—with depressing consequences for women.

A wife never fully belonged to her husband's family, nor was she a daughter to her father's family. She left her father's house young to marry whomever her parents chose. Her dowry was managed by her husband, and at her death it normally passed to her children by him.

A married woman's life was occupied nearly constantly with cycles of pregnancy, childbearing, and lactation. Women bore children through all the years of their fertility, and many died in childbirth. They were also responsible for raising young children up to six or seven. In the propertied classes that responsibility was shared, since it was common for a wet nurse to take over breast-feeding and for servants to perform other chores.

Women trained their daughters in the household duties appropriate to their status, nearly always tasks associated with textiles: spinning, weaving, sewing, embroidering. Their sons were sent out of the house as apprentices or students, or their training was assumed by fathers in later childhood and adolescence. On the death of her husband, a woman's children became the responsibility of his family. She generally did not take "his" children with her to a new marriage or back to her father's house, except sometimes in the artisan classes.

Women also worked. Rural peasants performed farm chores, merchant wives often practiced their husbands' trades, the unmarried daughters of the urban poor worked as servants or prostitutes. All wives produced or embellished textiles and did the housekeeping, while wealthy ones managed servants. These labors were unpaid or poorly paid but often contributed substantially to family wealth.

WOMEN'S ROLES: THE CHURCH. Membership in a household, whether a father's or a husband's, meant for women a lifelong subordination to others.

In western Europe, the Roman Catholic Church offered an alternative to the career of wife and mother. A woman could enter a convent, parallel in function to the monasteries for men that evolved in the early Christian centuries.

In the convent, a woman pledged herself to a celibate life, lived according to strict community rules, and worshiped daily. Often the convent offered training in Latin, allowing some women to become considerable scholars and authors as well as scribes, artists, and musicians. For women who chose the conventual life, the benefits could be enormous, but for numerous others placed in convents by paternal choice, the life could be restrictive and burdensome.

The conventual life declined as an alternative for women as the modern age approached. Reformed monastic institutions resisted responsibility for related female orders. The church increasingly restricted female institutional life by insisting on closer male supervision.

Women often sought other options. Some joined the communities of laywomen that sprang up spontaneously in the thirteenth century in the urban zones of western Europe, especially in Flanders and Italy. Some joined the heretical movements that flourished in late medieval Christendom, whose anticlerical and often antifamily positions particularly appealed to women. In these communities, some women were acclaimed as "holy women" or "saints," whereas others often were condemned as frauds or heretics.

In all, although the options offered to women by the church were sometimes less than satisfactory, they were sometimes richly rewarding. After 1520, the convent remained an option only in Roman Catholic territories. Protestantism engendered an ideal of marriage as a heroic endeavor and appeared to place husband and wife on a more equal footing. Sermons and treatises, however, still called for female subordination and obedience.

THE OTHER VOICE, 1300–1700

When the modern era opened, European culture was so firmly structured by a framework of negative attitudes toward women that to dismantle it was a monumental labor. The process began as part of a larger cultural movement that entailed the critical reexamination of ideas inherited from the ancient and medieval past. The humanists launched that critical reexamination.

THE HUMANIST FOUNDATION. Originating in Italy in the fourteenth century, humanism quickly became the dominant intellectual movement in

Europe. Spreading in the sixteenth century from Italy to the rest of Europe, it fueled the literary, scientific, and philosophical movements of the era and laid the basis for the eighteenth-century Enlightenment.

Humanists regarded the Scholastic philosophy of medieval universities as out of touch with the realities of urban life. They found in the rhetorical discourse of classical Rome a language adapted to civic life and public speech. They learned to read, speak, and write classical Latin and, eventually, classical Greek. They founded schools to teach others to do so, establishing the pattern for elementary and secondary education for the next three hundred years.

In the service of complex government bureaucracies, humanists employed their skills to write eloquent letters, deliver public orations, and formulate public policy. They developed new scripts for copying manuscripts and used the new printing press to disseminate texts, for which they created methods of critical editing.

Humanism was a movement led by males who accepted the evaluation of women in ancient texts and generally shared the misogynist perceptions of their culture. (Female humanists, as we will see, did not.) Yet humanism also opened the door to a reevaluation of the nature and capacity of women. By calling authors, texts, and ideas into question, it made possible the fundamental rereading of the whole intellectual tradition that was required in order to free women from cultural prejudice and social subordination.

A DIFFERENT CITY. The other voice first appeared when, after so many centuries, the accumulation of misogynist concepts evoked a response from a capable female defender: Christine de Pizan (1365–1431). Introducing her *Book of the City of Ladies* (1405), she described how she was affected by reading Mathéolus's *Lamentations*: "Just the sight of this book . . . made me wonder how it happened that so many different men . . . are so inclined to express both in speaking and in their treatises and writings so many wicked insults about women and their behavior."[4] These statements impelled her to detest herself "and the entire feminine sex, as though we were monstrosities in nature."[5]

The rest of *The Book of the City of Ladies* presents a justification of the female sex and a vision of an ideal community of women. A pioneer, she has

4. Christine de Pizan, *The Book of the City of Ladies*, trans. Earl Jeffrey Richards, foreword by Marina Warner (New York, 1982), 1.1.1, pp. 3–4.

5. Ibid., 1.1.1–2, p. 5.

received the message of female inferiority and rejected it. From the fourteenth to the seventeenth century, a huge body of literature accumulated that responded to the dominant tradition.

The result was a literary explosion consisting of works by both men and women, in Latin and in the vernaculars: works enumerating the achievements of notable women; works rebutting the main accusations made against women; works arguing for the equal education of men and women; works defining and redefining women's proper role in the family, at court, in public; works describing women's lives and experiences. Recent monographs and articles have begun to hint at the great range of this movement, involving probably several thousand titles. The protofeminism of these "other voices" constitutes a significant fraction of the literary product of the early modern era.

THE CATALOGS. About 1365, the same Boccaccio whose *Corbaccio* rehearses the usual charges against female nature wrote another work, *Concerning Famous Women*. A humanist treatise drawing on classical texts, it praised 106 notable women: ninety-eight of them from pagan Greek and Roman antiquity, one (Eve) from the Bible, and seven from the medieval religious and cultural tradition; his book helped make all readers aware of a sex normally condemned or forgotten. Boccaccio's outlook nevertheless was unfriendly to women, for it singled out for praise those women who possessed the traditional virtues of chastity, silence, and obedience. Women who were active in the public realm—for example, rulers and warriors—were depicted as usually being lascivious and as suffering terrible punishments for entering the masculine sphere. Women were his subject, but Boccaccio's standard remained male.

Christine de Pizan's *Book of the City of Ladies* contains a second catalog, one responding specifically to Boccaccio's. Whereas Boccaccio portrays female virtue as exceptional, she depicts it as universal. Many women in history were leaders, or remained chaste despite the lascivious approaches of men, or were visionaries and brave martyrs.

The work of Boccaccio inspired a series of catalogs of illustrious women of the biblical, classical, Christian, and local pasts, among them Filippo da Bergamo's *Of Illustrious Women*, Pierre de Brantôme's *Lives of Illustrious Women*, Pierre Le Moyne's *Gallerie of Heroic Women*, and Pietro Paolo de Ribera's *Immortal Triumphs and Heroic Enterprises of 845 Women*. Whatever their embedded prejudices, these works drove home to the public the possibility of female excellence.

THE DEBATE. At the same time, many questions remained: Could a woman be virtuous? Could she perform noteworthy deeds? Was she even, strictly speaking, of the same human species as men? These questions were debated over four centuries, in French, German, Italian, Spanish, and English, by authors male and female, among Catholics, Protestants, and Jews, in ponderous volumes and breezy pamphlets. The whole literary genre has been called the *querelle des femmes*, the "woman question."

The opening volley of this battle occurred in the first years of the fifteenth century, in a literary debate sparked by Christine de Pizan. She exchanged letters critical of Jean de Meun's contribution to *The Romance of the Rose* with two French royal secretaries, Jean de Montreuil and Gontier Col. When the matter became public, Jean Gerson, one of Europe's leading theologians, supported de Pizan's arguments against de Meun, for the moment silencing the opposition.

The debate resurfaced repeatedly over the next two hundred years. *The Triumph of Women* (1438) by Juan Rodríguez de la Camara (or Juan Rodríguez del Padron) struck a new note by presenting arguments for the superiority of women to men. *The Champion of Women* (1440–42) by Martin Le Franc addresses once again the negative views of women presented in *The Romance of the Rose* and offers counterevidence of female virtue and achievement.

A cameo of the debate on women is included in *The Courtier*, one of the most widely read books of the era, published by the Italian Baldassare Castiglione in 1528 and immediately translated into other European vernaculars. *The Courtier* depicts a series of evenings at the court of the Duke of Urbino in which many men and some women of the highest social stratum amuse themselves by discussing a range of literary and social issues. The "woman question" is a pervasive theme throughout, and the third of its four books is devoted entirely to that issue.

In a verbal duel, Gasparo Pallavicino and Giuliano de' Medici present the main claims of the two traditions. Gasparo argues the innate inferiority of women and their inclination to vice. Only in bearing children do they profit the world. Giuliano counters that women share the same spiritual and mental capacities as men and may excel in wisdom and action. Men and women are of the same essence: just as no stone can be more perfectly a stone than another, so no human being can be more perfectly human than others, whether male or female. It was an astonishing assertion, boldly made to an audience as large as all Europe.

THE TREATISES. Humanism provided the materials for a positive counterconcept to the misogyny embedded in Scholastic philosophy and law and inherited from the Greek, Roman, and Christian pasts. A series of humanist treatises on marriage and family, on education and deportment, and on the nature of women helped construct these new perspectives.

The works by Francesco Barbaro and Leon Battista Alberti—*On Marriage* (1415) and *On the Family* (1434–37)—far from defending female equality, reasserted women's responsibility for rearing children and managing the housekeeping while being obedient, chaste, and silent. Nevertheless, they served the cause of reexamining the issue of women's nature by placing domestic issues at the center of scholarly concern and reopening the pertinent classical texts. In addition, Barbaro emphasized the companionate nature of marriage and the importance of a wife's spiritual and mental qualities for the well-being of the family.

These themes reappear in later humanist works on marriage and the education of women by Juan Luis Vives and Erasmus. Both were moderately sympathetic to the condition of women without reaching beyond the usual masculine prescriptions for female behavior.

An outlook more favorable to women characterizes the nearly unknown work *In Praise of Women* (ca. 1487) by the Italian humanist Bartolommeo Goggio. In addition to providing a catalog of illustrious women, Goggio argued that male and female are the same in essence, but that women (reworking the Adam and Eve narrative from quite a new angle) are actually superior. In the same vein, the Italian humanist Mario Equicola asserted the spiritual equality of men and women in *On Women* (1501). In 1525, Galeazzo Flavio Capra (or Capella) published his work *On the Excellence and Dignity of Women.* This humanist tradition of treatises defending the worthiness of women culminates in the work of Henricus Cornelius Agrippa *On the Nobility and Preeminence of the Female Sex.* No work by a male humanist more succinctly or explicitly presents the case for female dignity.

THE WITCH BOOKS. While humanists grappled with the issues pertaining to women and family, other learned men turned their attention to what they perceived as a very great problem: witches. Witch-hunting manuals, explorations of the witch phenomenon, and even defenses of witches are not at first glance pertinent to the tradition of the other voice. But they do relate in this way: most accused witches were women. The hostility aroused by supposed witch activity is comparable to the hostility aroused by women. The evil deeds the victims of the hunt were charged with were exaggerations of the vices to which, many believed, all women were prone.

The connection between the witch accusation and the hatred of women is explicit in the notorious witch-hunting manual *The Hammer of Witches* (1486) by two Dominican inquisitors, Heinrich Krämer and Jacob Sprenger. Here the inconstancy, deceitfulness, and lustfulness traditionally associated with women are depicted in exaggerated form as the core features of witch behavior. These traits inclined women to make a bargain with the devil—sealed by sexual intercourse—by which they acquired unholy powers. Such bizarre claims, far from being rejected by rational men, were broadcast by intellectuals. The German Ulrich Molitur, the Frenchman Nicolas Rémy, and the Italian Stefano Guazzo all coolly informed the public of sinister orgies and midnight pacts with the devil. The celebrated French jurist, historian, and political philosopher Jean Bodin argued that because women were especially prone to diabolism, regular legal procedures could properly be suspended in order to try those accused of this "exceptional crime."

A few experts such as the physician Johann Weyer, a student of Agrippa's, raised their voices in protest. In 1563, he explained the witch phenomenon thus, without discarding belief in diabolism: the devil deluded foolish old women afflicted by melancholia, causing them to believe they had magical powers. Weyer's rational skepticism, which had good credibility in the community of the learned, worked to revise the conventional views of women and witchcraft.

WOMEN'S WORKS. To the many categories of works produced on the question of women's worth must be added nearly all works written by women. A woman writing was in herself a statement of women's claim to dignity.

Only a few women wrote anything before the dawn of the modern era, for three reasons. First, they rarely received the education that would enable them to write. Second, they were not admitted to the public roles—as administrator, bureaucrat, lawyer or notary, or university professor—in which they might gain knowledge of the kinds of things the literate public thought worth writing about. Third, the culture imposed silence on women, considering speaking out a form of unchastity. Given these conditions, it is remarkable that any women wrote. Those who did before the fourteenth century were almost always nuns or religious women whose isolation made their pronouncements more acceptable.

From the fourteenth century on, the volume of women's writings rose. Women continued to write devotional literature, although not always as cloistered nuns. They also wrote diaries, often intended as keepsakes for their children; books of advice to their sons and daughters; letters to family members and friends; and family memoirs, in a few cases elaborate enough to be considered histories.

A few women wrote works directly concerning the "woman question," and some of these, such as the humanists Isotta Nogarola, Cassandra Fedele, Laura Cereta, and Olympia Morata, were highly trained. A few were professional writers, living by the income of their pens; the very first among them was Christine de Pizan, noteworthy in this context as in so many others. In addition to *The Book of the City of Ladies* and her critiques of *The Romance of the Rose*, she wrote *The Treasure of the City of Ladies* (a guide to social decorum for women), an advice book for her son, much courtly verse, and a full-scale history of the reign of King Charles V of France.

WOMEN PATRONS. Women who did not themselves write but encouraged others to do so boosted the development of an alternative tradition. Highly placed women patrons supported authors, artists, musicians, poets, and learned men. Such patrons, drawn mostly from the Italian elites and the courts of northern Europe, figure disproportionately as the dedicatees of the important works of early feminism.

For a start, it might be noted that the catalogs of Boccaccio and Alvaro de Luna were dedicated to the Florentine noblewoman Andrea Acciaiuoli and to Doña María, first wife of King Juan II of Castile, while the French translation of Boccaccio's work was commissioned by Anne of Brittany, wife of King Charles VIII of France. The humanist treatises of Goggio, Equicola, Vives, and Agrippa were dedicated, respectively, to Eleanora of Aragon, wife of Ercole I d'Este, Duke of Ferrara; to Margherita Cantelma of Mantua; to Catherine of Aragon, wife of King Henry VIII of England; and to Margaret, Duchess of Austria and regent of the Netherlands. As late as 1696, Mary Astell's *Serious Proposal to the Ladies, for the Advancement of Their True and Greatest Interest* was dedicated to Princess Anne of Denmark.

These authors presumed that their efforts would be welcome to female patrons, or they may have written at the bidding of those patrons. Silent themselves, perhaps even unresponsive, these loftily placed women helped shape the tradition of the other voice.

THE ISSUES. The literary forms and patterns in which the tradition of the other voice presented itself have now been sketched. It remains to highlight the major issues around which this tradition crystallizes. In brief, there are four problems to which our authors return again and again, in plays and catalogs, in verse and letters, in treatises and dialogues, in every language: the problem of chastity, the problem of power, the problem of speech, and the problem of knowledge. Of these the greatest, preconditioning the others, is the problem of chastity.

THE PROBLEM OF CHASTITY. In traditional European culture, as in those of antiquity and others around the globe, chastity was perceived as woman's quintessential virtue—in contrast to courage, or generosity, or leadership, or rationality, seen as virtues characteristic of men. Opponents of women charged them with insatiable lust. Women themselves and their defenders—without disputing the validity of the standard—responded that women were capable of chastity.

The requirement of chastity kept women at home, silenced them, isolated them, left them in ignorance. It was the source of all other impediments. Why was it so important to the society of men, of whom chastity was not required, and who more often than not considered it their right to violate the chastity of any woman they encountered?

Female chastity ensured the continuity of the male-headed household. If a man's wife was not chaste, he could not be sure of the legitimacy of his offspring. If they were not his and they acquired his property, it was not his household, but some other man's, that had endured. If his daughter was not chaste, she could not be transferred to another man's household as his wife, and he was dishonored.

The whole system of the integrity of the household and the transmission of property was bound up in female chastity. Such a requirement pertained only to property-owning classes, of course. Poor women could not expect to maintain their chastity, least of all if they were in contact with high-status men to whom all women but those of their own household were prey.

In Catholic Europe, the requirement of chastity was further buttressed by moral and religious imperatives. Original sin was inextricably linked with the sexual act. Virginity was seen as heroic virtue, far more impressive than, say, the avoidance of idleness or greed. Monasticism, the cultural institution that dominated medieval Europe for centuries, was grounded in the renunciation of the flesh. The Catholic reform of the eleventh century imposed a similar standard on all the clergy and a heightened awareness of sexual requirements on all the laity. Although men were asked to be chaste, female unchastity was much worse: it led to the devil, as Eve had led mankind to sin.

To such requirements, women and their defenders protested their innocence. Furthermore, following the example of holy women who had escaped the requirements of family and sought the religious life, some women began to conceive of female communities as alternatives both to family and to the cloister. Christine de Pizan's city of ladies was such a community. Moderata Fonte and Mary Astell envisioned others. The luxurious salons of the French *précieuses* of the seventeenth century, or the comfortable English drawing rooms of the next, may have been born of the same impulse. Here women not only might escape, if briefly, the subordinate position that life in the family entailed but might also make claims to power, exercise their capacity for speech, and display their knowledge.

THE PROBLEM OF POWER. Women were excluded from power: the whole cultural tradition insisted on it. Only men were citizens, only men bore arms, only men could be chiefs or lords or kings. There were exceptions that did not disprove the rule, when wives or widows or mothers took the place of men, awaiting their return or the maturation of a male heir. A woman who attempted to rule in her own right was perceived as an anomaly, a monster, at once a deformed woman and an insufficient male, sexually confused and consequently unsafe.

The association of such images with women who held or sought power explains some otherwise odd features of early modern culture. Queen Elizabeth I of England, one of the few women to hold full regal authority in European history, played with such male/female images—positive ones, of course—in representing herself to her subjects. She was a prince, and manly, even though she was female. She was also (she claimed) virginal, a condition absolutely essential if she was to avoid the attacks of her opponents. Catherine de' Medici, who ruled France as widow and regent for her sons, also adopted such imagery in defining her position. She chose as one symbol the figure of Artemisia, an androgynous ancient warrior-heroine who combined a female persona with masculine powers.

Power in a woman, without such sexual imagery, seems to have been indigestible by the culture. A rare note was struck by the Englishman Sir Thomas Elyot in his *Defence of Good Women* (1540), justifying both women's participation in civic life and their prowess in arms. The old tune was sung by the Scots reformer John Knox in his *First Blast of the Trumpet against the Monstrous Regiment of Women* (1558); for him rule by women, defects in nature, was a hideous contradiction in terms.

The confused sexuality of the imagery of female potency was not reserved for rulers. Any woman who excelled was likely to be called an Amazon, recalling the self-mutilated warrior women of antiquity who repudiated all men, gave up their sons, and raised only their daughters. She was often said to have "exceeded her sex" or to have possessed "masculine virtue"—as the very fact of conspicuous excellence conferred masculinity even on the female subject. The catalogs of notable women often showed those female heroes dressed in armor, armed to the teeth, like men. Amazonian heroines romp through the epics of the age—Ariosto's *Orlando Furioso* (1532) and Spenser's *Faerie Queene* (1590–1609). Excellence in a woman was perceived as a claim for power, and power was reserved for the masculine realm. A woman who possessed either one was masculinized and lost title to her own female identity.

THE PROBLEM OF SPEECH. Just as power had a sexual dimension when it was claimed by women, so did speech. A good woman spoke little. Excessive speech was an indication of unchastity. By speech, women seduced men. Eve had lured Adam into sin by her speech. Accused witches were commonly accused of having spoken abusively, or irrationally, or simply too much. As enlightened a figure as Francesco Barbaro insisted on silence in a woman, which he linked to her perfect unanimity with her husband's will and her unblemished virtue (her chastity). Another Italian humanist, Leonardo Bruni, in advising a noblewoman on her studies, barred her not from speech but from public speaking. That was reserved for men.

Related to the problem of speech was that of costume—another, if silent, form of self-expression. Assigned the task of pleasing men as their primary occupation, elite women often tended toward elaborate costume, hairdressing, and the use of cosmetics. Clergy and secular moralists alike condemned these practices. The appropriate function of costume and adornment was to announce the status of a woman's husband or father. Any further indulgence in adornment was akin to unchastity.

THE PROBLEM OF KNOWLEDGE. When the Italian noblewoman Isotta Nogarola had begun to attain a reputation as a humanist, she was accused of incest—a telling instance of the association of learning in women with unchastity. That chilling association inclined any woman who was educated to deny that she was or to make exaggerated claims of heroic chastity.

If educated women were pursued with suspicions of sexual misconduct, women seeking an education faced an even more daunting obstacle: the assumption that women were by nature incapable of learning, that reasoning was a particularly masculine ability. Just as they proclaimed their chastity, women and their defenders insisted on their capacity for learning. The major work by a male writer on female education—that by Juan Luis Vives, *On the Education of a Christian Woman* (1523)—granted female capacity for intellection but still argued that a woman's whole education was to be shaped around the requirement of chastity and a future within the household. Female writers of the following generations—Marie de Gournay in France, Anna Maria van Schurman in Holland, and Mary Astell in England—began to envision other possibilities.

The pioneers of female education were the Italian women humanists who managed to attain a literacy in Latin and a knowledge of classical and Christian literature equivalent to that of prominent men. Their works implicitly and explicitly raise questions about women's social roles, defining problems that beset women attempting to break out of the cultural limits that had bound them. Like Christine de Pizan, who achieved an advanced education through her father's tutoring and her own devices, their bold questioning makes clear the importance of training. Only when women were educated to the same standard as male leaders would they be able to raise that other voice and insist on their dignity as human beings morally, intellectually, and legally equal to men.

THE OTHER VOICE. The other voice, a voice of protest, was mostly female, but it was also male. It spoke in the vernaculars and in Latin, in treatises and dialogues, in plays and poetry, in letters and diaries, and in pamphlets. It battered at the wall of prejudice that encircled women and raised a banner announcing its claims. The female was equal (or even superior) to the male in essential nature—moral, spiritual, and intellectual. Women were capable of higher education, of holding positions of power and influence in the public realm, and of speaking and writing persuasively. The last bastion of masculine supremacy, centered on the notions of a woman's primary domestic responsibility and the requirement of female chastity, was not as yet assaulted—although visions of productive female communities as alternatives to the family indicated an awareness of the problem.

During the period 1300–1700, the other voice remained only a voice, and one only dimly heard. It did not result—yet—in an alteration of social patterns. Indeed, to this day they have not entirely been altered. Yet the call for justice issued as long as six centuries ago by those writing in the tradition of the other voice must be recognized as the source and origin of the mature feminist tradition and of the realignment of social institutions accomplished in the modern age.

We thank the volume editors in this series, who responded with many suggestions to an earlier draft of this introduction, making it a collaborative enterprise. Many of their suggestions and criticisms have resulted in revisions of this introduction, although we remain responsible for the final product.

PROJECTED TITLES IN THE SERIES

Isabella Andreini, *Mirtilla*, edited and translated by Laura Stortoni

Tullia d'Aragona, *Complete Poems and Letters*, edited and translated by Julia Hairston

Tullia d'Aragona, *The Wretch, Otherwise Known as Guerrino*, edited and translated by Julia Hairston and John McLucas

Francesco Barbaro et al., *On Marriage and the Family*, edited and translated by Margaret L. King

Francesco Buoninsegni and Arcangela Tarabotti, *Menippean Satire: "Against Feminine Extravagance" and "Antisatire,"* edited and translated by Elissa Weaver

Rosalba Carriera, *Letters, Diaries, and Art*, edited and translated by Catherine M. Sama

Madame du Chatelet, *Selected Works*, edited by Judith Zinsser

Vittoria Colonna, Chiara Matraini, and Lucrezia Marinella, *Marian Writings*, edited and translated by Susan Haskins

Princess Elizabeth of Bohemia, *Correspondence with Descartes*, edited and translated by Lisa Shapiro

Isabella d'Este, *Selected Letters*, edited and translated by Deanna Shemek

Fairy Tales by Seventeenth-Century French Women Writers, edited and translated by Lewis Seifert and Domna C. Stanton

Moderata Fonte, *Floridoro*, edited and translated by Valeria Finucci

Moderata Fonte and Lucrezia Marinella, *Religious Narratives*, edited and translated by Virginia Cox

Catharina Regina von Greiffenberg, *Meditations on the Life of Christ*, edited and translated by Lynne Tatlock

In Praise of Women: Italian Fifteenth-Century Defenses of Women, edited and translated by Daniel Bornstein

Lucrezia Marinella, *L'Enrico, or Byzantium Conquered*, edited and translated by Virginia Cox

Lucrezia Marinella, *Happy Arcadia*, edited and translated by Susan Haskins and Letizia Panizza

Chiara Matraini, *Selected Poetry and Prose*, edited and translated by Elaine MacLachlan

Alessandro Piccolomini, *Rethinking Marriage in Sixteenth-Century Italy*, edited and translated by Letizia Panizza

Christine de Pizan, *Debate over the "Romance of the Rose,"* edited and translated by David F. Hult

Christine de Pizan, *Life of Charles V*, edited and translated by Nadia Margolis

Christine de Pizan, *The Long Road of Learning*, edited and translated by Andrea Tarnowski

Oliva Sabuco, *The New Philosophy: True Medicine*, edited and translated by Gianna Pomata

Margherita Sarrocchi, *La Scanderbeide*, edited and translated by Rinaldina Russell

Gabrielle Suchon, *"On Philosophy" and "On Morality,"* edited and translated by Domna Stanton with Rebecca Wilkin

Sara Copio Sullam, *Sara Copio Sullam: Jewish Poet and Intellectual in Early Seventeenth-Century Venice*, edited and translated by Don Harrán

Arcangela Tarabotti, *Convent Life as Inferno: A Report*, introduction and notes by Francesca Medioli, translated by Letizia Panizza

Laura Terracina, *Works*, edited and translated by Michael Sherberg

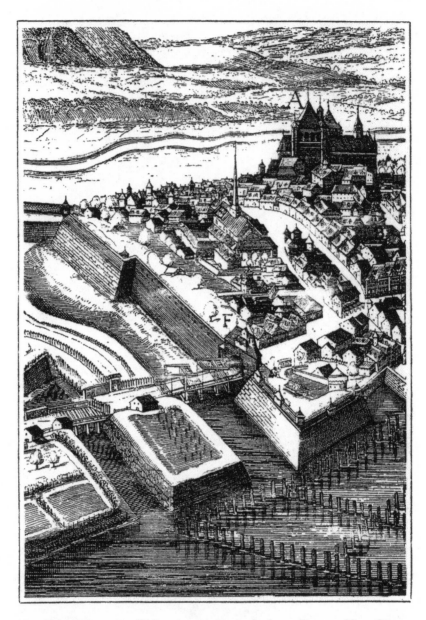

Pierre Chouet's engraving of Geneva in 1655 showing the former Convent of Saint Clare (by then a hospital) between the fortified wall and the cathedral. The convent buildings were demolished in 1709. Photograph by Carrie F. Klaus.

VOLUME EDITOR'S
INTRODUCTION

THE OTHER VOICE

A s the Protestant Reformation shook the foundations of early modern Europe, challenging ecclesiastical and secular authorities and reshaping social structures, a diverse collection of "other voices" emerged, both defending and denouncing traditional practice and belief. Jeanne de Jussie's is one of the most remarkable, and perhaps improbable, of these voices. Like her sisters in the Genevan Convent of Saint Clare, Jussie spent many hours of each day in silence, and yet, like the outspoken vicaress whom she describes so admiringly in her *Short Chronicle*, she drew upon her considerable talent for self-expression, as well as her deep religious conviction, to present the merits of her chosen way of life and to condemn what she saw as the unconscionable evils of the Reformation. Jussie's compelling story is significant for what it tells us about the Reformation's impact on the lives of the women who experienced it from inside the walls of their cloister and for the singular view it provides of struggles for political and religious power in early sixteenth-century Geneva.

Jeanne de Jussie writes of women who have since been relegated to the margins of history but who were absolutely at the center of events as they lived them. As we read her chronicle, we see many of the ways in which the Reformation affected women differently than men. Ever attentive to the specificity of women's experience both inside and outside her convent, Jussie writes of women who flee Geneva and then have to give birth in peasants' huts, of women who tear their babies from Reformed preachers' arms to prevent their children from being baptized in the "new" way, and of one woman who almost goes into premature labor after a heated confrontation with Reformers and civil authorities. Jussie describes husbands who beat their wives in an attempt to convert them, a father who banishes his daughter for her failure to convert, and three men who imprison their wives for their refusal to attend a Reformed celebration of the Lord's Supper. For the secluded women with whom Jussie lived, the Reformation amounted to a great sexual threat, and penetrations of cloister walls carried with them the terrifying possibility of physical violence to the nuns' own bodies, as Jussie shows repeatedly in her chronicle.

Throughout her narrative, Jussie writes of women's active participation in the battles of the Reformation on both sides of her convent's walls, often presenting women as even more ardently committed to their cause than their male counterparts—a disparity she underlines explicitly, noting, "[W]omen were always found to be much more steadfast and constant in the religion than men, and young girls and women were especially virile during those Lutheran errors."[1] Among the many visitors to her convent whom she describes are Reformed women who try to convert the cloistered nuns and lay Catholic women who offer their continual support (an echo of the Poor Clares' distant but powerful advocate, Beatrice of Portugal, Duchess of Savoy). Jussie records the acts of women—both Catholic and Reformed—who engage in the armed conflicts of the Reformation in countless ways, throwing rocks, ransacking a druggist's shop, even demonstrating early modern civil disobedience by doing laundry the day after Easter or by spinning wool conspicuously during a church procession.

Jeanne de Jussie chose to write, she tells us several times in her chronicle, so that the dramatic events she had experienced with her sisters in the Convent of Saint Clare would be remembered for all time. She brings these events and people to us in the lively and colorful language that is her "other voice," defending the traditional church, her way of life, and the women with whom she shared this life and making our picture of the Reformation richer, fuller, and more complete.

THE REFORMATION IN GENEVA

Geneva has long been identified as the city of John Calvin, as Calvin's prime location on the monumental Wall of the Reformers in Geneva makes eminently clear. The Reformation, however, was in full swing long before Calvin first came to the city on the lake in 1536.[2] From the beginning, the Reformation in Geneva was tied closely to struggles for political autonomy. In

---

1. P. 116.

2. For a detailed discussion of the Reformation in Geneva, see Henri Naef, *Les origines de la Réforme à Genève*, 2 vols. (Geneva: Droz, 1968). See also E. William Monter, *Calvin's Geneva* (New York: Wiley and Sons, 1967). On the spread of the Reformation through French-speaking lands, see Francis Higman, *La diffusion de la Réforme en France, 1520–1565* (Geneva: Labor et Fides, 1992).

the early sixteenth century, ecclesiastical authority broke down and Geneva, which had been an episcopal city-state ruled by a prince-bishop, came under the dominion of the House of Savoy. In 1526, the year in which Jussie's chronicle begins, Geneva was struggling for sovereignty against both the prince-bishop and the Duke of Savoy.[3] In 1526, in order to resist these powers, Geneva allied itself with the Swiss cantons of Bern and Fribourg, forming the *Combourgeoisie*.[4] Jussie begins her chronicle with a denunciation of this affront to ducal authority.

Jussie's affiliations were as political as they were religious. Like most of her sisters in the Convent of Saint Clare, she came from a land-owning noble family with close ties to the Duke of Savoy.[5] Supporters of the Swiss alliance, on the other hand, tended to be citizens and burghers[6] who lived within the Genevan city walls and were openly hostile to the duke. By and large, it was this second group, made up primarily of merchants and tradespeople, who welcomed the Reformation to Geneva—under the strong influence of Bern, which had accepted the Reformation in 1528. Not surprisingly, these political divisions amplified the Poor Clares' opposition to the Reformation, already partly determined, of course, by their vocation as monastic women.[7] Jussie's chronicle shows clearly the Poor Clares' support of the Duke of Savoy and the prince-bishop.

Struggles for control of Geneva and surrounding regions became especially significant on the European political stage because they served as a

---

3. The population of Geneva probably numbered around 12,000 at the time. Edmond Ganter says the population of the city was about 11,000 when the Convent of Saint Clare was established in 1473. *Les Clarisses de Genève: 1473–1535—1793* (Geneva: Société Catholique d'Histoire, 1949), 21. Monter puts the population of the city at about 10,300 in 1537. See Monter, *Calvin's Geneva*, 2. According to Alfred Perrenoud, there were 13,100 inhabitants in 1550. *La population de Genève du seizième au début du dix-neuvième siècle: Étude démographique* (Geneva: Jullien, 1979), 30, 37. For a consideration of the Genevans' origins and professions, see Monter, 4–5.

4. The term in German is *Eidgenossenschaft*, from which the term "Eidguenot" (cf. "Huguenot") is derived.

5. According to A.-C. Grivel, the only nonnoble nun in the Convent of Saint Clare in the years Jussie narrates was Sister Colette Masuere. "Notice sur l'ordre religieux de Sainte-Claire et sur la communauté des Clarisses de Genève" in the 1865 edition of Jussie's chronicle, *Le levain du Calvinisme, ou commencement de l'heresie de Geneve, faict par Reverende Soeur Jeanne de Jussie. Suivi de notes justificatives et d'une notice sur l'ordre religieux de Sainte-Claire et sur la communauté des Clarisses à Genève par Ad.-C. Grivel*, ed. Gustave Revilliod (Geneva: Fick, 1865), 267–93.

6. Ranking below the aristocracy, burghers (*bourgeois*) were either native or foreign-born inhabitants of Geneva who could purchase the right to become citizens (*citoyens*).

7. Interestingly, monastic women proved more resistant to the Reformed ideas than monastic men, perhaps because the Reformation did not offer the career options to women that it offered to men, who could become pastors of Reformed congregations and otherwise leaders in the church.

flashpoint for larger rivalries between the two major powers in Europe at the time: France and the Holy Roman Empire. The Duke of Savoy himself, Charles III, whom Jussie calls simply "monseigneur"[8] throughout her chronicle, had a complicated set of loyalties. He had political ties to the Holy Roman Emperor Charles V, but he also had family ties to French royalty, since he was the brother of Louise of Savoy and thus the uncle of the French king Francis I. France and the Empire were engaged in bitter struggles in the 1520s and 1530s, and settlements between the two powers—such as the treaty of Payerne in 1531, which Jussie describes in her chronicle—were short-lived.

Geneva's alliance with Bern and Fribourg altered the balance of power in the city.[9] Already in 1526, as Jussie writes in her chronicle, fifty-two prominent burghers who opposed the alliance with the Swiss Federation left Geneva, and in 1528, Prince-Bishop Pierre de la Baume fled as well. Bern's acceptance of the Reformation in 1528 had implications for Geneva. In 1532, the leaders of Bern sent Guillaume Farel to preach in the city, after the Reformer's success in Neuchâtel. At that time, as Jussie reports in her chronicle, Aymé de Gingis, abbot of the Cistercian Abbey of Bonmont in the canton of Vaud, drove Farel and his two associates[10] out of the city. In November or December of that same year, however, Reformed preacher Antoine Fromment[11] arrived and began to preach in Geneva, and from then on, the "Evangelical"[12] movement gained momentum in the city.

The year 1533 saw armed skirmishes and bloodshed in Geneva. The death of canon Peter Werle, killed by Reformed sympathizers one night

---

8. She calls the prince-bishop, Pierre de la Baume, "Monseigneur of Geneva."

9. See Helmut Feld's introduction to Jeanne de Jussie's, *Petite chronique*, ed. Helmut Feld (Mainz: von Zabern, 1996), xxxii.

10. Feld identifies these two men as Antoine Saunier and Pierre Robert, also called Olivetan. Introduction to the *Petite chronique*, xxxii.

11. A leading Reformer in Geneva in the pre-Calvin years, Fromment wrote his own chronicle of the Reformation of Geneva, from a Reformed perspective. This chronicle provides many useful comparisons with Jussie's. See Antoine Fromment, *Les actes et gestes merveilleux de la cité de Genève. Nouvellement convertie à l'Evangile faictz du temps de leur Reformation et comment ils l'ont receu redigez par escript en forme de Chroniques Annales ou Hystoyres commençant l'an MDXXXII*, ed. Gustave Revilliod (Geneva: Jules-Guillaume Fick, 1854). Fromment's wife, Marie Dentière, who appears in Jussie's chronicle, was also an active Reformer and a published writer. Dentière's work has been translated by Mary B. McKinley for the Other Voice series. See Marie Dentière, *Epistle to Marguerite de Navarre and Preface to a Sermon by John Calvin*, ed. and trans. Mary B. McKinley (Chicago: University of Chicago Press, 2004).

12. The term "Evangelical," which comes from the French *évangile* (Gospel), was used to describe Reformers because of their belief in the primacy of scripture.

during a battle between proponents of "old" and "new" beliefs, caused an uproar in the city, which Jussie records in great detail. In that same year, several leading supporters of the prince-bishop were beheaded, including Claude Pennet, Jean Portier, and Jacques Malbosson, all of whose executions Jussie mentions in her chronicle. In 1533, Prince-Bishop Pierre de la Baume returned to Geneva for the first time since 1528, but he met opposition when he preached in front of the cathedral and so fled again, never to return. In a last-ditch effort to thwart the Reformers, the Sorbonne in Paris sent theologian Guy Furbity to preach in Geneva during the Advent season. He was initially well received; when Fromment and an associate, Alexandre Canus, disrupted his preaching, they were banned from the city. Before long, however, the two outspoken Reformers returned with Farel and Pierre Viret, and Furbity found himself behind bars. Jussie laments Furbity's long imprisonment in her narrative.

In 1534, the Reformers began preaching in the Franciscan Rive Monastery, which was just next to the Convent of Saint Clare and contained one of the largest halls in Geneva. The Rive Disputation began on May 30, 1535, and lasted until June 24 of that year. In July, the Genevan city council[13] gave Farel and Viret permission to preach in the Convent of Saint Clare, which led to the most dramatic confrontation between Reformers and nuns described in the *Short Chronicle*. Soon afterward, Geneva definitively accepted the Reformation as preached by Farel, Viret, and their associates—and the House of Savoy lost its last hope of controlling the city. In August, the Poor Clares left Geneva to travel by foot to Annecy, under the protection of the Duke of Savoy, who invited them to live in the then-vacant Augustinian Monastery of the Holy Cross.

THE LIFE OF JEANNE DE JUSSIE

Jeanne de Jussie was born in 1503 in Jussy-l'Évêque, a village about fifteen kilometers from Geneva that still bears her family's name.[14] We know little

---

13. Genevan government at this time consisted of three major councils: the Small Council (an executive body including the four elected syndics), the Council of Two Hundred (an elected legislative body), and the General Council (all male heads of household).

14. The two spellings, "Jussie" and "Jussy," were used interchangeably. Biographical information on Jeanne de Jussie comes primarily from Helmut Feld (introduction to the *Petite chronique*); Edmond Ganter, *Les Clarisses*, and Henri Roth, "Une femme auteur du 16e siècle: Jeanne de Jussie," *Revue du Vieux Genève* 19 (1989): 5–13. See also Irena Backus, "Les clarisses de la rue Verdaine /

about her life before she entered the Convent of Saint Clare, and even then, we do not know much more than what she tells us in her chronicle. She was the youngest of the six children of Louis and Jeanne de Jussie to reach adulthood, the sister of Jean, Philibert, Nicolas, Guillaume,[15] and Madeleine. (Two of Jeanne's brothers, Pierre and François, died as minors. Louis de Jussie also had an illegitimate son named Antoine.) Jeanne's father, Louis, died before 1519. Her mother, also named Jeanne, died in 1535, the same year the nuns of the Convent of Saint Clare left Geneva for Annecy.

Louis de Jussie's family suffered considerable financial difficulties after his death, when his brother, Amédée, named his own son Georges heir to the family castle in Jussy-l'Évêque. When Louis's wife and children protested, Georges de Jussie filed a suit against them, beginning a costly legal battle that eventually forced the family to abandon the castle. Jeanne de Jussie's brothers sold off the remaining family property. Her family's financial troubles surely influenced her decision in 1521, at age eighteen, to take religious vows.

Although no record has been found of a girls' school in Geneva in this period, Jussie tells us in her chronicle that she attended school there. She reports that Reformers came to her convent one day specifically in search of those nuns who had attended school in Geneva: "[T]hey were mainly seeking the two from the city and the ones who had gone to school in their city," she writes, "and I, among them, was recognized by one of them."[16] It was likely at this school that Jussie learned to read and write, which resulted in her appointment as the convent's secretary by at least 1530.

In 1535, Jeanne de Jussie traveled by foot with the rest of the Poor Clares from Geneva to Annecy, where they settled in the Monastery of the Holy Cross. Jussie was elected abbess of her convent in Annecy in 1548. She died there on November 7, 1561.

The Poor Clares of the Rue Verdaine," in *Le guide des femmes disparues / Forgotten women of Geneva*, ed. Anne-Marie Käppeli (Geneva: Metropolis, 1993), 20–39; Théophile Dufour, "Notes sur le Couvent de Sainte-Claire à Genève," *Mémoires et documents publiés par la Société d'Histoire et d'Archéologie de Genève* 20 (1879–80): 119–45; Feld, "Jeanne de Jussie: Der Stand der Jungfräulichkeit und das große Gut der Ehe," in *Frauen des Mittelalters: Zwanzig geistige Profile* (Cologne: Böhlau, 2000), 309–25; Ganter, "Les Clarisses de Genève et d'Annecy," *La Revue Savoisienne* 90 (1949): 58–87; Louis Pfister, "En souvenir des Clarisses de Genève-Annecy," *La Revue Savoisienne* 90 (1949): 52–57; Albert Rilliet, "Notice sur Jeanne de Jussie et sur le livre intitulé le levain du Calvinisme," Jeanne de Jussie, *Le levain du Calvinisme*, 1–23 (numbered separately; not included in all copies of this edition); and Jules Vuy, *Jeanne de Jussie et les soeurs de Sainte-Claire* (Geneva: Trembley, 1881).

15. Guillaume de Jussie later became a Calvinist. Upon his death, after leaving five sols to each of his survivors, including his sister, Jeanne, he left all of his property to the hospital then housed in the former Convent of Saint Clare in Geneva. See Ganter, *Les Clarisses*, 207.

16. P. 132.

THE ORDER OF SAINT CLARE

The order of Saint Clare was founded in 1212 in Assisi, Italy, by Saint Clare of Assisi (1194–1253),[17] a noblewoman who took a vow of poverty and became a follower of Saint Francis of Assisi (1181/82–1226). First called the Second Franciscan Order of Poor Ladies and later renamed the Order of the Poor Clares, the order was established with Francis's support. It was reformed by Saint Colette of Corbie (1381–1447) in the fifteenth century.

The Poor Clares upheld strict vows of chastity, poverty, obedience, and enclosure.[18] Like all Franciscans, they were known, in particular, for their extreme poverty. They possessed no property, as individuals or as a community, except for the convent buildings and the land necessary to isolate the convent from the world. According to the Rule of Saint Clare, this land was to be used only to grow the fruits and vegetables necessary for the nuns' subsistence. No dowry was required to enter the convent, although novices or their families often made some kind of monetary contribution, which was then used to purchase objects necessary for the convent. Otherwise, the convent subsisted on alms and on payment received from time to time in exchange for prayers for the sick and the dead.

The Poor Clares were also known for their simplicity of dress. The Rule of Saint Clare called for the nuns to wear their hair cut short and to go barefoot. With her characteristic flair for the dramatic, and surely some exaggeration, Jussie reports in her chronicle that some of the Poor Clares did not know what to do with the shoes given to them for the long walk from Geneva to Annecy, and that, bewildered, they tied them to their belts instead of putting them on their feet! The Poor Clares wore loose-fitting garments made of rough wool—gray, black, or undyed—and had coats of the same fabric. A plain linen hood and a headband covered most of each woman's face—at least her forehead, part of her cheeks, and her chin—and hung down to her waist. Each nun also wore a simple rope belt, wrapped around her waist twice, one end of which hung down almost to her feet and had four equally spaced knots, said to represent the four vows. A rosary hung down on the left side of this rope belt. The Poor Clares of Geneva may or may not have worn scapulars.

---

17. For the writings of Saint Clare and documents relative to her canonization, see Père Damien Vorreux, ed., *Sainte Claire d'Assise, documents: Biographie, écrits, procès et bulle de canonisation, textes de chroniqueurs, textes législatifs et tables* (Paris: Les Éditions franciscaines, 2002).

18. Information on the Order of Saint Clare comes primarily from Ganter, *Les Clarisses;* Feld (introduction to the *Petite chronique*); and Grivel, "Notice," 274.

The Poor Clares would likely have slept on simple pine beds with straw mattresses, although aged or ailing nuns would have been allowed to have feather pillows and wool blankets if necessary. They fasted at all times, except at Christmas, when they could eat two meals; even at Christmas, however, they ate no meat. According to the Rule of Saint Clare, the abbess could punish sinful nuns by giving them only bread and water and making them sit on the floor of the refectory to eat instead of at the table. Despite these ascetic practices, however, the abbess was also charged with making sure that excessive physical suffering was avoided. Nuns could be excused from fasting if they were ill, for example. Jussie writes that before their departure from Geneva, the abbess gave all the nuns permission to have an extra meal so that they would have strength for the journey, although she adds that most of the women were too upset to eat. Later on, she recalls with satisfaction that a man named Burdet offered the Poor Clares a "nice round loaf of white bread and some good, aged cheese, and a cup of the best wine he could find"[19] after the nuns had left Geneva and crossed the bridge into the territory of the Duke of Savoy. The Rule of Saint Clare is silent with regard to self-inflicted physical punishment. The *Vie de Sainte Claire* (Life of Saint Clare), however, contains numerous accounts of Saint Clare's own self-mortification, and Jussie says three times in her chronicle that the nuns "disciplined themselves."[20]

According to the Rule of Saint Clare, the Poor Clares confessed at least twelve times each year. They received the sacrament of the Eucharist seven times: on Christmas, Holy Thursday, Easter, Pentecost, the Assumption, the Feast of Saint Francis, and All Saints' Day. As we see in Jussie's chronicle, the passing of the year was marked for the nuns more by saints' days and church festivals than by months and seasons, a system of timekeeping that surely affected the women's view of the world. Although describing an event that occurred "on the Feast of Monseigneur Saint Francis" may have been as automatic to Jussie as saying "on October 4," the constant evocation of the saints in the commonest of settings must have made these figures seem very close in both time and space. In the cloister, at least, Saint Francis was likely as real to the Poor Clares as was Peter Werle or Jacques Malbosson, whose deaths Jussie laments in her chronicle.

Just as their years were marked by church festivals, so the nuns' days were punctuated by the canonical hours. Jussie and her sisters in the Con-

---

19. P. 172.

20. See especially chap. 11, nos. 17–18. See also Vorreux, *Sainte Claire d'Assise*, 55–57; and Grivel, "Notice," 274.

vent of Saint Clare would have recited prayers, or offices, at the following times: matins at midnight, lauds at 3 a.m. or at dawn, prime at 6 a.m., terce at 9 a.m., sext at noon, nones at 3 p.m., vespers at 6 p.m. or at sunset, and compline at 9 p.m. or just before bedtime.[21] Jussie mentions matins, vespers, and compline specifically in her chronicle. Following the Rule of Saint Clare, the Poor Clares would have used the Franciscan breviary, and they would have chanted, rather than sung, the Divine Office. They would have observed the "great silence" from compline until terce, as well as silence in the choir, in the dormitory, and during meals. Between their prayers, the nuns would have been kept busy cooking, cleaning, doing dishes, mending their simple clothing, attending to the daily offices, and taking care of any other tasks required for life in community. The youngest nuns would have been assigned the more strenuous chores in order to spare the older women, and the most menial tasks would have been done by the tertiary sisters.

THE GENEVAN POOR CLARES

The Convent of Saint Clare, properly known as the "Monastère Jésus de Bethléem," was the only women's religious house inside the Genevan city walls. It was established by Yolande of Savoy—another reason for the nuns' fidelity to the Duke of Savoy—who received authorization from Pope Sixtus IV in 1473 to set up a convent in Geneva.[22] Yolande, the widow of Duke Amédée IX of Savoy, the daughter of King Charles VII of France, and the sister of King Louis XI of France, had founded a Clarissen convent in Chambéry a few years earlier. At the time, there were also Clarissen convents in nearby Orbe and Vevey, both mentioned in the *Short Chronicle*, the Order of Saint Clare having received a new burst of energy in Savoy and the surrounding regions through the reformation of Colette of Corbie in the fifteenth century.[23]

The convent in Geneva was situated at the top of the Rue Verdaine on the busy Place du Bourg-de-Four, not far from the cathedral, on the site now occupied by the Palais de Justice. This location was desirable both because of its proximity to the main episcopal buildings of Geneva and because of its

21. There was some variation from convent to convent, and offices such as matins and lauds, prime and terce, or sext and nones were sometimes combined.

22. Details of the history of the convent in Geneva come primarily from Feld's introduction to the *Petite chronique*; Ganter *Les Clarisses*; Grivel, "Notice"; and Roth, "Une femme auteur." For more information on events preceding the convent's establishment in Geneva, see Ganter.

23. According to Ganter, *Les Clarisses*, all fifteen of the nuns who first came to live in the Genevan Convent of Saint Clare had known Colette of Corbie.

visibility to the Christians on whose alms the Poor Clares depended for their survival. Part of the land for the convent was donated in 1473 by François, Count of Gruyère and Marshall of Savoy, who owned a house and garden on the Rue Verdaine. Additional land was obtained by the purchase of two adjacent houses, owned by André Baudichon and Claude Granger. Construction on the convent began in 1474. The first fifteen nuns to live in the Convent of Saint Clare in Geneva arrived from Seurre, Poligny, Chambéry, Vevey, and Orbe in 1477.

Above the main entrance to the convent on the Place du Bourg-de-Four, Jussie tells us, hung a handsome crucifix. Inside this entrance was a long corridor decorated with colorful frescos and statues of saints. Just inside the entrance, on the right, was a door to the lay brothers' portion of the convent, which occupied the whole right wing of the convent. On the left was a door into the church. Further down the hallway on the right, the lay brothers' garden was visible through a set of arcades. At the end of the hallway on the left was a locked door into the cloister.

The church and cloister, the areas Jeanne de Jussie knew best, occupied the left wing of the convent. Visitors could enter the church to hear offices or Mass, but the cloister was sealed off completely from the outside world. The church itself was a plain rectangular shape, without any pillars or columns. It consisted of a chancel, a nave, and two chapels, as well as a sacristy that was separated from the chancel by a rood screen. Near the entrance to the church was a stairway that led up to the nuns' choir, which hung over the back part of the nave. An iron grille separated a landing at the top of this staircase from the choir. Through this grille, the priest could pass the Eucharist to the nuns and visitors to the convent could speak to the cloistered women. A thin curtain hung inside the grille, and there was also a wooden door that the nuns could close.

The heavy walnut door that led from the central corridor into the cloister was opened only on the most solemn occasions: to admit a novice, for example, to administer the last sacraments or when a sovereign—such as the Duchess of Savoy—came to visit. The chapter room, infirmary, kitchen, refectory, and workrooms made up the ground floor of the cloister; they lay around a courtyard with a well in the middle. The nuns' dormitory was upstairs. Their garden was outside the courtyard on the side opposite the church. It was much larger than the lay brothers' garden and was not visible from the public areas of the convent. The city walls formed the outer side of the garden, assuring relative tranquility (except when men climbed up on these walls to taunt the nuns, as Jussie records in her chronicle). The

Poor Clares could thus garden, gather herbs, and enjoy the fresh air while remaining in seclusion.[24]

If a visitor wished to speak to a nun, he or she would go to the turning window, which was located near the entrance to the cloister. The turning window served as a means of communication between inside and outside the cloister and was attended by a portress. The portress would ask for the visitor's intentions. If the portress granted the visitor permission to speak to the nuns, the visitor would enter the church and climb the stairs up to the grille and the nun would appear inside, always accompanied by at least three discreets, nuns appointed as advisors to the abbess.

The abbess of the convent—the aged Louise Rambo during the years that Jussie narrates—was elected by the community of Poor Clares to govern the convent. She was assisted by the vicaress—the energetic and outspoken Pernette de Montluel during most of the period about which Jussie writes—who was second in charge. In accordance with the Rule of Saint Clare, there were also eight discreets. Jussie also mentions in her text a few portresses, a bursar,[25] cooks, and a nurse. Although Jussie does not refer to them specifically, there may also have been a laundress, a sacristan,[26] and a gardener. Finally, there was the convent secretary,[27] who took care of any necessary written correspondence with the outside world and who signed receipts for donations to the convent and for any other items. We know from the *Short Chronicle* that Jussie was drafting pleas on her convent's behalf by at least 1530. Receipts in her handwriting are currently in archives in Geneva and in Annecy.[28]

There were also lay sisters in the convent, although Jussie makes no specific reference to them. These women, who would have come from families lower in rank than the nuns' families, were not cloistered and would

---

24. Roberta Gilchrist has analyzed the significance of the design of medieval English convents, which bore many similarities to the Convent of Saint Clare in Geneva. See *Gender and Archaeology: Contesting the Past* (New York: Routledge, 1999); and *Gender and Material Culture: The Archaeology of Religious Women* (New York: Routledge, 1994).

25. The bursar would have overseen the few funds necessary for daily purchases.

26. The sacristan would have attended to the ceremonial vestments.

27. Jussie calls herself the *écrivaine*. The term *écrivaine*, a feminist one by the standards of modern French, was in common usage at the time and not marked as particularly feminist.

28. A receipt dated October 11, 1533, in Jussie's handwriting and signed by Abbess Louise Rambo, is in the Genevan Archives d'État (P.H. no. 1089). A similar receipt dated April 17, 1538, is in Annecy in the Archives départementales de la Haute Savoie (35, H. 3). See Feld's introduction to the *Petite chronique*, lxiii—lxv. The facsimile of another receipt is reproduced in Du Four, "Notes," facing p. 126.

have attended to such tasks as keeping the chapel in order and running errands. The convent also provided for tertiary sisters, who would have acted as servants. Jussie mentions the tertiaries once in her narration of the Poor Clares' journey to Annecy. Along with the women, there were two or three lay brothers who, in addition to participating in the convent's spiritual life, would have served as kind of early modern handymen, seeing to heavier domestic tasks. Finally, there were two convent confessors from the reformed Franciscan order.

Twenty-four nuns lived in the Convent of Saint Clare in Geneva during the period Jussie narrates. All these women except one—the apostate Blaisine Varembert—left Geneva at dawn on August 30, 1535. They traveled on foot to Annecy, spending one night (August 30) in Saint-Julien, four nights (August 31 through September 3) in Viry at the Castle of La Perrière, hosted by Michel, Baron of Viry, the cousin of vicaress Pernette de Montluel, and one night (September 4) at the Abbey of Bonlieu. They arrived in Annecy late in the evening on September 5. In Annecy, Duke Charles III of Savoy turned over to the Poor Clares the unoccupied Augustinian Monastery of the Holy Cross.

Louise Rambo served as abbess of the Convent of Saint Clare for almost three more years after the Poor Clares' resettlement in Annecy. She died in 1538 and was succeeded—not surprisingly—by the former vicaress Pernette de Montluel. Jeanne de Jussie was elected abbess in 1548. After her death in 1561, she was succeeded by Claude de Pierrefleur, who died in 1565. Although the Poor Clares spent more than two centuries in Annecy—far more than their fifty-eight years in Geneva—they always referred to themselves as the "Sisters of Saint Clare of Geneva in refuge in Annecy." Their convent was officially dissolved on July 8, 1793, in the aftermath of the French Revolution.[29]

Their convent building in Geneva was turned into a hospital for the poor in September 1535, almost immediately after the nuns' departure from the city. In November of that same year, it became a general hospital. The building was razed in 1709. In 1865, the current Palais de Justice was built on the foundations of the former convent. The convent building in Annecy was occupied by a cotton mill soon after the dissolution of the convent. In 1949, a plaque commemorating the Poor Clares, and Jeanne de Jussie in particular, was placed on the building, which was still standing at the end

---

29. For further information on the history of the Convent of Saint Clare in Annecy until its dissolution in 1793, see Ganter, *Les Clarisses*, 117–53.

of the Rue Sainte Claire just next to the Porte Sainte Claire.[30] In the 1970s, the structure was demolished and a parking garage and shops were built on the site. The plaque was saved and placed on the wall of the new building in 1979, where it remains. It bears the following inscription:

> "Cotton mill established after the Revolution in the former Monastery of the Holy Cross of Annecy, built in 1490, where the Poor Clares, established in Geneva in 1477 by Duchess Yolande of Savoy, took refuge in 1535 and remained until 1793. // Jeanne de Jussie, author of the tale of the sorrowful departure, was abbess of this monastery from 1548–1561. // Inscription placed through the care of the learned societies of Annecy and the Catholic historical society of Geneva. // June 19, 1949."

Below the first plaque was added a second one, which bears this inscription: "This plaque, affixed on the wall of the former chapel of the Poor Clares, was attached to this new structure built on the site of the Convent of Saint Clare 30 years later, on June 19, 1979."

THE "SHORT CHRONICLE"

Although the task of the *écrivaine* consisted mainly of signing receipts and attending to correspondence between the convent and the outside world, Jeanne de Jussie took it upon herself to compose a narrative of the Reformation's turbulent arrival in Geneva, leading up to her convent's departure from the city in 1535.[31] The chronicle begins with the *Combourgeoisie* between

---

30. Pfister, "En souvenir des Clarisses de Genève-Annecy," 52–57, describes the dedication of the plaque. The inscriptions on both plaques are in French; translations given below are mine.

31. Although the rich record she left of her experiences of the Reformation from behind convent walls is unique in the French language, Jussie does have some counterparts, especially in German-speaking lands. Caritas Pirckheimer (1467–1532), abbess of a Convent of Saint Clare in Nuremberg and a woman with a humanist background and close ties to humanist circles— including her brother, Willibald Pirckheimer (1470–1530)—defied Reformers in Nuremberg and refused to allow her convent to be closed. She left letters and a journal. See Caritas Pirckheimer, *Briefe der Äbtissin Caritas Pirckheimer des St. Klara-Klosters zu Nürnberg nach der Erstveröffentlichung von Josef Pfanner, übertragen von Benedicta Schrott*, ed. P. Georg Deichstetter (St. Ottilien: EOS Verlag, 1984); *Denkwürdigkeiten aus dem Reformationszeitalter: Charitas Pirckheimer*, ed. Constantin Höfler (Osnabrück: Otto Zeller, 1984); Georg Deichstetter, ed., *Caritas Pirckheimer: Ordensfrau und Humanistin: ein Vorbild für die Ökumene: Festschrift zum 450. Todstag* (Cologne: Wienand, 1982). See also Charlotte Woodford, *Nuns as Historians in Early Modern Germany* (Oxford: Oxford University Press, 2002). Katherine Rem, a nun in the Katherine convent in Augsburg, sent a letter to her brother Bernard explaining her reasons for rejecting the Reformation. Her letter and his answer to her, printed

Geneva, Bern, and Fribourg in 1526, as Jussie outlines briefly key events of the first few years of the alliance: opposition from nobles, the flight of Prince-Bishop Pierre de la Baume, the murder of François Ternier, Lord of Pontverre, and the arrival of Swiss troops. She covers the years 1530 to 1534 in greater detail, describing escalating conflicts between defenders of the traditional religion and advocates of the Reformation as the battle for control of Geneva becomes more theological and less political, at least on the surface. She then devotes more than half of her text to what are, for her, the tragic events of the year 1535. The *Short Chronicle* concludes with a brief epilogue in which Jussie describes the misfortunes suffered by the House of Savoy in 1536.

Jussie's narrative takes place in several overlapping spheres. She writes not only of the Reformation's effects in her convent, but also of events in Europe (the spread of Lutheranism, battles between Christians and Turks, negotiations among France, the Empire, and Rome), in the Swiss-Savoy borderlands (the duke's attempt to assert his authority, iconoclastic acts, burning of castles), and in Geneva (fighting in the streets, public executions, the Rive Disputation). Her sources are seldom explicit. She often makes comments such as "I heard it from a respectable man" or "It was said" or "People said," so it is clear, at any rate, that she had continual access to news of current events. Indeed, despite their seclusion, the Poor Clares had many ways of learning what was happening outside their convent. Reports from distant lands, such as the Grand Turk's exploits in Hungary and the miracle of the Virgin Mary in Picardy, may have been among narratives that were passed from convent to convent.[32] In addition, there were at least two confessors from the reformed Franciscan order in the convent who could come and go as they pleased and who no doubt communicated with other Franciscan monasteries and convents as well as other clerics and prominent persons.[33] Although Jussie does not mention him by name, one of the confessors at the Genevan Convent of Saint Clare during the years she narrates was Jean Gacy,[34] who had published anti-Reformist treatises and was a known opponent of Erasmus. In addition to the confessors, there were two or three lay brothers. Jussie

---

in 1523, are included in both German and in English in Merry Wiesner-Hanks, *Convents Confront the Reformation: Catholic and Protestant Nuns in Germany* (Milwaukee: Marquette University Press, 1996), 27–37.

32. See Ganter, *Les Clarisses*, 212.

33. See Feld's introduction to the *Petite chronique*, xlviii—liii.

34. Gacy was the author of the *Trialogue nouveau contenant lexpression des erreurs de Martin Luther* ([Geneva]: [Wygand Köln], 1524) and the lesser-known *Deploration de la cité de Genesve*, ed. Jules Vuy (Geneva: Tremblay, 1882). According to Vuy, Gacy published the *Deploration* shortly after the Poor Clares' departure for Annecy.

refers explicitly to one of these lay brothers, Nicolas des Arnox, who, near the beginning of the chronicle, protects the nuns from the soldiers who try to break into the cloister and who, near the end of the text, despite his own illness, arranges for a wagon to carry the older and weaker nuns on their journey from Geneva to Annecy. Finally, many Genevan townspeople visited the convent regularly, as Jussie relates in her chronicle. Many of these women were close relatives of the nuns and surely shared with them news of current events in the city, both ordinary and extraordinary.

MIRACULOUS MOMENTS AND DIVINE INTERVENTION

These separate spheres—the ordinary and the extraordinary—often converge in Jussie's narrative, and the lines separating the material from the spiritual world seem to disappear altogether. Jussie actively seeks connections between these two worlds, searching the heavens, and even the weather, for divine significance. She writes of two comets, one of which, she says, predicted the death of Louise of Savoy and the other whose meaning she does not—yet—know.[35] She writes of the cold winter of 1532 as well, the coldest in twenty-five years, which afflicts Geneva just after the Duke of Savoy has forbidden anyone to take provisions into the city. According to Jussie, the harsh cold is God's punishment for the heresy into which the city is falling.

A strong sense of the miraculous pervades much of Jussie's text. She includes reports of numerous modern-day miracles, many of which have biblical precedents. There is, for example, the multiplication of the bread that should have only lasted for two days but that nourishes Jussie and her sisters for twelve whole days and is even enough for them to share with their confessors, the lay brothers and sisters, and visitors. Then there is the woman long past her child-bearing years who, like the biblical Elizabeth, becomes pregnant as compensation for her piety and bears a daughter after thirty-one years of childless marriage. Other miracles echo the incorruptibility of the body of Christ. In two cases, the sacred host disappears to avoid profanation: once when an iconoclast tries to throw it on the ground in a churchyard and later when another tries to feed it to his horse. Reports of devout Christians killed for their beliefs whose bodies do not rot also echo Christ's incorruptible flesh. In perhaps the most remarkable of these stories, the body of a Christian woman who has been on the gibbet for about a

---

35. One of these comets was Halley's comet. For the interpretations of Halley's comet during the Reformation, see Julius Rauscher, "Der Halleysche Komet im Jahre 1531 und die Reformatoren," *Zeitschrift für Kirchengeschichte* 32 (1911): 259–76.

year turns over and bites a dead heretic on the chin. Still other miracles show a particular concern for women's experiences, such as the story of the prostitute in Tournai who is near a public fountain—recalling, perhaps, the Samaritan woman at the well[36] —and who, when beaten by a drunkard, cries out for help to an image of the Virgin Mary, which sheds tears of blood in sympathy.

Jussie also writes of cases in which God is seen to intervene directly in the course of human events, punishing the wicked or foiling them. Seven hundred Christians defeat nine thousand heretics at the Battle of Kappel;[37] a sudden storm afflicts only the Turks in a battle against the Hungarians; a heretic dies after poking out the eyes of an image of Saint Anthony of Padua; and cannons misfire in an attack on the Castle of Peney. God is also seen to intervene to reward or protect the righteous. Mysterious knights appear at the door of the Convent of Saint Clare to shield it from the plague; the nuns avoid all physical harm as they leave Geneva despite mobs in the streets; Jeanne de Jussie herself is healed of a high fever when the Poor Clares kiss the relics of Saint Romanus at the Castle of La Perrière; and a stillborn child comes back to life when the nuns say a "Salve Regina" at the church of Notre Dame de Liesse in Annecy.

In all these cases, the report of divine intervention illustrates God's continuing interest in devoted Christians. The status of miracles was, of course, intensely disputed during the Reformation, and Jussie's reports of miracles must therefore not be read innocently. In his own chronicle of the Reformation of Geneva, *Les actes et gestes merveilleux de la cité de Genève* (The Marvelous Acts and Gestures of the City of Geneva), Reformer Antoine Fromment rejects miracles as inventions of avaricious clerics, and he tries to demystify some of them by exposing the trickery behind them. He writes, for example, of a relic in Geneva that was said to be Saint Anthony's arm but that turned out to be the "natural virile member" of a deer and of voices of the dead that were discovered to be wind blown through pipes.[38] As her depictions of confrontations between Reformers and the Poor Clares—with the vicaress as their mouthpiece—make absolutely clear, Jussie was aware of key theological differences between advocates of "old" and "new" belief. By relating these miraculous events, Jussie is therefore not only providing proof of the side favored by God in the ongoing battles, but is implicitly expressing her allegiance to the traditional church.

---

36. See Jn 4:6–30.

37. It was at the Battle of Kappel on October 11, 1531, that Ulrich Zwingli was killed.

38. Fromment, *Les actes et gestes merveilleux de la cité de Genève*, 146–50 (my translation).

Perhaps above all, Jeanne de Jussie writes of a world in which, despite the horrific acts of violence going on all around her, things make sense. She never doubts God's complete control of events. Whether or not they can yet put all the pieces together—and the *Short Chronicle* is surely an attempt to do just that—Jussie and her sisters in the Convent of Saint Clare are protagonists in a story with a plot, and their experiences are meaningful in it. From start to finish, Jussie's chronicle has a strong sense of narrative. Despite a few detours, the action of the story is largely unified. Jussie begins and ends her tale with the House of Savoy, first presenting the duke and duchess as the rightful leaders of the good people, then later regretfully relating their sad fate: Savoy's capitulation to France, the exile of the duke, and the death of the duchess and of three of their children. To conclude, she brings up the last glimmer of hope that remains: the duke's son Emmanuel-Philibert, who is in the service of Emperor Charles V. Jussie must have felt some degree of vindication when, more than twenty years later (and not long before her own death in 1561), this same Emmanuel-Philibert, Duke of Savoy since 1553, regained his lands in the 1559 Treaty of Cateau-Cambresis and negotiated a reconciliation with France through his marriage to Marguerite, the youngest daughter of King Francis I and sister of King Henry II.

THE BATTLE BETWEEN GOOD AND EVIL

Just as Jussie makes little distinction between spiritual and material worlds, so religion and politics converge in her text. The protagonists in the *Short Chronicle*, usually called simply "the good people" or "the Christians," are the supporters of the Duke of Savoy ("Monseigneur"), the prince-bishop ("Monseigneur of Geneva"), and the traditional church. The antagonists are the Genevans who have made an alliance with Bern and Fribourg and who subsequently usher the Reformation into their city; they are "heretics," "evangelicals," or more often, "Lutherans." (Martin Luther's only role in the Reformation of Geneva was, of course, as a distant inspiration, rivaled by the much closer Ulrich Zwingli in Zurich, who was killed in 1531, and, of course, Guillaume Farel.) Even worse than the heretics are Jews and Turks, but they seem less like real people in the text than like abstract figures of evil invoked for rhetorical effect.

As she tells us explicitly in her chronicle, Jussie is living through a time of persecution. This persecution, however, has a meaning, and Jussie has full confidence in divine justice. She provides numerous examples of heretics who are either punished by God or struck with contrition and repent and of Christians who hold fast to their religion and are then rewarded. The

Poor Clares are, of course, the leading example of constancy in the text. Jussie alludes frequently to her convent's privileged place among Christians in Geneva; the phrase "except in the Convent of Saint Clare" is a frequent refrain. When Swiss troops come to Geneva in 1530, Jussie writes, all masses and divine service cease inside the city walls, and yet, they continue in her convent. Jussie often emphasizes the Poor Clares' service to the Genevan community, underlining the fact that they not only use their sanctuary for their own prayers, but open it to all who wish to hear Mass or the Divine Office. The Convent of Saint Clare is the only religious house in Geneva in which there are no "perversions" from the traditional faith, says Jussie—conveniently dismissing the apostate Blaisine Varembert by saying she was not sincere about her vows in the first place. After August 8, 1535, when the Reformation has gained a definitive hold on Geneva but before the nuns have left the city, Jussie reports that no Mass or divine service is celebrated in the whole city, "except at the Convent of Saint Clare, where the poor sisters still observ[e] the canonical hours, but with the doors closed."[39] The nuns' prayers are of little use to the Genevan community at this point, however. Although they continue to recite the Divine Office, the Poor Clares' departure—or dissolution—has become inevitable. Their situation is bearable only because they know God will reward their constancy in the end.

WOMEN'S INVOLVEMENT

Throughout her account, Jussie makes a point of describing both men's and women's participation in the events she relates. She paints a vivid picture of good men and women attending Reformers' sermons and leaving scandalized, resisting Farel's attempts to convert them, participating in church processions, preparing to fight at the Place du Molard, and, finally, watching the Poor Clares leave the city. One of the most remarkable aspects of her tale is the rare glimpse it offers of women fighting both for and against the Reformation in Geneva, even outside the walls of the Convent of Saint Clare. Jussie describes women throwing rocks at Fromment and at other Reformers. Their bitterest violence, however, seems to be directed against other women. In one memorable scene, a group of women, furious over the fatal blow that has been dealt to a "good Christian merchant," seeks revenge on a Reformed apothecary's wife and tries to throw her into the Rhone. The woman is likely Claudine Levet (wife of Aymé Levet), who later tries to convert Jussie and

39. P. 138.

her sisters by preaching in the Convent of Saint Clare. Unable to find her, the women ransack the apothecary shop instead.[40]

When Guy Furbity, the theologian sent to Geneva by the Sorbonne, is imprisoned, Jussie reports that it is the devout "Christian" women of Geneva who are the most outraged and who do all they can to ease his suffering, offering vows, prayers, and pious acts in exchange for his release and coming often to the Convent of Saint Clare to have masses to the Virgin recited for him. The good Christian wife of Furbity's heretical prison guard slips jam and other good things to him secretly until she is discovered and denounced. The Poor Clares themselves do what they can, Jussie tells us, by writing letters of comfort—surely penned by Jussie herself—and sending Furbity candles, ink, and paper so that he might respond. However, the women's pleas with the Bernese for Furbity's release are to no avail.

The Catholic women of Geneva show the same concern for the Poor Clares during their troubles. Jussie refers several times to their visits to the Convent of Saint Clare to exhort the nuns to remain strong. Perhaps the most dramatic example of women's support of the Poor Clares occurs on August 24, 1535, the fateful day when an iconoclastic horde finally enters the convent, smashing statues and burning paintings, and then departs, leaving the convent wide open. After this catastrophe, Jussie writes, God inspires two prominent burgher women—Lady Guillaume de la Rive and Lady Leonarde Vindrette—to come to the convent and assist the nuns. These burgher women offer their sympathy and then stay with the distraught nuns as the apostate Blaisine Varembert is finally removed from the convent. At one point, one of the women even hides a young nun beneath her skirts. After the traumatic events of that day, Jussie reports, one of the women, who is pregnant, has to have her dress and cloak loosened, and she narrowly avoids going into premature labor. Women continue to support the Poor Clares during their journey from Geneva to Annecy. Jussie mentions explicitly the noble and burgher women who greet them in Saint-Julien and in Annecy. Their chief supporter is, of course, the Duchess of Savoy herself, or at least Jussie finds it expedient to say so. Jussie describes the duchess's devotion at

40. Natalie Zemon Davis describes similar acts by other Catholic women in French-speaking lands: "On the lowest level, [organized group action among women] was reflected in the violent activity of all-female Catholic crowds—throwing stones at Protestant women, throwing mire at pastors, and, in the case of a group of female butchers in Aix-en-Provence, beating and hanging the wife of a Protestant bookseller" (*Society and Culture in Early Modern France* [Stanford: Stanford University Press, 1975], 92–93). On pp. 74–77, Davis discusses the activities of Catholic city women just prior to the Reformation.

great length at the end of her chronicle as she mourns her untimely death in January 1538.

Even more vivid are Jussie's portraits of the women who champion the Reformation and who are therefore the Poor Clares' enemies. She describes with contempt anonymous "Lutheran" women who express their opposition to church ceremonies by sitting in their windows doing needlework during processions and by doing laundry on the feast days after Easter and Pentecost. She also describes visits by Reformed women who attempt to preach to the nuns in the convent. Hemme Faulson appears several times in the chronicle as she tries—successfully, in the end—to remove her sister Blaisine Varembert, whom she claims entered the convent against her will. Faulson, Jussie says, "could not hold back her venom, but poured it out on the poor nuns' hearts," and she denounces transubstantiation, saying the sacrament is "nothing but a wafer."[41]

Jussie also describes visits by Marie Dentière and Claudine Levet, both of whom preach to the nuns. Dentière, once an Augustinian nun in Tournai, had left her convent in the 1520s and married Simon Robert, himself a former priest, also from Tournai. The two of them were active in the French-speaking Reformed community in Strasbourg in the late 1520s and came to the Valais region in 1528 as followers of Guillaume Farel. Robert died in 1533; soon afterward, Dentière married Antoine Fromment, the author of the *Actes et gestes merveilleux de la cité de Genève* mentioned above. Another follower of Farel, Fromment became a leading Reformer in Geneva in the 1530s. Dentière penned at least two published texts relative to the Reformation in Geneva, the *Epistre très utile* (Very Useful Epistle) addressed to Marguerite de Navarre in 1539[42] and a preface to a sermon by John Calvin advocating modesty in women's dress, published in 1561.[43] A third text, the anonymous *Guerre et deslivrance de la ville de Genesve* (War and Deliverance of the

---

41. Pp. 100, 101.

42. *Epistre très utile, faicte et composée par une femme chrestienne de Tornay, envoyée à la Royne de Navarre, seur du Roy de France, contre les Turcs, Juifz, Infideles, Faulxchrestiens, Anabaptistes et Lutheriens, [à Anvers, chez Martin l'empereur]* (Geneva: Jean Girard, 1539). Recently translated into English and edited by Mary B. McKinley in *Epistle to Marguerite de Navarre and Preface to a Sermon by John Calvin;* see above, note 11.

43. "Preface to a Sermon by John Calvin," printed in *Les conditions et vertus requises en la femme fidèle et bonne mesnagere: Contenues au xxxi. Chapitre des Proverbes de Salomon. Mis en forme de cantique, par Théodore de Besze. Plus, un sermon de la modestie des femmes en leurs habillemens, par. M. Jean Calvin. Outre, plusieurs chansons spirituelles, en Musique* (1561). Also recently translated into English and edited by Mary B. McKinley in *Epistle to Marguerite de Navarre and Preface to a Sermon by John Calvin;* see above, note 11.

City of Geneva),[44] has also been attributed to her, but more tenuously.[45] In her chronicle, Jussie calls Dentière a "false, wrinkled abbess with a devilish tongue,"[46] and she reports that the nuns spit on her in scorn when she praises marriage and family. Levet, most likely the apothecary's wife mentioned above, also preaches to the nuns, even though, Jussie says, "she did not know how."[47] Like Dentière, she praises marriage and condemns the cloistered life. The nuns spit on her as well, Jussie tells us, to the evident amusement of the syndics who accompany her, although they try to hide their mirth.

STYLE

Despite the serious and deeply spiritual nature of her story, Jussie's narrative is lively, even humorous at times. Her style is unpretentious and direct, bearing imprints of oral speech and storytelling such as incomplete sentences,

---

44. *La guerre et deslivrance de la ville de Genesve [composée et publiée en 1536 par Marie Dentière de Tournay, ancienne abbesse et femme d'Antoine Froment]*, ed. Albert Rilliet, in *Mémoires de la Société d'Histoire et d'Archéologie de Genève* 20 (Geneva: Charles Schuchardt, 1881). The original title of the work as it appeared in 1536 was *La guerre et délivrance de la ville de Genesve fidèlement faicte et composée par un Marchand demourant en icelle.*

45. Dentière, *Epistle to Marguerite de Navarre* (above, note 11). See McKinley's introduction to that volume for a detailed bibliography of Dentière and an analysis of her work. In recent years, Dentière has gained increasing critical attention as both a feminist and an eloquent defender of Reformed theology. See Irena Backus, "Marie Dentière: Un cas de féminisme théologique à l'époque de la Réforme?" *Bulletin de la Société de l'Histoire du Protestantisme Français* 137 (1991): 177–95; Jane Dempsey Douglass, "Marie Dentière's Use of Scripture in Her Theology of History," in *Biblical Hermeneutics in Historical Perspective: Studies in Honor of Karlfried Froehlich on his Sixtieth Birthday*, eds. Mark Burrows and Paul Rorem (Grand Rapids, Mich.: William B. Eerdmans, 1991), 227–44; Cynthia Skenazi, "Marie Dentière et la prédication des femmes," *Renaissance and Reformation / Renaissance et Réforme* 21, no. 1 (1997): 5–18. See also Thomas Head, "A Propagandist for the Reform: Marie Dentière," in *Women Writers of the Renaissance and Reformation*, ed. Katharina M. Wilson (Athens: University of Georgia Press, 1987), 260–83; Catherine M. Bothe, "Écriture féminine de la Réformation: Le témoignage de Marie Dentière," *Romance Languages Annual* 5 (1993): 15–19. William Kemp and Diane Desrosiers-Bonin have considered Dentière's connections to Marguerite de Navarre in "Marie d'Ennetières et la petite grammaire hébraïque de sa fille d'après la dédicace de l'*Epistre* à Marguerite de Navarre," *Bibliothèque d'Humanisme et Renaissance* 50, no. 1 (1998): 117–34. Madeleine Lazard and Elisabeth M. Wengler have both discussed this encounter between Dentière and the Poor Clares. Madeleine Lazard, "Deux soeurs ennemies, Marie Dentière et Jeanne de Jussie: Nonnes et réformées à Genève," in *Les réformes: Enracinements socio-culturels*, ed. B. Chevalier and C. Sauzat (Paris: La Maisnie, 1985), 233–49; Elisabeth M. Wengler, "Women, Religion, and Reform in Sixteenth-Century Geneva" (Ph.D. diss.,Boston College, 1999), see especially 99–101.

46. P. 151.

47. P. 159.

loose organization (particularly at the beginning of the chronicle, when she quickly reviews for her audience key events of the years 1526 to 1530), and reported dialogue that a modern theorist of discourse might label free indirect speech. She uses colorful, image-filled language. She calls heretics repeatedly "disloyal dogs," and she condemns Martin Luther, the worst heretic of all, as "that pestiferous dragon with the venomous tail".[48] It is with obvious delight that she relates the words of the vicaress who, in response to the lieutenant who accuses the nuns of hoarding a dagger (he is actually referring to a treasure the nuns call the "bishop's relic"), insists that the Poor Clares "never waged war except on fleas and houseflies."[49] Jussie puts such speech into her own mouth, as well, as she tells us that in an effort to stop council member Claude Bernard from trying to convert her, she retorts, "it does as much good for you to preach to me as to beat yellow bile to make butter."[50]

The *Short Chronicle* also contains comic and satirical elements. Perhaps most notably, Jussie does not hesitate to use obvious exaggeration to make her point. In one passage, she imagines a Reformed reenactment of the Last Supper taking place in Geneva. She writes, "A homicidal and murderous criminal pretending to be Jesus Christ washed the others' feet, and then as a sign of peace and union, one after the other, they all bit off pieces of bread and cheese."[51] Jussie would certainly have known that no Reformed denial of transubstantiation would have extended to such a sacrilege, but the moral of the story was more important to her than strict "truth." Interpretation prevails over mere fact in her tale.[52] Later, in her description of the Poor Clares' journey on foot from Geneva to Annecy, Jussie explains how bewildering it is for women who have been secluded for decades to find themselves in the world again. Some of them, she claims, are so frightened and confused that they think the cows in the fields are bears and the sheep are ravenous wolves. Furthermore, she says, when the vicaress gives the normally barefoot nuns shoes for the journey, some of the women are so baffled that they do not know what to do with them, and so they tie the shoes to their rope belts

---

48. P. 62.

49. P. 150.

50. P. 154.

51. P. 82.

52. Irena Backus, one of the few to appreciate fully the craft of Jussie's writing, commented, "Here, Jeanne describes a practice that Protestants as well as Catholics would have found blasphemous. Did she really believe that Farel's partisans engaged in such practices? Certainly not. But the aim of the chronicle was not so much to describe events as they took place as to alert young nuns to the dangers of the 'Lutheran' religion. Thus, satire supersedes history." "Les clarisses de la rue Verdaine" (The Poor Clares of the Rue Verdaine), 32.

instead of placing them on their feet. Surely these women of noble birth, who had spent at least their childhood outside the convent, had worn shoes before! Even if they had not, and if they had never noticed the shoes worn by visitors to the convent, the capable vicaress would have explained how to wear the shoes and the few, mystified nuns would have seen the rest of the Poor Clares putting on their travel shoes. However, the goal of the passage is, of course, not to create a strictly accurate historical record, but to illuminate the contrast between the safe haven of the cloister and the perils of the world to which the Reformers have exposed the nuns and to emphasize the arduousness of the journey. Jussie therefore succeeds brilliantly in her description.

Although Jussie's language demonstrates the orthographical diversity typical of the early sixteenth century, her lexicon is, in fact, much more conventional than it may seem at first glance. Almost all the words she chooses that have disappeared from modern French usage can be found in a dictionary of the period such as Huguet.[53] There seems to be little interference from local dialects such as Savoyard. The most intriguing aspect of her orthographical diversity are the idiosyncratic spellings that may provide clues to her interpretation of persons and events. By spelling *erreur* ("error") most frequently as *herreur*, for example, Jussie reinforces the connection between *herreur* and *hérésie*, error and heresy, and between *herreur* and *hérétique*, error and heretic. Similarly, when she spells *syndic* as *saintique*, she suggests a conflation of religious and secular authority in Geneva. In another instance, when she describes the band of iconoclastic Reformers that storms the convent, smashing statues and burning paintings, she refers in a single breath to their violations of the *cueur* ("choir") of the church and the anguish in the nuns' *cueur* ("heart"), thereby bringing together two sacred spaces, both of which had previously been off limits to the marauders. It is impossible to convey this irregular spelling, of course, in an English translation of the text. Whenever a particular spelling seems potentially significant, I have included a footnote with a reference to the original French.

COMPOSITION AND RECEPTION

Jeanne de Jussie probably began writing her chronicle not long after she experienced the events it contains, perhaps soon after the Poor Clares' re-

---

53. Edmond Huguet, *Dictionnaire de la langue française du seizième siècle*, 7 vols. (Paris: Didier, 1925–1967). Vuarnet published a "glossary" of Jussie's language: E. Vuarnet, "Glossaire du Livre de Jeanne de Jussie," *Revue Savoisienne* 43 (1902): 290–93.

settlement in Annecy. Helmut Feld suggests that she began writing the text in 1535, perhaps incorporating pieces she had written as early as 1532, and that she completed it before 1547.[54] As she composed her narrative, she may well have used copies she had saved of letters she had written previously, such as the detailed account of the Poor Clares' journey from Geneva to Annecy that she apparently sent to the Duke and Duchess of Savoy, as well as to Philippe de Gheldres, a staunch supporter of the convent, after the nuns' arrival in Annecy.[55] Jussie states several times that her main goal in writing the chronicle is historical: she does not want these important events to be forgotten. "I promise that I write nothing I do not know to be true," she says at one point, adding, "and still I do not write a tenth of it, but only a very small part of the main events so that they will be remembered, so that in the future those who suffer for the love of God in this world will know that our ancestors suffered as much as we do, and as people after us will, and always, to varying degrees, in the example of Our Lord and Redeemer who suffered the first and the most."[56] Jussie almost certainly did not intend to publish her text, but rather expected for it to remain as a record for her present and future sisters in the Convent of Saint Clare.

Jussie's chronicle was likely read aloud in the convent, perhaps during meals, a time when early modern monastic men and women often heard readings intended for their spiritual edification.[57] Another handwritten copy of the text produced later in the sixteenth century was perhaps made in order to spare the original, which was becoming worn from its heavy use in the convent; alternatively, it may simply be the one remaining example of multiple copies that were made for distribution in the region, as Ganter suggests.[58] Both of these manuscripts are now in the collections of the Bibliothèque Publique et Universitaire in Geneva. In his edition of Jussie's text, Feld labels the manuscripts A and B, respectively. Manuscript A, which has served as the basis for this English-language translation, is a 285-page double-sided document presumably in Jussie's own hand. It bears later inscriptions that identify the text and its author. On the reverse side of the first blank page, an unknown hand has written in ink, "The original of the chronicle of Geneva belonging to the poor nuns of the Convent of the Holy Cross, of Saint Clare, in Annecy." (Inscriptions are in French; translations are mine.) Below this

---

54. Feld's introduction to the *Petite chronique*, xxiii—xxiv. See also Rilliet, "Notice," 21–22.

55. See Ganter, *Les Clarisses*, 212.

56. P. 90.

57. See Feld's introduction to the *Petite chronique*, xxv.

58. See Ganter, *Les Clarisses*, 215.

inscription, a second hand has added, "Composed by the Reverend Mother Jeanne de Jussie Abbess of this convent, who was in Geneva during all the troubles and was exposed to all the misfortunes." Another set of inscriptions attests to the perceived value of the chronicle in the convent. On the front of the next page, an inscription reads "We must be very careful not to take this book out of the convent, but to take very special care of it and preserve it carefully for always," followed by another, on the back: "Take good care of this book and never take it out of the convent." Fortunately, someone did remove the manuscript before the convent archives were burned just after the French Revolution.

Even before the Revolution, however, at least four editions of Jussie's chronicle had been published. The text was first published in 1611 by the Catholic press of the Frères Du Four in Chambéry, under the somewhat misleading title *Le levain du Calvinisme, ou commencement de l'heresie de Geneve* (The Leaven of Calvinism, or Beginning of the Heresy of Geneva).[59] Calvin does not, of course, figure in Jussie's text. On the other hand, the title may not be completely inappropriate, if the editor is suggesting that the events Jussie narrates in her chronicle gave rise to Calvinism in subsequent years. The prefatory matter in the 1611 edition shows that Jussie suffered the fate of so many early modern women writers, as even her most admiring editor failed to recognize the craft of her work. In a dedicatory epistle addressed to Prince Victor-Aymé, Prince of Savoy and of the Piedmont, signed V.E.I.H.D.F. ("Valet et imprimeur Hubert du Four"),[60] Jussie's editor calls her text a "naive Tableau,"[61] and in a letter to the reader that follows the dedication, he suggests that Jussie composed her text without any attention to her language, which he describes as "utterly bare,"[62] that is, a transparent reflection of what her eyes and ears revealed to her. He asks his readers for their indulgence, advising them to "gather the roses without being stuck by the thorns."[63] The letter to the reader also reveals the editor's strongly partisan position, as Du Four calls Jussie's text "a Tragic Story, source of Lutheranism, Calvinism,

---

59. *Le levain du Calvinisme, ou commencement de l'heresie de Geneve. Faict par Reverende Soeur Jeanne de Jussie, lors religieuse de Saincte Claire de Geneve, & apres sa sortie Abbesse au Convent d'Anyssi* (Chambéry: Du Four, 1611).

60. Ganter, *Les Clarisses*, 216.

61. *Le levain du Calvinisme* (1611), "A Illustrissime Prince Victor Amé, Prince de Savoye, et de Piedmont," a2v. This and all translations from the prefatory matter in the 1611 volume are mine.

62. *Le levain du Calvinisme* (1611), "L'imprimeur au lecteur," unnumbered recto.

63. "L'imprimeur au lecteur," unnumbered verso.

Bezaism and ten thousand other heresies."[64] He mentions that a Capucin monk had been entrusted with the text, and he says that since Jussie is no longer living, there is no indiscretion in publishing her text.

Jeanne de Jussie had already been dead for a half century, however, when her text first appeared. Albert Rilliet has proposed a specific polemical motivation for the text's initial publication in 1611. Rilliet suggests that after the death of King Henry IV of France in May 1610, Charles-Emmanuel, then Duke of Savoy, was contemplating an attack on Geneva. According to Rilliet, by publishing Jussie's text in 1611 and dedicating it to Victor-Aymé, the duke's eldest son, and by telling Victor-Aymé to bring down his "victorious arm" on the enemies of the holy church, Du Four was encouraging the duke to carry out his plans.[65] In the end, the duke did not go through with the attack.

Although the 1611 Du Four edition contains most of Jussie's original manuscript, there are a few key changes and omissions. For one, the editor leaves out the introductory passage in which Jussie announces her subject matter and lists the religious and political leaders with whom she identifies, namely, Pope Clement VII and Duke Charles III of Savoy and his family. The editor omits similar remarks that appear from time to time when Jussie begins a new section in the narrative—remarks that generally begin "Sensuyt apres . . ." (The following is . . .)—as well as her concluding reference to a record of the convent's benefactors. There are numerous small changes, as the editor deletes incomplete sentences, condenses lengthy passages, corrects dates, and reorders sections to make them appear chronologically in the text. The most significant omission is Jussie's long description of the "conduct and customs of the Turks," which disappears with no explanation. Jussie's description of the Baron of Viry taking the nuns to visit his castle, including the secret chamber containing all his treasures, is also missing.

The 1611 edition of *Le levain du Calvinisme, ou commencement de l'heresie de Geneve* was followed by at least three more editions in the seventeenth century, all based on the 1611 edition, although with small changes. One edition came off the presses of Jacob Garnich in Nancy in 1626 and another off the presses of the Frères Du Four in Chambéry in 1649, both with the same title. An edition called the *Relation de l'apostasie de Genève* (Relation of the Apostasy

---

64. "L'imprimeur au lecteur," unnumbered recto.

65. Rilliet, "Notice," 7. The author of the introduction to the excerpts from Jeanne de Jussie published in *La France franciscaine* in 1913 makes the same argument. "Les clarisses de Genève-Annecy et les Protestants (1530–1535), d'après la relation de l'Abbesse Jeanne de Jussie," *La France franciscaine* 2 (1913): 20.

of Geneva) was published by René Guinard in Paris in 1682. An undated edition, also published by the Frères Du Four in Chambéry, was identical to the 1649 edition with the exception of the title page.[66]

Portions of Jussie's chronicle were translated into both German and Italian in the nineteenth century.[67] Two critical editions in French also appeared, both reproductions of the 1611 Du Four edition and both published by Jules-Guillaume Fick in Geneva.[68] The 1853 edition includes a new introduction, notes, and twenty-eight woodcut illustrations by A. Gandon. The 1865 edition includes excerpts from council registers relevant to the chronicle as well as background on the convent and biographical information on Jeanne de Jussie. Even these critical editions, however, dismiss Jussie's intentionality as a writer. Rilliet, who wrote the biographical note in the 1865 edition, sounds much like Jussie's first editor as he still calls her writing naive and un-self-conscious. "She creates," he observes, "simply by the naiveté of her narrative, picturesque effects that she in no way intended."[69] Other comments on excerpts from Jussie's text published in the nineteenth and early twentieth centuries echo these judgments. Jean-Marie-Vincent Audin, who included passages from Jussie's chronicle in a biography of John Calvin in 1856, seems more aware of Jussie's skill, but he still attributes her writing not to her head but to her heart, from which, he says, her chronicle "fell." He introduces her work with these words: "In the convent of Saint Clare . . . lived a holy girl whose mission was not limited to praying to God, consoling the afflicted, and clothing prisoners; the Lord had reserved another role for her." He continues, "Under a nun's habit, Providence had placed the heart of an artist, whom the spectacle of Bernese profanations against the material representations of art moved to tears and who, gifted with a woman's imagination, was able to transmit to the reader's soul the suffering of all kinds

66. *Le levain du Calvinisme ou commencement de l'heresie de Geneve. Faict par Reverende Soeur Jeanne de Jussie, lors religieuse à Saincte Claire de Geneve, & apres sa sortie Abbesse au Convent d'Anyssi* (Nancy: Garnich, 1626); *Histoire veritable de tout ce qui est passé dés le commencement de l'heresie de Geneve. Ensembles la sortie des Prestes[sic], Moynes, Religieux, & Religieuses. Le tout Recueilly par le R. A. P. Chanoine de l'Eglise Cathedrale de Sainct Pierre* (Chambéry: Du Four, 1649); *Relation de l'apostasie de Geneve, Par Soeur Jeanne de Jussie, pour lors religieuse du Convent de Sainte Claire de Geneve* (Paris: Guinard, 1682).

67. "Auszug aus dem Tagebuch der Schwester Johanna von Jussie, einer Nonne im St. Clara-kloster zu Genf, beim Beginn der Reformation daselbst," *Der Pilger* 2 (1843): 256–59, 364–66, 372–75; *Istoria memorabile del principio dell'eresia di Genevra per Suor Giovanna di Jussie Monaca Francescana,* ed. and trans. Marcellino da Civezza (Prato: Ranieri Guasti, 1882).

68. *Le levain du Calvinisme, ou commencement de l'heresie de Geneve. Faict par Reverende Soeur Jeanne de Jussie, lors religieuse à Saincte Claire de Geneve, et apres sa sortie Abbesse au Convent d'Anyssi,* ed. Gustave Revilliod (Geneva: Jules-Guillaume Fick, 1853); *Le Levain du Calvinisme,* 1865 (cited above, note 5).

69. Rilliet, "Notice," 16 (my translation).

that she had to endure." He concludes, "Let Geneva dig through its library, it will never find more poignant pages than those that fell from the pen—or rather, the heart—of this pious nun."[70] In 1913, *La France franciscaine* published about a hundred pages from the 1682 edition of the chronicle, with similar introductory comments.[71] It is only in recent years that scholars have begun to give Jussie's work the critical reading it merits.[72]

In 1974, excerpts from Jussie's narrative were published along with pieces of other chronicles of sixteenth-century French-speaking Switzerland written by Bonivard, Pierrefleur, and Fromment.[73] Until recently, however, none of Jussie's early editors had published her text in its entirely. With his critical edition of the text in 1996, titled simply the *Petite chronique*, Helmut Feld finally made Jeanne de Jussie's full chronicle available to the public.[74] It is his edition of the text that has served as the basis for this English-language translation.

70. Jean-Marie-Vincent Audin, *Histoire de la vie, des ouvrages et des doctrines de Calvin* (Paris: L. Maison, 1856), 1: 172–73 (my translation).

71. "Les clarisses de Genève-Annecy et les protestants (1530–1535)", 15–117. The editor of the text for *La France franciscaine* also refers to excerpts published in a short history of the Order of Saint Clare written by an abbess in Lyons, *Histoire abrégée de l'Ordre de Sainte-Claire*, 2: 184–207. Cited in *La France franciscaine*, 25.

72. One monograph-length study has been devoted to Jussie, Henri Roth, "Jeanne de Jussie et le *Levain du Calvinisme*: Attitudes mentales d'une clarisse du XVIe face à la Réforme" (M.A. thesis, Université de Genève, 1983).

73. Maurice Bossard and Louis Junod, eds., *Chroniqueurs du XVIe siècle: Bonivard, Pierrefleur, Jeanne de Jussie, Fromment* (Lausanne: Bibliothèque romande, 1974). That same year, Robert M. Kingdon published brief excerpts translated into English by Raymond A. Mentzer, Jr., "Jeanne de Jussie, Calvinist Germs or the Beginning of Heresy in Geneva," in *Transition and Revolution: Problems and Issues of European Renaissance and Reformation History*, ed. Robert M. Kingdon (Minneapolis: Burgess, 1974), 87–95.

74. Feld also published a German translation of the text that same year. *Kleine Chronik* (Mainz: von Zabern, 1996).

VOLUME EDITOR'S
BIBLIOGRAPHY

EDITIONS AND TRANSLATIONS OF JEANNE DE JUSSIE'S CHRONICLE (IN CHRONOLOGICAL ORDER)

Le levain du Calvinisme, ou commencement de l'heresie de Geneve. Faict par Reverende Soeur Jeanne de Jussie, lors religieuse de Saincte Claire de Geneve, & apres sa sortie Abbesse au Convent d'Anyssi. Chambéry: Du Four, 1611.

Le levain du Calvinisme, ou commencement de l'heresie de Geneve. Faict par Reverende Soeur Jeanne de Jussie, lors religieuse à Saincte Claire de Geneve, & apres sa sortie Abbesse au Convent d'Anyssi. Nancy: Garnich, 1626. (This edition is very similar, but not identical, to the 1611 edition.)

Histoire veritable de tout ce qui est passé dés le commencement de l'heresie de Geneve. Ensembles la sortie des Prestes[sic], Moynes, Religieux, & Religieuses. Le tout Recueilly par le R. A. P. Chanoine de l'Eglise Cathedrale de Sainct Pierre. Chambéry: Du Four, 1649. (Some copies of this edition, which may have appeared before 1649, have an undated title page.)

Relation de l'apostasie de Geneve, Par Soeur Jeanne de Jussie, pour lors religieuse du Convent de Sainte Claire de Geneve. Paris: Guinard, 1682. (This edition is also very similar, but not identical, to the 1611 edition.)

"Auszug aus dem Tagebuch der Schwester Johanna von Jussie, einer Nonne im St. Clarakloster zu Genf, beim Beginn der Reformation daselbst." *Der Pilger* 2 (1843): 256–59, 364–66, 372–75.

Le levain du Calvinisme, ou Commencement de l'heresie de Geneve. Faict par Reverende Soeur Jeanne de Jussie, lors religieuse à Saincte Claire de Geneve, et apres sa sortie Abbesse au Convent d'Anyssi. Edited by Gustave Revilliod. Geneva: Jules-Guillaume Fick, 1853. (This edition is essentially a reprint of the 1611 edition, with a new introduction by Revilliod, illustrations by A. Gandon, and notes.)

"La Soeur Jeanne de Jussie." *Histoire de la vie, des ouvrages et des doctrines de Calvin,* Jean-Marie-Vincent Audin. Vol. 1, pp. 172–91. Paris: L. Maison, 1856.

Le levain du calvinisme, ou commencement de l'heresie de Geneve, faict par Soeur Jeanne de Jussie. Suivi de notes justificatives et d'une notice sur l'ordre religieux de Sainte-Claire et sur la communauté des Clarisses à Genève par Ad.-C. Grivel. Edited by Gustave Revilliod. Geneva: Jules-Guillaume Fick, 1865. (This edition is another reprint of the 1611 edition, with notes, excerpts from the registers of the Genevan city council, and notices on the convent and on Jeanne de Jussie.)

Istoria memorabile del principio dell'eresia di Genevra per Suor Giovanna di Jussie Monaca Francescana. Edited and translated by Marcellino da Civezza. Prato: Ranieri Guasti, 1882.

"Les clarisses de Genève-Annecy et les protestants (1530–1535), d'après la relation de l'Abbesse Jeanne de Jussie." *La France franciscaine* 2 (1913): 15–117.

"Jeanne de Jussie." *Chroniqueurs du XVIe siècle: Bonivard, Pierrefleur, Jeanne de Jussie, Fromment.* Edited by Maurice Bossard and Louis Junod, 151–214. Lausanne: Bibliothèque romande, 1974.

Petite chronique. Edited by Helmut Feld. Mainz: Von Zabern, 1996.

Kleine Chronik. Edited and translated by Helmut Feld. Mainz: Von Zabern, 1996.

PRIMARY SOURCES

Augustine of Hippo. *The City of God against the Pagans.* Translated by Robert W. Dyson. Cambridge: Cambridge University Press, 1998.

Dentière, Marie. *Epistle to Marguerite de Navarre and Preface to a Sermon by John Calvin.* Edited and translated by Mary B. McKinley. Chicago: University of Chicago Press, 2004.

———. *Epistre très utile, faicte et composée par une femme chrestienne de Tornay, envoyée à la Royne de Navarre, seur du Roy de France, contre les Turcs, Juifz, Infideles, Faulxchrestiens, Anabaptistes et Lutheriens, [à Anvers, chez Martin l'empereur].* Geneva: Jean Girard, 1539.

———. "Preface to a Sermon by John Calvin." Printed in *Les conditions et vertus requises en la femme fidèle et bonne mesnagere: Contenues au xxxi. Chapitre des Proverbes de Salomon. Mis en forme de cantique, par Théodore de Besze. Plus, un sermon de la modestie des Femmes en leurs habillemens, par. M. Jean Calvin. Outre, plusieurs chansons spirituelles, en Musique.* 1561.

Friedberg, Aemilius, ed. *Corpus Iuris Canonici.* Leipzig, 1879.

Fromment, Anthoine. *Les actes et gestes merveilleux de la cité de Genève. Nouvellement convertie à l'Evangile faictz du temps de leur Reformation et comment ils l'ont receu redigez par escript en forme de Chroniques Annales ou Hystoyres commençant l'an MDXXXII.* Edited by Gustave Revilliod. Geneva: Jules-Guillaume Fick, 1854.

Gacy, Jean. *Deploration de la cité de Genesve.* Edited by Jules Vuy. Geneva: Tremblay, 1882.

———. *Trialogue nouveau contenant lexpression des erreurs de Martin Luther.* Geneva: Wigand Köln, 1524.

La guerre et deslivrance de la ville de Genesve [composée et publiée en 1536 par Marie Dentière de Tournay, ancienne abbesse et femme d'Antoine Froment.] Edited by Albert Rilliet and included in volume 20 of the *Mémoires de la Société d'Histoire et d'Archéologie de Genève.* Geneva: Charles Schuchardt, 1881. Originally published in 1536 as *La guerre et délivrance de la ville de Genesve fidèlement faicte et composée par un Marchand demourant en icelle* [The war and deliverance of the city of Geneva, faithfully told and written by a merchant living in that city].

Pirckheimer, Caritas. *Briefe der Äbtissin Caritas Pirckheimer des St. Klara-Klosters zu Nürnberg nach der Erstveröffentlichung von Josef Pfanner, übertragen von Benedicta Schrott.* Edited by P. Georg Deichstetter. St. Ottilien: EOS Verlag, 1984.

———. *Denkwürdigkeiten aus dem Reformationszeitalter: Charitas Pirckheimer.* Edited by Constantin Höfler. Osnabrück: Otto Zeller, 1984.

Qur'an Translation. Translated by Mahomodali H. Shakir. Elmhurst, N.Y.: Tahrike Tarsile Qu'ran, 1985.

Rem, Katherine, and Bernhart Rem. "Antwurt zwayer Closter frauen im Katheriner Closter zu Augspurg an Bernhart Remen Und hernach seyn gegen Antwurt / The Answer of Two Nuns in the Katherine Convent of Augsburg to Bernhart Rem and afterwards His Answer to This." In *Convents Confront the Reformation: Catholic and Protestant Nuns in Germany.* Edited by Merry Wiesner-Hanks, 27–37. Milwaukee: Marquette University Press, 1996.

SECONDARY SOURCES

Backus, Irena. "Les clarisses de la rue Verdaine / The Poor Clares of the Rue Verdaine." In *Le guide des femmes disparues / Forgotten Women of Geneva.* Edited by Anne-Marie Käppeli, 309–25. Geneva: Metropolis, 1993.

————. "Marie Dentière: Un cas de féminisme théologique à l'époque de la Réforme?" *Bulletin de la Société de l'Histoire du Protestantisme Français* 137 (1991): 177–95.

Barnaud, Jean. *Pierre Viret: Sa vie et son oeuvre.* Saint-Amans: G. Carayol, 1911. Nieuwkoop: B. de Graaf, 1973.

Blackburn, William M. *William Farel and the Story of the Swiss Reform.* Philadelphia: Presbyterian Board of Publication, 1865.

Blaisdell, Charmarie Jenkins. "Religion, Gender, and Class: Nuns and Authority in Early Modern France." In *Changing Identities in Early Modern France.* Edited by Michael Wolfe, 147–68. Durham, N.C.: Duke University Press, 1999.

Bothe, Catherine M. "Écriture féminine de la Réformation: Le témoignage de Marie Dentière." *Romance Languages Annual* 5 (1993): 15–19.

Cross, F. L., ed. *The Oxford Dictionary of the Christian Church.* 3d ed. Oxford: Oxford University Press, 1997.

Davis, Natalie Zemon. *Society and Culture in Early Modern France.* Stanford: Stanford University Press, 1975.

Deichstetter, Georg, ed. *Caritas Pirckheimer: Ordensfrau und Humanistin: ein Vorbild für die Ökumene: Festschrift zum 450. Todstag.* Cologne: Wienand, 1982.

Douglass, Jane Dempsey. "Marie Dentière's Use of Scripture in Her Theology of History." In *Biblical Hermeneutics in Historical Perspective: Studies in Honor of Karlfried Froehlich on his Sixtieth Birthday.* Edited by Mark Burrows and Paul Rorem, 227–44. Grand Rapids, Mich.: William B. Eerdmans, 1991.

Dufour, Théophile. "Notes sur le Couvent de Sainte-Claire à Genève." *Mémoires et Documents publiés par la Société d'Histoire et d'Archéologie de Genève* 20 (1879–1880): 119–45.

Eire, Carlos M. N. *War against the Idols: The Reformation of Worship from Erasmus to Calvin.* Cambridge: Cambridge University Press, 1986.

Elwood, Christopher. *The Body Broken: The Calvinist Doctrine of the Eucharist and the Symbolization of Power in Sixteenth-Century France.* Oxford: Oxford University Press, 1999.

Feld, Helmut. Introduction to the *Petite chronique* by Jeanne de Jussie. Edited by Helmut Feld, xiii—lxxv. Mainz: Von Zabern, 1996.

————. "Jeanne de Jussie: Der Stand der Jungfräulichkeit und das große Gut der Ehe." In *Frauen des Mittelalters: Zwanzig geistige Profile.* Edited by Helmut Feld, 309–25. Cologne: Böhlau, 2000.

Gaberel, Jean. *Histoire de l'eglise de Genève depuis le commencement de la Réformation jusqu'en 1815.* Geneva: Cherbuliez and Jullien, 1853.

Ganter, Edmond. *Les Clarisses de Genève: 1473–1535—1793.* Geneva: Société Catholique d'Histoire, 1949.

————. "Les Clarisses de Genève et d'Annecy." *La Revue Savoisienne* 90 (1949): 58–87.

Gilchrist, Roberta. *Gender and Archaeology: Contesting the Past*. New York: Routledge, 1999.

——. *Gender and Material Culture: The Archaeology of Religious Women*. New York: Routledge, 1994.

Godefroy, Frédéric. *Dictionnaire de l'ancienne langue française et de tous ses dialectes du IXe au XVe siècle*. 10 vols. Geneva: Slatkine, 1982.

Grivel, Ad.-C. "Notice sur l'ordre religieux de Sainte-Claire et sur la communauté des Clarisses de Genève." In *Le levain du Calvinisme, ou commencement de l'heresie de Geneve, faict par Reverende Soeur Jeanne de Jussie. Suivi de notes justificatives et d'une notice sur l'Ordre religieux de Sainte-Claire et sur la communauté des Clarisses à Genève par Ad.-C. Grivel*, by Jeanne de Jussie, 267–93. Geneva: Jules-Guillaume Fick, 1865.

Guillaume Farel, 1489–1565: Biographie nouvelle écrite d'après les documents originaux par un groupe d'historiens, professeurs et pasteurs de Suisse, de France et d'Italie. 1930. Geneva: Slatkine Reprints, 1978.

Head, Thomas. "A Propagandist for the Reform: Marie Dentière." In *Women Writers of the Renaissance and Reformation*. Edited by Katharina M. Wilson, 260–83. Athens: University of Georgia Press, 1987.

Higman, Francis. *La diffusion de la Réforme en France, 1520–1565*. Geneva: Labor et Fides, 1992.

Hillerbrand, Hans J., ed. *The Oxford Encyclopedia of the Reformation*. 4 vols. Oxford: Oxford University Press, 1996.

Huguet, Edmond. *Dictionnaire de la langue française du seizième siècle*. 7 vols. Paris: Didier, 1925–1967.

Kemp, William, and Diane Desrosiers-Bonin. "Marie d'Ennetières et la petite grammaire hébraïque de sa fille d'après la dédicace de l'*Epistre* à Marguerite de Navarre." *Bibliothèque d'Humanisme et Renaissance* 50, no. 1 (1998): 117–34.

Kingdon, Robert M. "Was the Protestant Reformation a Revolution? The Case of Geneva." In *Transition and Revolution: Problems and Issues of European Renaissance and Reformation History*. Edited by Robert M. Kingdon, 53–107. Minneapolis: Burgess, 1974.

Klaus, Carrie F. "Architecture and Sexual Identity: Jeanne de Jussie's Narrative of the Reformation of Geneva." *Feminist Studies* 29, no. 2 (2003): 279–97.

Langbein, John H. *Torture and the Law of Proof*. Chicago: University of Chicago Press, 1977.

Lazard, Madeleine. "Deux soeurs ennemies, Marie Dentière et Jeanne de Jussie: Nonnes et réformées à Genève." In *Les réformes: Enracinements socio-culturels*. Edited by B. Chevalier and C. Sauzat, 233–49. Paris: La Maisnie, 1985.

Monter, E. William. *Calvin's Geneva*. New York: Wiley and Sons, 1967.

Naef, Henri. *Bezanson Hugues: Patriote et homme d'état*. Geneva: Jullien, 1933.

——. "Claude d'Estavayer, Évêque de Belley, Confident de Charles II Duc de Savoie (1483?—1534)." *Revue d'Histoire ecclésiastique suisse* 50 (1956): 85–137.

——. *Les origines de la Réforme à Genève*. 2 vols. Geneva: Droz, 1968.

Newman, Barbara. *From Virile Woman to WomanChrist*. Philadelphia: University of Pennsylvania Press, 1995.

Perrenoud, Alfred. *La Population de Genève du seizième au début du dix-neuvième siècle: Étude démographique*. Geneva: Jullien, 1979.

Pfister, Louis. "En souvenir des Clarisses de Genève-Annecy." *La Revue Savoisienne* 90 (1949): 52–57.

Rauscher, Julius. "Der Halleysche Komet im Jahre 1531 und die Reformatoren." *Zeitschrift für Kirchengeschichte* 32 (1911): 259–76.

Rilliet, Albert. "Notice sur Jeanne de Jussie et sur le livre intitulé Le Levain du Calvinisme." In *Le levain du Calvinisme, ou commencement de l'heresie de Geneve, faict par Reverende Soeur Jeanne de Jussie. Suivi de notes justificatives et d'une notice sur l'Ordre religieux de Sainte-Claire et sur la communauté des Clarisses à Genève par Ad.-C. Grivel.* Edited by Gustave Revilliod, 1–23 (numbered separately; not included in all copies of this edition). Geneva: Jules-Guillaume Fick, 1865.

Roth, Henri. "Jeanne de Jussie et le *Levain du Calvinisme:* Attitudes mentales d'une clarisse du XVIe face à la Réforme." M.A. thesis, University of Geneva, 1983.

———. "Une femme auteur du 16e siècle: Jeanne de Jussie." *Revue du Vieux Genève* 19 (1989): 5–13.

Saincte-Marthe, Scévole de, and Louis de. *Histoire généalogique de la Maison de France.* Paris: N. Buon, 1628.

Schwoebel, Robert. *The Shadow of the Crescent: The Renaissance Image of the Turk (1453–1517).* New York: Saint Martin's, 1967.

Skenazi, Cynthia. "Marie Dentière et la prédication des femmes." *Renaissance and Reformation/Renaissance et Réforme* 21, no. 1 (1997): 5–18.

Valensi, Lucette. *The Birth of the Despot: Venice and the Sublime Porte.* Translated by Arthur Denner. Ithaca, N.Y.: Cornell University Press, 1993.

Vorreux, Père Damien, ed. *Sainte Claire d'Assise, Documents: Biographie, écrits, procès et bulle de canonisation, textes de chroniqueurs, textes législatifs et tables.* Paris: Éditions franciscaines, 2002.

Vuarnet, E. "Glossaire du Livre de Jeanne de Jussie." *Revue Savoisienne* 43 (1902): 290–93.

Vuy, Jules. *Jeanne de Jussie et les soeurs de Sainte-Claire.* Geneva: Trembley, 1881.

Wengler, Elisabeth M. "Women, Religion, and Reform in Sixteenth-Century Geneva." Ph. D. diss.,Boston College, 1999.

Woodford, Charlotte. *Nuns as Historians in Early Modern Germany.* Oxford: Oxford University Press, 2002.

NOTE ON TRANSLATION

I am deeply grateful to Helmut Feld for his painstaking transcription of both sixteenth-century manuscripts of Jussie's text and for the extensive documentation he provides, particularly for all the work he did to identify persons, verify dates, and check events. This English translation of Jussie's chronicle is based almost exclusively on manuscript A, the one presumed to be in Jussie's own hand, as it appears in Feld's edition. I have used manuscript B only as an aid for clarifying obscure passages. At times, the second manuscript was helpful, since the early modern copyist's instinctive sense for the idioms of sixteenth-century French was surely more reliable than my own. In many cases, however, the copyist seems to have been as confused as I was and chose to revise or simply omit a difficult passage. In addition to these revisions and omissions, the writer of manuscript B made many deliberate stylistic and orthographical changes. I have tried to identify in notes any potentially significant discrepancies between the two manuscripts, and I have included a note anytime I had to make a choice in the translation in order to resolve an ambiguity in the original French.

I have followed Jussie's original French text closely and aimed for accuracy and clarity above all else. I have tried to convey in English Jussie's conversational style as much as possible, although whenever a choice had to be made between accuracy and style, I have opted for accuracy. Jussie's syntax is typical of middle French. She uses the present participle where the simple past or the imperfect would be found in modern French, composes very long sentences, and uses many doubled expressions ("wisely and sensibly," "quickly and in great haste," "destroyed and demolished"). I have attempted to convey the liveliness and richness of her language without preserving elements that would add a false archaism. Thus, I have often translated present participles with the past tense and I have occasionally broken up very long sentences. I have retained the doubled near synonyms as much as possible. I have occasionally clarified antecedents in pronoun-heavy passages.

There are, of course, no paragraph divisions in the original text. In most, although not all, cases, I have followed Feld's paragraph divisions. I have used the conventions of punctuation characteristic of modern English. As mentioned above, a modern English translation cannot reflect the orthographical diversity of middle French. For personal names, I have chosen a spelling that most resembles modern French and used it consistently throughout the text. I have left titles such as "Monseigneur" and "Madame" in French in an attempt to convey the flavor of the original. Jussie uses very few capital letters in her text. To maintain this relatively unmarked style, I have capitalized proper nouns only, including references to God and related figures, again following conventions of modern English.

Helmut Feld chose *Petite chronique* as a title for Jussie's text, a phrase that comes from her introductory passage to the narrative, a passage omitted in 1611 and in subsequent editions of the text. The introduction begins, "Sensuyt une petite cronique contenant ung petit en partie de ce qua aeste fait dens genesve . . ." (The following is a short chronicle containing a small part of what was done in Geneva . . .). Following Feld, I have called Jussie's narrative simply the *Short Chronicle*.

Unless otherwise indicated, all dates, identification and background of persons, and references to scripture and canon law come from Feld. Feld also has rich information from Genevan council registers, which was unfortunately too lengthy to include in this English translation. All other notes are my own.

Numbers in brackets refer to page numbers in Feld's edition.

Carrie F. Klaus

THE SHORT CHRONICLE

PROLOGUE

Jesus Maria Franciscus Clara

The following is a short chronicle containing a small part of what was done in Geneva because of Eidguenotry[1] and heretics and the Lutheran sect,[2] beginning in 1526, when the Holy Father Pope Clement VII[3] was in the Holy Apostolic See, and the most illustrious, most high, powerful, and formidable Lord Charles III,[4] and the most illustrious, excellent Lady Madame Beatrice of Portugal,[5] his most noble wife, and the most excellent Louis, Monseigneur the Prince of the Piedmont,[6] Philibert Emmanuel, Monseigneur the Lord of Bresse,[7] and [4] the most excellent Lady Catherine Charlotte,[8] their most noble children, were in the magnificent Duchy of

---

1. *Eidguenots* (also *Eyguenots, Eydgenos, Anguenotz, Enguenotz,* etc., from the German *Eidgenossen,* "confederates"; cf. *Huguenot*) refers to partisans of the Swiss cantons of Bern and Fribourg in the struggle for political control of Geneva. The pejorative term *Mammelukes* (also *Mammellus, Malmellus, Mamelus, Mamelucz, Mammelucz,* etc., from the Arabic *Mamluk,* literally "slave", but used to refer to Christians who had converted to Islam) was applied by their detractors to the supporters of the House of Savoy, implying that they were traitors to Christianity.

2. Throughout her chronicle, Jussie uses the term "Lutheran" indiscriminately to describe any Christian of Reformed persuasion, especially the followers of Guillaume Farel, Pierre Viret, and Antoine Fromment in Geneva.

3. Giulio de' Medeci, pope (1523–34).

4. Charles III (1486–1553) became Duke of Savoy in 1504. When Jussie uses the term *Monseigneur* in her chronicle, it is almost invariably in reference to Charles III. *Monseigneur of Geneva* refers to Pierre de la Baume, the Bishop of Geneva (see below, note 11).

5. Beatrice of Portugal (1504–38), daughter of King Emmanuel I of Portugal and of Maria of Castile.

6. Louis of Savoy, Prince of the Piedmont (1523–36).

7. Emmanuel-Philibert of Savoy, Prince of the Piedmont (1528–80), who succeeded his father as Duke of Savoy in 1553.

8. Catherine of Savoy (1529–36).

Savoy. Also, the most high illustrious Count of the Genevois, Monseigneur Philippe of Savoy, the Duke of Nemours.[9]

ALLIANCE AMONG GENEVA, BERN, AND FRIBOURG

In the year of the incarnation of Our Lord 1526, in the month of March, ambassadors from Bern and Fribourg renewed longstanding alliances with the town of Geneva,[10] which was wickedly rebelling against the illustrious Prince of Savoy, completely rejecting his power and lordship and spurning all the nobles. At that time the Bishop of Geneva was a powerful lord named Pierre de la Baume,[11] of the House of Montrevel in Bresse. People were saying he had agreed [5] to the alliance, which he suffered for later, along with the rest of the country, as you will see written below in part and in brief, since it is impossible to write even half of what happened.

FIFTY-TWO NOBLE BURGHERS OF GENEVA LEAVE
THE CITY

The most prominent townspeople, wisely and sensibly considering the damage that could come from such an arrangement, did not agree to it, so at least fifty-two noble burghers, wealthy merchants, and lawyers left town, which greatly upset the citizens, and to get revenge they looted their houses and shops and sold all their property, furnishings, large wares, inheritances, and other priceless goods, to the great detriment and damage of the lords, merchants, and honorable people. And they[12] called them[13] traitors, saying they wanted to surrender the city to monseigneur and had written treacherous letters, which was not true. And they accused them of worse, saying they had made false measures for wheat and wine. But they could not prove it, and so to remain loyal to monseigneur, they left the city and were called

9. Philippe of Savoy, younger brother of Duke Charles III of Savoy, Duke of Nemours (1490–1533), Bishop of Geneva 1495–1509. (Incomplete sentence in manuscript A.)

10. The first treaty was signed in 1477 between the Bishop of Geneva and the victors over Charles the Bold. In 1518, the citizens of Geneva signed a treaty with Fribourg that was directed against the Duke of Savoy. The treaty of 1526 was ratified on February 24 and 25 by the Council of Two Hundred. Ambassadors from Bern and Fribourg arrived in Geneva on March 11.

11. Pierre de la Baume (1477–1544), Bishop of Geneva (1522–43). Revilliod includes a biography of Pierre de la Baume in his 1853 edition of Jussie's chronicle, i–viii. See also Monter, *Calvin's Geneva*, 38–39.

12. Opponents of the Duke of Savoy who favored the alliances with Bern and Fribourg.

13. Supporters of the Duke of Savoy who opposed the alliances.

banished and Mammelukes,[14] the clergy and other people. And [6] from then on, more and more people started to hold grudges against monseigneur and to spurn the nobles and the clerics.

EVENTS OF THE YEARS 1526-28

In the year 1527,[15] monseigneur forbade all of his subjects in all his lands, under great penalty, to bring any kind of supplies into the town. And that interdiction lasted from the Feast of Saint Luke until the Feast of the Conception of Our Lady,[16] when all was dropped at the request of Bern and Fribourg and supplies returned as before. That whole year there was great dissension and hatred among the citizens and their neighbors. At that time, in the month of December, a very old and honorable burgher was put in prison, a rich merchant named Sire François Cartelier, who was accused of being a Mammeluke and held prisoner until the next March.[17] He was ransomed at a high cost to Monseigneur of Geneva,[18] and it was said that [7] the money was paid in measures of wheat. Nevertheless, he was condemned as a traitor by the judge of the high court of the city[19] and sentenced to have his head cut off and his body quartered and put in the four corners of the city. And, indeed, he was turned over to the hangman, who promptly put a rope around his neck. But Monseigneur of Geneva's chief steward[20] delivered him from the hands of the people who wished to slay him, and he was put back in prison villainously at the high court judge's orders and stripped of his robe and his cap, and the executioner was ordered to wear them as if they were his own, out of mockery. His family tried to buy them back for 13 écus au soleil,[21] but the executioner would not give them up.

14. See above, note 1.

15. Actually 1526. See Feld's edition of the *Petite chronique*, 6, n. 12.

16. October 18–December 8, 1526.

17. François Cartelier, syndic (1516–21), was arrested on December 13, 1526. See Feld's edition of the *Petite chronique*, 6, n. 15.

18. Bishop Pierre de la Baume.

19. Cartelier was actually sentenced by the Small Council. See Feld's edition of the *Petite chronique*, 7, n. 17.

20. Probably Carolus de Fago, also known as Chiveluto, abbot from San Mauro (near Turin). See Feld's edition of the *Petite chronique*, 7, n. 18.

21. There were many different coins in circulation in sixteenth-century Geneva. At this time, the écu was worth about six florins. See Jean Gaberel, *Histoire de l'Église de Genève depuis le commencement de la Réformation jusqu'en 1815* (Geneva: Cherbuliez and Jullien Frères, 1853), vol. 1, pt. 2, p. 30. The *écu au soleil*, the only gold coin minted in France after 1484, had the image of the sun stamped on it.

During Holy Week, they took the merchant out of prison and dragged him through the city by a halter, and little children mocked him and threw mud at him and spat in his face just like the Jews[22] did to Our Lord. And, as [8] it was God's will, he escaped from their hands, and, old and feeble as he was, he fled, and no one could catch him. His family paid five thousand écus of ransom for him, and all his property was confiscated: his house, furnishings, fabric shop, and other possessions inside the city walls. He took refuge with his wife and children in Bourg-en-Bresse, and he died there in 1531. And he was found innocent of all the crimes he had been accused of by immoral envy.

That same year on the night of the Feast of Saint Peter ad Vincula,[23] Monseigneur of Geneva, seeing the coming troubles, stole across the lake to take refuge in his Abbey of Saint Claude.[24]

EVENTS OF THE YEAR 1529

Afterward, in the year 1529, some gentlemen formed a brotherhood they called the Brotherhood of the Spoon[25] [9], and the leader of this group was Monseigneur [François de Ternier] of Pontverre, a noble knight, valiant and hardy in chivalry. Those gentlemen gathered in Nyon to pray to God for the service of the church and the deliverance of all their ancestors. And the week after Our Lord's birth, on a Saturday, the Feast of the Octave of Saint John [January 3], the Knight and Lord of Pontverre, Messire François, bid the nobles farewell to return home to Madame his wife, and he set off for Geneva with no ill intentions. When he was on the bridge over the Rhone, he was treacherously accosted and was unable to defend himself. His men fled. Seeing that he could not escape, he surrendered and begged them humbly for mercy. But the brazen Genevan men struck him all over and dealt him more than fifteen mortal blows to the stomach and then carried him to the chapel of a nearby hospital and killed him. It was said that after he was dead they cut him all to pieces and stuck three swords into his lower and private parts in

22. Like many writers of her time, Jussie compares her enemies to Jews in order to rally her audience against them. Protestants and Catholics alike shared a common enmity of Jews—and of Turks—in this period.

23. August 1, the feast of the patron of the cathedral of Geneva, also known as Lammas Day and the Feast of Saint Peter's Chains.

24. Pierre de la Baume had been Abbot of Saint Claude since March 5, 1511. After this nighttime departure from Geneva on August 1, 1528, he did not return again until July 1, 1533.

25. An association of some of the nobles from around Geneva against the city. For more information, see Monter, *Calvin's Geneva*, 46.

great insult and mockery. He stayed there that whole night and the next day, which was Sunday [January 4], all day long until four o'clock in the evening, when he was taken and buried at the Franciscan monastery[26] without [10] any rites because his family, mourning his death, did not come. After that terrible act a great disturbance and uproar arose among messieurs the nobles, not only his family but all the nobles of the land, against the Genevans, and so merchants did not dare leave the city to go about their business for fear they would be killed or robbed by those gentlemen and their men. However, the good prince saw to it that the merchants, who could hardly bear it, were not harmed as they came and went in his lands.

GARRISON OF THOSE FROM BERN AND FRIBOURG IN GENEVA

The next Lent eight hundred allied soldiers from Bern and Fribourg arrived. And they arrived in Geneva on Shrove Sunday[27] and set up their garrison because the Genevans were afraid the people in the surrounding country would harm them, and they ate meat and all kinds of food during Lent, just like at other times, and they drove up the prices of all supplies. At that time, an agreement was reached [11] among monseigneur and the city and the Swiss, and everyone returned to their cities, including messieurs the nobles who had gathered in Gaillard[28] to resist the Swiss at great expense to the surrounding countryside.

Also, from that first Sunday on, the clergy of the cathedral, parishes, and religious houses inside the city walls were forbidden to ring any bells from seven o'clock in the evening until seven o'clock in the morning, and they could not even sound the city clock. They did not ring the bells or say the "Ave Maria"[29] after compline,[30] which was very strange and seemed like a time of darkness.[31]

---

26. The Rive Monastery in Geneva.

27. February 14, 1529. Shrovetide is traditionally the three days preceding Ash Wednesday.

28. Approximately ten kilometers southwest of Geneva.

29. "Hail Mary," the first words of a common prayer in honor of the Virgin Mary.

30. The last of the canonical hours, a liturgical office traditionally recited just before bedtime.

31. "From noon on, darkness came over the whole land until three in the afternoon" (Mt 27:45); "He opened the shaft of the bottomless pit, and from the shaft rose smoke like the smoke of a great furnace, and the sun and the air were darkened with the smoke from the shaft" (Rv 9:2); "The fifth angel poured his bowl on the throne of the beast, and its kingdom was plunged into darkness" (Rv 16:10). These and all subsequent citations from the Bible come from the *New Revised Standard Version*.

GATHERING OF THE NOBLES IN GAILLARD

On Holy Wednesday [March 24, 1529] a great company of gentlemen gathered at the Castle of Gaillard, and they plotted among themselves to scale the city walls secretly at night. To do it they sent many soldiers out to the roads to detain everyone leaving the city and not let them go back in. [12] They were planning to attack the city at two o'clock in the morning on Holy Thursday, the Feast of the Annunciation of Our Lady.[32] Monseigneur was warned about it, and the good, peace-loving prince sent out Monseigneur of Balleyson[33] quickly and in great haste, and he went so swiftly that he reached Gaillard around midnight; he presented and showed the gentlemen his letters from monseigneur, which forbade anyone to proceed any further under penalty of death, which upset the nobles, for there were already at least ten thousand men ready to take action, on horse and on foot, and, very upset, they all followed the orders and went home, including the ones who were guarding the roads. From then on, the sisters of Saint Clare were not allowed to ring bells for matins,[34] although they recited them[35] at the usual hour of midnight, until the following Christmas [1529], when they asked messeigneurs of the Council[36] to allow them to ring bells for matins, and their request was granted under the following conditions: that they not ring them very long and not as a signal. The poor[37] sisters lived in great fear and subjection. God alone knows. [13]

SIEGE OF GENEVA BY THE NOBLES OF THE LAND

In the year 1530, in the month of September, the gentlemen gathered again, and without monseigneur's knowledge, they decided to frighten the city. They attacked the town on both sides of the Rhone and pillaged and carried off everything they could find that belonged to the Genevans known as Eidguenots. That is a German word, which means in French "good

---

32. March 25, 1529. Also called Maundy Thursday.

33. Balleyson is in Savoy.

34. The first of the canonical hours, a liturgical office traditionally recited during the night.

35. In accordance with the Rule of Saint Clare (chap. 3, no. 1), the Poor Clares recited the office instead of singing it. See Vorreux, *Sainte Claire d'Assise*, 111.

36. See the volume editor's introduction, note 13.

37. Jussie uses the adjective "poor" (*povre*) liberally, not only to evoke the Poor Clares' rejection of material possessions but also to refer figuratively to the state of Christians (e.g., "the poor world", *le povre monde*), who are in dire need of salvation.

allies."[38] And they also took away their livestock and caused great damage. The Genevans, who had been warned, prepared to defend themselves and quickly destroyed the bridge over the Arve. But it was soon repaired by the gentlemen who came in force to the faubourg[39] of La Corraterie, near the Dominican monastery and next to Notre Dame de Grâce,[40] and to [14] the faubourg of Saint Antoine, and they laid siege to the city from all sides, so that no one was able or dared to go out, although they did not hurt them because monseigneur, who had been warned, quickly sent out several lords of his house to put an end to the actions under penalty of death. At his orders the gentlemen left without doing any other harm. But, alas, it was to the great detriment of the land, as you will see. Because the Swiss Germans had already been told about the gathering, and according to honorable people, about twenty-five thousand of them, all warriors, came directly to Savoy in great fury and haste to help their allies in Geneva.

THE SWISS TROOPS DEVASTATE THE AREA
AROUND GENEVA

On the Feast of Monseigneur Saint Francis [October 4, 1530] on a Tuesday at ten o'clock in the morning, the Swiss quartermaster arrived in Morges, a small city in the Vaud, to seek housing for the army, and when the soldiers arrived, they immediately went to the lake and drew in a huge ship loaded with at least a thousand golden écus worth of city property, which was being taken to the other side of the lake to Nyon and Thonon. But it was captured by the Swiss [15] and taken to Lausanne under their protection. On Wednesday, Thursday, and Friday [October 5–7], the two cantons of Bern and Fribourg arrived in Morges and did much damage. For when they left their lands and entered monseigneur's, they began to pillage, rob, and plunder the poor people, and they did not leave any wheat, wine, food, or furnishings in the houses, which was a very piteous thing. They pillaged and then burned the houses and castles of nobles everywhere, which was no small loss.

When the Bernese were in Morges, some of them were housed in the Franciscan monastery, and they did many great unspeakable evils and injus-

---

38. See above, note 1.

39. A neighborhood just outside the city walls.

40. The Augustinian monastery Notre Dame de Grâce was founded in the late fifteenth century. For information on this monastery and on the lively neighborhood around it, see Revilliod's 1853 edition of Jussie's chronicle, x–xi.

tices. They profaned the holy ground by keeping up to two hundred cart horses in the cloister and the church. They slept in the dormitory of the monastery, and the poor monks slept on the cold ground. That night those Bernese, like evil heretics, figured out how to get into the choir of the church, and they went inside and built a big fire in the middle of the nave. Then, like disloyal dogs who were mad and out of their minds, they took the ciborium that held the most worthy sacrament of the precious body of Jesus Christ Our Redeemer and put it all in that big fire,[41] and so they villainously scorned the price paid for our Redemption, just like Caiaphas' agents did when they [16] spat in His precious face[42] and like Pilate's devilish minions did when they whipped and crucified Him so ignominiously.[43]

Also, they destroyed the very lavish painting on the main altar and burned all the wooden statues. They smashed the window behind the main altar, which was beautiful and ornate. And in all the chapels where there were carved statues of the glorious saints,[44] they destroyed and ruined everything, which was a lamentable thing to see. They did the same thing in all of the

41. The question of how to interpret the Eucharist was a key theological issue dividing Reformers from adherents to traditional belief. Following the doctrine of transubstantiation, traditional Catholics believed that the bread and wine blessed by a priest in the sacrament of the Eucharist *became* the body and blood of Christ. Reformers, particularly those influenced by Swiss theologian Ulrich Zwingli, believed that the bread and wine only *represented* Christ's body and blood. In this passage, as in others, Jussie draws her readers' attention to these disputes over the nature of the Eucharist. The act of burning the sacramental bread that Jussie describes here would have been scandalous to traditional Christians for it would have been tantamount to burning the body of Christ. With this provocative act, the Reformers were demonstrating that they believed the bread to be merely bread, with no literal connection to Christ's body. For a detailed discussion of the doctrine of the Eucharist during the Reformation, see B. A. Gerrish's entry on the Eucharist in Hans J. Hillerbrand, ed., *The Oxford Encyclopedia of the Reformation*, 4 vols. (New York and Oxford: Oxford University Press, 1996), s.v. "Eucharist"; see also s.v. "Transubstantiation." For a brief overview of the Eucharist in Christian theology, see F. L. Cross, ed., *The Oxford Dictionary of the Christian Church*, 3d ed (Oxford: Oxford University Press, 1997), s.v. "Eucharist." See also Cross, *The Oxford Dictionary of the Christian Church*, s.v. "Transubstantiation." For an in-depth study of the Eucharistic controversy, particularly in French Protestantism and in later Calvinist theology, see Christopher Elwood, *The Body Broken: The Calvinist Doctrine of the Eucharist and the Symbolization of Power in Sixteenth-Century France* (Oxford: Oxford University Press, 1999).

42. "Then they spat in his face and struck him; and some slapped him" (Mt 26:67); "Some began to spit on him, to blindfold him, and to strike him, saying to him, 'Prophesy!' The guards also took him over and beat him" (Mk 14:65); "They struck his head with a reed, spat upon him, and knelt down in homage to him" (Mk 15:19).

43. "So he released Barabbas for them, and after flogging Jesus, he handed him over to be crucified" (Mt 27:26); "So Pilate, wishing to satisfy the crowd, released Barabbas for them; and after flogging Jesus, he handed him over to be crucified" (Mk 15:15).

44. Jussie refers explicitly to both male and female saints here: *des glorieulx sains et saintes.*

churches they could get into.[45] Still not satisfied with those great injustices, those heretics smashed the sacristy and all the brand-new cabinets that were so well built as decorations for a house dedicated to God. They removed all the locks and ironwork and took all the decorations they found and carried off everything, including the convent clock and all the friars' dishes and linen, so that nothing remained but the empty building.

Also, they stripped and beat all the priests they found wearing long robes.

With the tips of their spears and swords, they poked out the eyes of all of the flat images in paintings and murals that they could not burn, and they [17] spat on them to efface and disfigure them; it was a shocking thing to see. They burned all the parchment books, the cantor's and others, and they plundered all the priests' houses and stole everything. What is more, they burned the monastery's lectern, which was very handsome. And in that city of Morges, and in others, they did more great injustices than anyone can tell or write.

Also, they pillaged and then burned the castle of Monseigneur of Vufflens, the Castle of Allaman, the Castle of Perroy, the one in Begnins, and a house belonging to Lord Andrieu Feste, who had a castle in Nyon. And on Saturday the seventh of October,[46] that army left its quarters and headed straight for Rolle, two leagues from Geneva. They pillaged and burned the castle, which was very fine. Then on Sunday [October 9] they spent the

---

45. Veneration of the saints, and of their images, came under fierce attack during the Reformation. Traditional Catholic belief holds that saints play an important intercessory role, since their holiness gives them privileged access to God, while the human lives they led makes them equally accessible to Christians. Reformed theology, on the other hand, holds that all Christians have direct access to God and do not need the mediation of a saint (or priest). For many Reformers, to venerate a saint was to misplace adoration rightly due to God alone. Images of the saints were thus seen as blasphemous, and iconoclasm, the destruction of these images, was viewed as an attempt to rid the church of corruption. In the early 1520s, Ulrich Zwingli preached in Zurich against the veneration of the saints and against images. Acts of iconoclasm began in Zurich in 1523 and 1524 and spread quickly across Switzerland in the late 1520s and 1530s. These iconoclastic acts were not confined to images of the saints. In this passage, Jussie goes on to accuse the "heretics" of outright pillaging. For a consideration of sainthood and the cult of saints during the Reformation, see the entries on these topics in Hillerbrand, ed., *The Oxford Encyclopedia of the Reformation*, s.v. "Saints." See also Cross, *The Oxford Dictionary of the Christian Church*, s.v. "Saints, devotion to the." For a detailed discussion of the history and significance of iconoclasm during the Reformation and its role in different countries and regions, see Carlos M. N. Eire's entry in Hillerbrand, *The Oxford Encyclopedia of the Reformation*, s.v. "Iconoclasm." For an in-depth study of images and iconoclasm during the Reformation, with particular attention to Geneva, see Eire, *War against the Idols: The Reformation of Worship from Erasmus to Calvin* (Cambridge: Cambridge University Press, 1986).

46. Saturday was October 8.

night in Nyon, and they pillaged the churches and the Franciscan monastery there and burned and destroyed all the images. That Saturday [October 8] [18] evening some wicked Genevan men brought a company of those Swiss to plunder the Cistercian Abbey of Bellerive near Geneva, and they stole everything, even the church bell.[47] Then they set fire to it, but Our Lord stopped them. The church did not catch fire but remained standing despite their efforts. The poor nuns escaped, disguised as poor wayward women, each to her family's house. Afterward the nuns came back to their convent to serve God as before. The poor nuns of Saint Clare in Geneva saw the abbey burning from their garden, and there can be no doubt but that it was a very piercing and painful sword to them[48] and that they expected nothing less to happen to themselves. For those dogs desired nothing but to harass pious people and to abolish the state of virginity and divine worship.

On the following Sunday afternoon [October 9] a great proclamation was made to the sound of a trumpet [19] that all bakers should bake a great abundance of bread and that butchers should kill animals and get meat and necessary supplies ready.

On that Sunday evening the clergy decided to close the cathedral church of Saint Peter's and all the other churches and not to open them again to celebrate Mass or any other service until the Swiss went away, which is what was done. Monseigneur the vicar[49] ordered all the treasures of the parish churches, convents, and monasteries to be carried to the cathedral church and hidden in the crypt so that the heretics could not get them, for it was well known that they would have destroyed everything. Brazen Genevan men got up on the city walls to look at the fire and smoke coming from the castles and churches burning around Geneva, coming from the Vaud because even though the air was fine and clear, it was clouded by the dark smoke. Some of them were upset and felt pity, others were joyful and laughed wickedly at it. [20]

PLEA FROM THE NUNS OF SAINT CLARE TO THE SYNDICS AND THE COUNCIL

The poor secluded ladies, the nuns of Madame Saint Clare, terribly frightened by those people and afraid they would hurt them, with the fury they

---

47. The Abbey of Bellerive was founded in the mid-twelfth century. For information on the abbey, see Revilliod's 1853 edition of Jussie's chronicle, ix.

48. "and a sword will pierce your own soul too" (Lk 2:35).

49. Aymé de Gingins, vicar (1527–35).

were showing toward pious people, prayed tearfully night and day, and they gathered together in the chapter room to decide what to do about it. And they made a very humble plea to messieurs the syndics[50] and councilors written by myself[51] in the following manner and substance:

"Our magnificent and most honored lords, fathers, and good protectors, we have heard of the arrival of God's enemies in your town and of the evil and disrespectful things they are doing in the church of God and to pious people, and we are very afraid. We therefore beg you very humbly, kneeling prostrate on the ground with our hands folded in honor of Our Redeemer and His sorrowful passion and of His Virgin Mother and of Monsieur Saint Peter, Monsieur Saint Francis, and Madame Saint Clare and of all the saints in paradise, please to keep us in your safeguard and protection so that those enemies of God do not [21] violate or disturb us. For we do not want any innovation of religion or law or to turn away from divine service, but we are determined to live and die in our holy vocation here in your convent praying to Our Lord for the peace and preservation of your noble town, if you lords will agree to preserve and protect us all here as your ancestors have done; and if not, let us leave our convent and your town, to save ourselves and seek refuge elsewhere to observe divine service, and we will keep you, as our fathers, in our prayers there, and we ask you for your good will and for an answer."

The letter was presented on Thursday evening [October 6]. On Friday morning [October 7], three of the aldermen came to hear Mass at the convent, and after Mass they asked the father confessor[52] and his associates[53] to give the sisters their answer, saying, "Messieurs and the council have seen and considered the ladies' humble request, and they should not worry about anything because the city will take care of them and make sure that no harm comes to them, and they should also have no fear for their religion, for the city does not want to be Lutheran." [22]

The sisters were a bit cheered and, in this hope, remained in their convent.

---

50. The four syndics were the highest elected officials in Geneva and served as representatives of the people before the bishop. Here, as elsewhere, Jussie spells "syndics" as "sainctiques," suggesting that she may see a conflation of religious and secular authority.

51. This passage is the first of many in which Jussie refers to herself in the first person (she also sometimes uses the third person). See especially pp. 113–14, 131, 156, 200, 242–44, 292, and 309 in Feld's edition of the *Petite chronique.*

52. Jean Gacy. See Feld's introduction to the *Petite chronique*, xlviii–li.

53. Pierre Gautier and Philibert Dubois.

DIVINE SERVICE AT SAINT CLARE

The next Monday [October 10], early in the morning, all the churches in town were closed, and there was no Mass or divine service, high or low, observed in them while those false heretical Swiss were there, except in the convent of Madame Saint Clare, whose church was closed to no one. The father confessor and his associates said Mass with open doors, and many good chaplains came secretly, carrying their priests' robes under their arms and putting them on in the convent, and all the clerics and monks carried weapons and arms to be first in the battle. Almost the whole city came there in great piety. The sisters still said divine service at the accustomed hours. But they did it hurriedly and without recitation, and the first two days they said it secretly in the refectory. But afterward they took heart and said it in the church because it was very strange to worship God in hiding and see Him reviled in [23] public. It is no wonder that the holy church allowed a ciborium to be placed in the hand of the statue of Madame Saint Clare because it was to her glory once again that no Mass or service was celebrated in any church inside the Genevan city walls except in her convent, where it was done without any opposition.

OCCUPATION OF GENEVA BY TROOPS FROM BERN AND FRIBOURG

On that Monday [October 10] at eight o'clock in the morning, the Swiss quartermaster came to find housing for the army, and he marked down a number for each house. At the poor sisters' convent he marked down three hundred. But the sisters wisely returned to the head captain[54] and begged him to keep them away from those men and humbly reminded him of the danger he was putting them in, and out of pity he reduced the number and said they would have to house and feed thirty-five men and six horses. But Our Lord made sure they were all good Catholics from Fribourg, and they listened willingly to Mass and in great piety, and at the sisters' request they all stood at the door with their weapons to keep the heretics away so they would not hurt them during Mass, and they followed orders to let the people in.[55] But although they were [24] Christians, they were also good plunderers, and they injured the poor people just like the others. The head captain

54. Bezanson Hugues, a leading advocate of the *Combourgeoisie* in Geneva. See Henri Naef, *Bezanson Hugues: Patriote et homme d'état* (Geneva: Jullien, 1933). See also Monter, *Calvin's Geneva,* 48–49.

55. That is, people who were coming to hear Mass.

of Geneva, named Bezanson, told the sisters to take down the large cross in front of the convent and the handsome crucifix above the door at the entrance to the convent and to hide them because those dogs would have chopped them to pieces. It was a very strange thing to hide the sign of our redemption.

Also, on the previous Saturday [October 8], the Genevans went with weapons to the village of Meyrin. They met a company of good peasants there who were all armed. The peasants began to defend themselves and fought so hard that at least forty of them died, as did one Genevan. At Lord Michel Nergue's house, the Genevans cruelly killed one of his sons who had never hurt anyone. The poor child knelt down humbly and surrendered to their pity and mercy. But they very cruelly beheaded him out of spite toward his father because he was one of the fugitives from the city, which was a dreadful thing for [25] the poor father. They plundered everything in that house and in the whole village. The poor people were utterly destroyed and left to starve.

On Monday [October 10] around noon the army entered Geneva. They brought nineteen large cannons, some of which they left at Saint-Gervais and the others at Plainpalais near a small church called the Oratory. The canton of Bern was housed in the Rue de la Rivière and the Corraterie, near the bridge over the Arve. At the Dominican monastery were housed six troops of foot soldiers, all Lutherans. The monks were forced to leave the monastery and take refuge in the city. The church remained locked, and they did no damage to it, except for burning and cutting the heads off all the statues that were outside it and in the monastery, which were handsome. In the square, where the monks preached, and in the cemetery and cloister they kept at least two hundred of the army's horses, and they did not leave any supplies. Many were housed at the Augustinian monastery of Notre Dame de Grâce [26], and there were at least 120 at the Franciscan monastery. They used up the supplies just like at the Dominican monastery.

At the Convent of Saint Clare there were thirty men and six horses, which caused the sisters great expense. The men gave the whole pasture to their horses for grazing, and they let their comrades who were housed in the city have some of it. They burned all the firewood, and the poor sisters gave them everything they had to support them and keep them from robbing the poor. But they still had a hard time feeding them, and there were only a few peas to make soup. The men could not believe that the sisters were so poor, so they tried to break into and enter the women's residence. Some brazen men, on nights when they were drunk, tried to come in with the women and harm and violate them. But Our Lord always caused some impediment, with the help of a good young man, a lay brother named Nicolas des Arnox, who dealt with them and soothed their fury, as it was God's will. He had removed his habit so that he could walk more safely in the city, since he was not required to wear it.

The sisters, warned that they were in great danger, asked [27] their guests to go up to the grille.[56] When everyone was there, and with a great many tears and in deep humility, the sisters commended themselves to the men and asked them for mercy and to protect them from the heretics. Then the men all started to weep and said, "Fine ladies, may God comfort and preserve you as His handmaidens, for we cannot protect you if they want to harm you. We have sworn not to hurt anyone. But although we meant it, they are stronger than we are, and, indeed, they have a keen desire to find you here, and we have already kept them away several times."

Then the poor sisters were half-dead with anguish and fear. The men felt such pity for them that they promised to protect them and to risk death for them if necessary. From then on they stayed at the convent to protect them from the heretics. God never allowed anyone to come in. The abbess at that time was the venerable Sister Louise Rambo, and the [28] venerable, very wise Sister Pernette de Montluel[57] was portress, and they knew well how to deal with the men and to satisfy them with words.

When they were in town, all the priests and monks took off their habits and dressed like laymen so that you could not tell them from married men, and they all wore the sign of war, a white cross,[58] on their stomachs and behind their shoulders, and none of the clerics dared appear in robes. However, the sisters' father confessor and his associate never removed their habits, nor did a priest named Messieur Claude Cartody, who took refuge in the convent with the brothers and said Mass piously there every day.

GUILLAUME FAREL'S FIRST SERMON AT SAINT PETER'S CATHEDRAL

The next Tuesday [October 11] at eight o'clock in the morning the Lutherans had Saint Peter's church opened. When they were inside they rang

---

56. The *treille* or *treillie* was an iron grille that separated the nuns' choir from the church itself at the top of a staircase in the nave. A thin curtain hung on the choir side of the grille, and there were wooden doors that the nuns could close. An officiating priest would pass the bread of the Eucharist to the nuns through the grille, and visitors were occasionally allowed to speak to the nuns through it.

57. Pernette de Montluel, who later became vicaress, plays an important role in the second half of the *Petite chronique*. She became abbess of the convent in Annecy in 1535.

58. The white or silver cross on a red background was the symbol of the Duke of Savoy and the military symbol of the Holy Roman Empire.

the bishop's bell for the sermon because they had brought their accursed preacher, Master Guillaume Farel. [29] He got up in the pulpit and preached in German.[59] His audience leaped onto the altar like goats and brutish beasts, with great contempt for the images of Our Redemption and of the Virgin Mary and all the saints. They stayed there all day, preaching and ringing the bell. No other bell, large or small, was rung in Geneva.

PILLAGING AROUND GENEVA BY THE SWISS

On that Tuesday after dinner they gathered to go out and pillage monseigneur's lands. They pillaged and burned the Castle of Saconnex and a fine house nearby and pillaged the whole village and led away all the livestock. They took all the food, wheat, wine, meat, and all the furnishings that they found everywhere they went, and they burned the church.

Also, on that same day, in another village, named Cologny, they pillaged the house of Lord Louis Montion, where they found many valuable items. The house was not burned, although it was in danger. They did a lot of damage that day. [30]

On Wednesday [October 12] they went out and pillaged the city of Gaillard and burned monseigneur's castle. They plundered the castle of Monseigneur of Villette. Then they burned it and did much damage. They did the same thing to Madame of Saint-Genix and Madame of Rossylon, widows whose lords, their sons, were still innocent young orphans.[60] Afterward they pillaged and burned the church in Villette, the one in Annemasse, and the surrounding villages. Ten people in Ville-la-Grand were killed and thrown into a hole like disreputable dogs in a field.

On that same day they pillaged the Castle of Confignon but did not burn it because the captain[61] did not let them since he was related to its

---

59. Farel most likely did not come to Geneva until 1532. On his first visit and the question of whether he spoke German, see Feld's introduction to the *Petite chronique*, li–liii. According to Bossard and Junod, the Reformer to whom Jussie refers was actually a German-speaking preacher by the name of Gaspard Grossman. Bossard and Junod, eds., *Chroniqueurs du XVIe siècle*, 174, n.1. For background on Guillaume Farel and his contributions to the Reformation in French-speaking Switzerland, the two following classic studies remain valuable: William M. Blackburn, *William Farel and the Story of the Swiss Reform* (Philadelphia: Presbyterian Board of Publication, 1865); *Guillaume Farel, 1489–1565: Biographie nouvelle écrite d'après les documents originaux par un groupe d'historiens, professeurs et pasteurs de Suisse, de France et d'Italie* (1930; Reprint Geneva: Slatkine, 1978). Kingdon also discusses Farel's role in the Reformation of Geneva: *Tradition and Revolution*, 53–77.

60. Orphans because their fathers had died.

61. According to Feld, this captain was most likely Hans von Erlach, commander of the Bernese troops. See Feld's edition of the *Petite chronique*, 30, n. 15.

lord. But they left only the walls standing. And they continued to ravage the poor land.

In the evening the captain announced that no one should go out and pillage anymore. But that did not stop them. The poor people ran from them like sheep from wolves. Poor gentlewomen hid in the woods and mountains; they had to spend the winter in poor peasants' houses, and several of them gave birth in those miserable conditions. It was a piteous thing to hear tell of. [31]

TREATIES BETWEEN THE DUKE OF SAVOY AND THE SWISS

Monseigneur, who heard about that piteous situation from his city of Chambéry, was very upset and immediately sent the Reverend Father Bishop of Belley[62] and several of the leading lords of his house to speak to the Swiss and to find out why they were wreaking havoc on his lands and destroying the poor people. When they arrived in Saint-Julien, a short distance from Geneva, they ordered the captains and all the leaders of the army to come to them. On Thursday morning [October 13] they proclaimed to the sound of a trumpet that, under penalty of the rope,[63] no one should go out and pillage. But it did no good because there were plenty of them outside the city. The captains discussed the matter with monseigneur's ambassadors until Sunday. Then they returned and ordered their followers [32] not to do any more damage or harm in monseigneur's lands and they said they should all pay for the expenses they had caused in those lands, which they did.[64] But the Genevans were not able to raise enough money to satisfy the great amount they had promised. The town was in great danger of being burned and pillaged because people were angry at them for ravaging the countryside for no good reason. [33]

THE SWISS ARMY LEAVES GENEVA

During that time the poor people were paralyzed with fear, and, as it was God's will, the Genevans promised the Swiss enough to convince them to leave. The next Thursday, the eve of the Feast of the Thousand Virgins,[65]

---

62. Claude d'Estavayer. See Henri Naef, "Claude d'Estavayer, Évêque de Belley, Confident de Charles II Duc de Savoie (1483?–1534)," *Revue d'Histoire ecclésiastique suisse* 50 (1956): 85–137.

63. Possibly hanging or, more likely, the *strappado* (*trait de corde*). See below, note 128.

64. That is, the payments were made.

65. The eve of the Feast of Saint Ursula, October 20, 1530. See below, note 248.

that huge army left town at the same time it had arrived, and they all left at once and returned to their cantons. But, alas, because of that war, food was very expensive in the land all year long. May God in His goodness spare us from such misfortune forevermore.

SACRILEGIOUS AND ICONOCLASTIC ACTIONS BY THE SWISS

Those Swiss Germans who had attacked the country did unspeakable harm to the land, and like disloyal, heretical dogs, they pillaged and burned all the churches, monasteries, and convents everywhere they went. They smashed all the ciboria that held Our Lord's body.

They took the sacred host and trampled it under their feet, and some of them threw it into the fire or mud. They also took [34] the blessed ointment for the sacrament of baptism and the blessed oil with which all good Christians are anointed in the last days of their illness, and they poured them on the ground in great horror and contempt—the Mohammedan Turks and infidel Jews could not have done worse—and they emptied the holy fonts. They spat on and shamefully wiped their noses and bodies[66] with the holy relics.

It was said that in a church in the Vaud they took the sacred host of the body of Jesus Christ and fed it to a goat, a poor brutish beast. Then they said in great scorn, "Go and die whenever you like, for you have your sacraments."

A good Christian was in a church they pillaged, and he watched carefully to see what they did with the blessed sacrament. They smashed the ciborium and took its custodial and threw the sacred host spitefully on the ground in the cemetery. When they had left, that good Christian went to look at the place where he had seen the sacred host fall, to cover it with a white cloth, out of piety, until it could be taken back by the church. But he never saw it again and could find no sign of it. That good man declared that he firmly believed the angels had lifted it up from that place and called it back to an honorable place unknown to us. [35]

Those dogs who kept watch by night over the cannons in the oratory [in the Plainpalais] tore down the altar in the chapel and smashed the windows on which the images of Monseigneur Saint Anthony the Abbot and Saint

---

66. According to the writer of manuscript A, they *crachoient et ce mouchoint . . . et tourchoiens* with the relics; the writer of manuscript B deletes *et tourchoiens*.

Sebastian were painted. They completely destroyed a very fine stone cross, and from its pieces they made stools for sitting by the fire.

Also, they destroyed many fine images at the Augustinian monastery and very fine stone ones at the Dominican monastery, and they burned the image of Saint Crispin and his followers and committed many other grave and serious insults against God.

THE CONVENT OF SAINT CLARE DURING THE OCCUPATION

While the Swiss were in Geneva, which was for eleven days [October 10–20], no bells were rung, except to announce their devilish sermons, and no Mass or divine service was celebrated, except at the Convent of Madame Saint Clare, where Our Lord did not allow any abuses, nor did his enemies [36] ever come in, although it was said later that several brazen men of the city tried to get in. But when they came in the first door, they were immediately struck with such terror that they quickly ran away. They often came sneaking around the convent. But Our Lord filled them with fear, and they could never get in. The poor nuns watched for them every night, praying to God for the holy religion and for the poor world, and they all disciplined themselves[67] after matins and asked God for mercy. Then they lit wax candles and some of them recited the fine "Benedicatur,"[68] bowing all the way down to the ground in the name of Jesus Christ. Others knelt and recited the "Ave benigne Jesu."[69] Others hailed Our Lord's wounds and the Virgin Mary's tears and said other fine [37] prayers aloud. Every day they made a procession into the garden, and often twice a day, reciting the holy litany and stepping with bare feet[70] on the white frost, begging for mercy for the poor world and for themselves, who were in piteous danger. Our Lord protected and nourished them with his grace and worked a miracle so that the bread that by all reason should have lasted only two days was multiplied by God's will so that they lived for twelve days on it, with their good fathers

---

67. That is, they committed acts of self-mortification. The writer of manuscript B deleted the reference to mortification. The Rule of Saint Clare is vague on the topic, but the *Vie de Sainte Claire* (especially chap. 11, nos. 17–18) contains numerous accounts of Saint Clare's own self-mortification. See Vorreux, *Sainte Claire d'Assise, documents*, 55–57. See also Grivel, "Notice," 274.

68. "Benedicatur Dominus / Natus ex Annae filia" (Let the Lord be blessed / He is born of the daughter of Anne). See Feld's edition of the *Petite chronique*, 36, n. 30.

69. "Hail, Blessed Jesus", the first words of a prayer to Jesus Christ and a salutation sometimes added to the beginning of the "Hail, Mary" (see above, note 29).

70. The Poor Clares normally went barefoot.

and servants,[71] and they gave some of it to their visitors and still had plenty to eat.[72]

GENERAL PARDONS BY POPE CLEMENT VII AT THE CONVENT OF SAINT CLARE

In the year 1530, at the request of Monseigneur of Caserta, Master Pierre Lambert[73] and, without the sisters' knowledge or application, the Holy Father Pope Clement [VII] declared general pardons at the Convent of Saint Clare, on the Feast of the Annunciation of Our Lady [March 25, 1530], and it was published throughout the land.[74] [38]

The poor people came there in great piety. But the Genevans closed the city gates and would not let them in, which greatly upset the poor people, for they had come from faraway. People from the area around Foucigny forced them to open the gate, and they narrowly avoided great bloodshed. At vespers,[75] with fine unsheathed swords and heavy weapons, the syndics came with the sentinels and sergeants,[76] and they angrily threw out all the

---

71. That is, the confessors and the lay brothers and sisters.

72. "When it was evening, the disciples came to him and said, 'This is a deserted place, and the hour is now late; send the crowds away so that they may go into the villages and buy food for themselves.' Jesus said to them, 'They need not go away; you give them something to eat.' They replied, 'We have nothing here but five loaves and two fish.' And he said, 'Bring them here to me.' Then he ordered the crowds to sit down on the grass. Taking the five loaves and the two fish, he looked up to heaven, and blessed and broke the loaves, and gave them to the disciples, and the disciples gave them to the crowds. And all ate and were filled; and they took up what was left over of the broken pieces, twelve baskets full. And those who ate were about five thousand men, besides women and children. (Mt 14:15–21). See also Mk 6:35–44, Lk 9:10–17 and Jn 6:15–21. (Scriptural references are mine.)

73. Bishop of Caserta (d. 1541).

74. In the practice of pardons, also known as indulgences, the church allowed Christians who had confessed their sins to a priest and had been absolved to make partial or complete retribution for these sins through monetary gifts to ecclesiastical institutions or projects. Following an official declaration of pardons at the Convent of Saint Clare, Christians from the surrounding region would have traveled to Geneva to visit the convent and its relics and to make donations. The church began to grant pardons in the eleventh and twelfth centuries; the practice became more common in the late medieval period, as did abuses. Both Reformers and Catholics spoke out against the corruption of the practice. Luther decried it famously in his ninety-five theses. See Hillerbrand, *The Oxford Encyclopedia of the Reformation*, s.v. "Indulgences." See also Cross, *The Oxford Dictionary of the Christian Church*, s.v. "Indulgences" and "Pardon."

75. A canonical hour recited in the late afternoon or evening. Jussie also uses the term *vespres* simply to mean "evening."

76. Men charged with maintaining public order; law officers; police.

people who were worshiping in the church. It made the poor people very upset. The poor nuns did not profit much from it.

The holy father pope heard what had happened and learned of the sisters' poverty, which was caused by the diminution of piety and devotion in the world. He published yet another bull declaring general pardons at the convent, without the sisters' knowledge or request, but by divine inspiration, and he ordered that, under penalty of excommunication, no one should oppose it or cause any obstruction. Monseigneur of Geneva and the other bishops approved the pardons and published them in their dioceses. The [39] Genevans did not dare oppose them. But they came with weapons and kept watch. When the pardons were finished the syndics came to the convent. They wanted to take all the offerings. But some honorable men saw to it that the trunks were put inside the convent and securely locked, and they forbade the sisters to touch them. Messieurs wanted to be sure they knew what became of them, so they took the keys away and the sisters did not have access to a single maille.[77]

The next Sunday[78] two syndics came to the convent to see the sisters, along with four notaries who were good Christian burghers. They counted all the money and forbade the sisters to use any of it outside the city. But the mother abbess and her portress responded wisely, "Messieurs, so that you will not think we want any harm to come to the city, we ask you to manage this money, to pay our fathers what we owe them for the wheat and wine we have received for our nourishment and to use the rest to provide us with such things as you deem necessary for our life of poverty, which you see here." [40]

But when the syndics saw there was not much money, they were fully satisfied and left.

THE PLAGUE IN GENEVA

That whole year there were many deaths caused by the plague because some people who were already heretics had plotted to kill all the leaders of the town so that they would then be lords over the whole town, and they took the infection and rubbed it on the locks of doors and threw it in the street in fruits and in handkerchiefs and in other pretty little things they dropped. Everyone who picked those things up was stricken, and so many honorable people died.

77. A small coin, worth one-half or one-quarter denier. Jussie uses the term figuratively to refer to a very small amount of money, much as the word sou is used in modern French.

78. Date unknown, according to Feld. See his edition of the *Petite chronique*, 39, n. 41.

In the month of May, God allowed some of them to be punished, and in the whole city and in every street flesh was burned with great, red-hot irons,[79] which was a piteous thing. A priest who had agreed to that evil plot was drawn and quartered and met his rightful end.[80] One stubborn woman died without ever repenting or recognizing her sin.[81]

A man named Michel Caddo, a native of Geneva, was tortured with irons on his whole body.[82] [41] He confessed and freely accepted martyrdom. He confessed their whole enterprise and plans and said they had started the plague two years earlier. He confessed that they had done everything they could to poison and kill the sisters of Saint Clare and their good fathers and that they had planned to turn the convent into a fine castle and live in it. They had often come all the way up to the convent door with the infection, but when they tried to get in, they suddenly saw three very fine and excellent knights in front of them, standing at the door, and they were amazingly fine and formidable, and each one had a fine shining cross in front of him, which frightened them so much that they were never able to harm the sisters or the convent. He confessed that during the pardons he had come in with the others, pretending to come for the pardons, and had rubbed and infected the trunk, the bull, and the reliquary, so that they should all have been infected. But by the grace of God no one was ever touched. Honor and praise be to God the Father, the Son, and the Holy Spirit, One God in the Trinity, forever and ever. Amen. [42]

DIPLOMATIC CONFERENCE IN PAYERNE

Afterward, in the year 1531 in the month of January, monseigneur's ambassadors gathered in Payerne.[83] The illustrious prince Monseigneur the High

79. Branding irons, used to mark the flesh of convicted criminals.

80. Jean Dufour.

81. Probably Jeanne, wife of Jean Placet, according to Feld. See his edition of the *Petite chronique*, 40, n. 43.

82. As John Langbein has shown, "judicial torture" was employed commonly in the investigation and prosecution of crime in late medieval and early modern Europe. Langbein examines origins of the practice of the Roman canon law of proof, principles used to regulate it, key aspects of its use in England and in continental Europe, and reasons for its disappearance in the eighteenth century. John H. Langbein, *Torture and the Law of Proof* (Chicago: University of Chicago Press, 1977). For a description of principles that would likely have regulated judicial torture in Geneva in the period of which Jussie writes, see 12–17. Langbein also includes eighteenth-century engravings of modes and implements of torture (18–26).

83. In fact, the conference began in December 1530.

Marshal of Savoy and Count of Challant[84] was there and other powerful lords of monseigneur's house. Ambassadors of the most excellent Emperor Charles V and the very Christian king of France Francis I and from all the Swiss cantons and German lands came to negotiate some kind of treaty.[85] But it did not last long, as you will see later, because of the Genevans. Monseigneur proclaimed throughout the land that the Genevans should come and go [43] as they please and that no one should harm any of them, low or high. Likewise, it was proclaimed in Geneva, under penalty of death, that no one should harm any of monseigneur's subjects and that everyone should be able to go about and conduct business safely. But the gentlemen did not dare to trust in those assurances because of the treachery that had been done to Monseigneur of Pontverre,[86] and they stopped coming into town for any reason, especially the members of the Brotherhood of the Spoon, who knew well that they were in disgrace. And so it did not do much good to trust, with things as they were.

VIOLATION OF THE TREATY OF PAYERNE
BY THE GENEVANS

The following July, some Genevans went to dine on the bridge in Étrembières[87] at the home of Monseigneur of Thorens, a member of their [44] group and an ally. After dinner on their way back to Geneva they stopped in the city of Gaillard. One of them shot the church bell with his harquebus.[88] They smashed a handsome statue of Our Lady. Then out of mockery and scorn toward monseigneur and all the nobles they used a piece of charcoal to draw a bear soiling with its filth the noble white cross that was the battle emblem and sign of monseigneur and of the land of Savoy, as everyone knows.

Monseigneur was told about those things done so disrespectfully. He immediately sent word to Bern and Fribourg that their allies in Geneva had

---

84. René, Count of Challant, Marshal of Savoy (1527), Lieutenant General of Savoy (1529), died 1565.

85. The records of the negotiations at Payerne do not name an ambassador of Charles V among the representatives from Savoy until July 31, nor do they mention an envoy of the King of France. (A messenger of the French king was, however, in Bern on October 29 and in Fribourg on October 31, 1530.) The records do mention representatives of the cities of Bern and Fribourg, of the Duke of Savoy, and of Geneva. See Feld, nn.47–49.

86. See above, note 25 and related text.

87. A bridge over the Arve in Étrembières, near Gaillard.

88. A heavy matchlock gun.

committed injuries and insults against God, His Virgin Mother, and all the saints and that they had also tainted His Excellency and his land, and he asked that justice be done by him and promises kept. For in the Treaty of Payerne it had been decided that if monseigneur's subjects caused any disturbances, fights, or arguments, the whole land of Vaud would be seized by Bern and Fribourg and the Barony of Gex would go to the Genevans and that if the Genevans started it, they would lose their sovereignty and citizenship, which is why the abovementioned injuries caused a great stir in the [45] land and why the cantons were very upset with the Genevans. No good intentions could excuse them.

DEMOLITION OF CHURCHES AND ICONOCLASTIC ACTS IN GENEVA

The next August during the octave of the Assumption of Our Lady [August 15–22, 1531] the Genevans took down the bells at the Priory of Saint Victor,[89] and then they destroyed and demolished, all the way to their foundations, the whole monastery and a fine house at the monastery's entrance where the priory steward stayed. In that same month on the day of the beheading of Saint John the Baptist [August 29], they tore down a small and very pretty church in Saint Laurent,[90] and one of the disloyal Lutherans took the statue of the blessed saint and cut its arms off with his sword and then threw it in [46] the ditch. But the man who committed that villainous act did not remain unpunished by divine justice for long because he died of the plague soon afterward in a hospital outside the city. But Our Lord, who does not desire the sinner's death,[91] struck his heart with contrition, and he confessed and received the Holy Sacrament and returned to God, and for that we must thank Our Lord.

On that same Feast of Saint John they tore down the church of Madame Saint Margaret, where a woman recluse lived all alone out of love for God, doing penance. She took refuge in her daughter's house and soon afterward

---

89. One of the oldest religious buildings in Geneva, the Church of Saint Victor was constructed in the late fifth century. For a history of this church and the neighborhood surrounding it, see Revilliod's 1853 edition of Jussie's chronicle, xii–xiv.

90. See Revilliod's 1853 edition of Jussie's chronicle, xiv.

91. "Have I any pleasure in the death of the wicked, says the Lord God, and not rather that they should turn from their ways and live?" (Ez 18:23); "Say to them, As I live, says the Lord God, I have no pleasure in the death of the wicked, but that the wicked turn from their ways and live; turn back, turn back from your evil ways; for why will you die, O house of Israel?" (Ez 33:11).

went to Chambéry to make her plea to monseigneur, and the good prince benevolently gave her a house and a living in Chambéry.

A wooden cross that stood in front of the convent of Madame Saint Clare was pulled up and thrown into the well by a wretch who had been at the destruction of the churches and holy places. He did not remain unpunished, for in the month of November three of those profaners were struck with the plague and [47] died in the hospital. Two of them returned to God and publicly confessed to throwing down the cross and to other crimes, and they asked for forgiveness and ended up as good Christians. The third one never recognized his God and died in his heresy and stubbornness.

DEATH OF MADAME LOUISE OF SAVOY

In the month of August a giant comet was seen in the sky,[92] giant and with a flaming tail visible in France. It was said to be a sign of the death of madame the regent, Lady Louise of Savoy, who was, through her father, the sister of Monseigneur the Duke Charles and of the Count of the Genevois the Duke of Nemours and the mother of King Francis I. She died the following twenty-second of September and was buried in a royal tomb at Saint-Denis. [48]

BATTLE OF KAPPEL

In the following month of October a great war was waged among those heretics near the city of Zurich.[93] Our Lord granted the Christians such great courage and force that seven hundred of them miraculously defeated nine thousand.

MARTIN LUTHER AND HIS HERESY

The prince and grand heresiarch of that damnable sect was an Augustinian monk named Martin Luther. In the year 1518, filled with wickedness and great self-pride, he set his mind to all sorts of malice and error, and he revived all the heresies and errors that had existed ever since the apostles' death, and he had them printed in [49] Basel and carried straightaway through almost all of Christendom, and so his pestiferous venom poisoned all the kingdoms and

92. Halley's comet. See volume editor's introduction, note 35.
93. Jussie is referring to the battle near Kappel on October 11, 1531, in which Ulrich Zwingli was killed.

lands of the Catholic Church. If kings and princes had not severely punished people who followed that accursed sect, the souls bought with the precious blood of Jesus Christ Our Lord would have been in grave danger of eternal damnation. But God, who never forsakes His bride the church, inspired our Holy Father Pope Leo X to declare Luther a disloyal heretic and an enemy of the holy Catholic religion before the consistory and college of messeigneurs the cardinals, pronouncing a sentence of excommunication and anathema on that disloyal dog Luther and excommunicating and anathematizing all men and women who believe, defend, maintain, or favor those heresies, no matter what their estate, rank, or worth, making no exception for anyone. He sent that bull to all kingdoms and lands and throughout all of Christendom. [50]

Another thing, out of loathing for his vile body they burnt him in effigy in the Campo di Fiori in Rome as a despicable heretic and corrupter of holy Christendom.[94] For because of him many noble countries, flourishing in piety, turned away from the true religion and fell into his heresies. The Prince and Duke of Saxony and his whole country followed him and protected him so that he would not be killed and could teach that devilish heresy better and so that other princes would not harm him. The town of Basel was perverted, and the bishop was run out of town and banished from the town of Strasbourg, from the city of Bern and all its domains, from Zurich and two other cantons,[95] and from the county of Neuchâtel and several other German-speaking cities, towns, and lands whose names I do not know. And now it is happening again, in the town of Geneva in Savoy, even though there have always been so many fine people and good Catholics here, and for this reason many people have left town, and everyone is divided, and the land too, [51] as has already been shown above and as I will make even plainer. Because of those scoundrels, all the sacraments of the holy church have been abolished and all piety and decency. They have also removed and destroyed all the images, whether painted or standing or other, of all the glorious saints[96] and especially of Our Redeemer and His Virgin Mother, and they have burned parish churches and monasteries and convents. They have pillaged all the treasures of those places and stripped them of all their furnishings and completely abolished the commandments of the holy church and all its fine ceremonies, all the divine service and the worship of God.

94. On whether Luther was burnt in effigy in Rome, see Feld's introduction to the *Petite chronique*, liii–lx.

95. Saint Gallen and Schaffhausen.

96. Once again, Jussie refers explicitly to both male and female saints: *tous les glorieulx sains et sainctes*.

Not satisfied with his own perdition, that pestiferous dragon with the venomous tail[97] tried to bring people of every estate down with him. That is why he pursued and pestered people who had consecrated and dedicated themselves to God with a holy vow of chastity and tried to get them to marry, and he himself and his disciples were married in the ordinary manner. Numerous priests and monks, ungrateful and lacking respect for their holy vocation, followed him.[98]

Clerics were not allowed to remain where that heresy was introduced and reigned unless they removed their habits, and they were all hunted down and sent away from their lands, so they had no place of their own. They suffered greatly. That time could well be called "the time of persecution of the holy church."[99]

It is, indeed, true that prelates and clerics at that time did not respect [52] their vows and estates but used the advantages of the church immorally for their own pleasure, keeping women and children in wantonness and adultery, and almost the whole world was infected with that loathsome, abominable sin; it is piteously to be believed that the sins of the world that abounded in people of all estates provoked God's anger and caused Him to use those false, disloyal agents of the devil, disguised as men, to inflict divine punishment.[100] Good monks and nuns were persecuted and experienced the secret judgment of God along with the guilty ones. But it is to be believed that it aided in their salvation and multiplied their merits before God. Many good and pious monasteries were ruined and destroyed, but their inhabitants were not perverted by it, but took refuge in the world wherever they could to continue in their holy vocation. Even in Bern several Dominican

---

97. That is, Martin Luther.

98. The question of whether or not clerics should marry was frequently disputed during the middle ages, until the Second Lateran Council came down firmly against it in 1139. Even then, however, opinion remained mixed, and by the fifteenth and early sixteenth centuries, abuses such as clerical concubinage were common. Reformers, including Martin Luther, to whom Jussie refers here, believed that the prohibition of clerical marriage led to corruption and that the existence of this corruption proved that celibacy was not ordained by God. They, therefore, encouraged clerics to marry and to raise families. In 1525, Luther married Katharina von Bora, a former nun. The Council of Trent (1545–63) reaffirmed the official prohibition of clerical marriage. For a detailed discussion of the question of marriage during the Reformation, see Hillerbrand, *The Oxford Encyclopedia*, s.v. "Marriage." For a brief history of the doctrine of clerical celibacy and a consideration of the importance of this doctrine during the Reformation, see Hillerbrand, *The Oxford Encyclopedia*, s.v. "Celibacy and Virginity." See also Cross, *The Oxford Dictionary*, s.v. "Celibacy of the Clergy."

99. "That day a severe persecution began against the church in Jerusalem, and all except the apostles were scattered throughout the countryside of Judea and Samaria" (Acts 8:1).

100. Manuscript B omits the reference to divine punishment.

nuns returned to their families and served as servants so that they would not have to renounce their estate. Others got married: Carthusians, Augustinians, Cistercians, and Franciscans, and [53] even Observant Franciscans and Dominicans. There were perversions among all the orders of the world, except among the nuns of Madame Saint Clare of the Reformation of the Blessed Colette, where not a single nun was ever perverted or unfaithful, except for one[101] who had not entered the convent through the proper door of good intentions, but by feigned and wicked hypocrisy. She was not truly worthy of Our Lord and was easily led astray and removed from the order and convent in Geneva, and it was because of her sister, a member of that sect; she was taken out violently despite the strong resistance that the nuns put up for her, and I will show below exactly what happened.

PERSECUTION OF THE POOR CLARES IN ORBE

The order of Madame Saint Clare was greatly bothered by those heresies, especially the convents in Vevey and Orbe and Geneva, which were surrounded by [54] the evildoers. The time of persecution of the nuns in Orbe, which affected the nuns and the lay brothers in their service, began in the year 1521,[102] on the Feast of the Annunciation of Our Lady, during Lent, when their father confessor, Friar Michel Julien, who preached against those heresies in the convent and praised virginity, was removed from the pulpit and replaced by a wretched Lutheran of the city, Christophe Hollard, whose brother was a married priest. The women could not bear the injury to God but seized that wicked man by his hair and dragged him out of the church in contempt. But the bailiff ordered the father confessor to be put in prison, to the poor sisters' immense sorrow. They took up ink and paper right away and wrote a letter on behalf of the convent and the region expressing the grief and [55] danger they were in, begging for aid and comfort and offering the prayers and merits of the convent, with the good advice and aid of the prelate. Our Lord allowed the good father to be released from prison, but he was banished from the city and never dared set foot there again, for which the poor sisters were very sorry and upset.

The following April the heretical preacher was sent to Orbe by messieurs of Bern to preach and pervert the poor city.[103] But Our Lord did not

---

101. Blaisine Varembert. See below, text at note 292.

102. Actually 1531.

103. Guillaume Farel came to Orbe on April 22, 1531. Bern had officially adopted the Reformation in 1528.

allow it. Most of them remained constant and put up great resistance, and even though he preached for a long time, the city was never led completely astray. The women bore it heroically. The bailiff had him preach in the convent for a long time, and the sisters were forced to ring the bell for the sermon and to listen at the grille with the curtain raised, which caused them much grief, there can be no doubt. The sisters in Geneva, with much compassion for them [56], begged their father confessor[104] to go see them and comfort them, which he did willingly;[105] he stayed there at least ten weeks to confess and console them, with the consent of his daughters in Geneva, until the prelates could take charge and care of them. They gave those poor ladies such a hard time that, to avoid worse danger and out of obedience to the prelate, seventeen of the youngest ones left the convent on the Feast of Saint Pantaleon [July 22, 1531] at eleven o'clock at night, accompanied by the guardian father of Nozeroy[106] and other good monks, and they took refuge in Nozeroy under the protection of Madame the Princess of Orange [Philiberte of Luxembourg], who took them in benevolently, put them up in a house near her castle, and fed and provided for them there until the following tenth of May, when the heretics' furor was abated and the city remained under Christian control. Then the sisters returned to their convent with their good mothers to continue serving God together. But five of them did not return. There were the two nieces of the aforementioned lady of the noble House of Challon[107] and one from Orbe named [57] Sister Claire Gryvat. They were taken to the convent in Poligny in Burgundy. The other two were taken to Chambéry; one was Sister Jeanne from Arbi, and the other was Sister Claire Tavel from Orbe. Our Lord did not allow any of them to be perverted or separated, but all returned to worship God in their convent. Our Lord protected and preserved them in good comfort and safety, even though, as long as those heresies lasted, they and the others were never safe, but always in grave danger, because those heretics were great enemies of the perfect religion and of God.

EVENTS OF THE YEAR 1531 (1532)

Also, in the year 1531, a noble burgher woman, because of her piety, gave birth to a daughter miraculously, for she had lived with her husband for thirty-one years without any descendants and was very old. [58]

---

104. Jean Gacy.
105. Manuscript B adds "out of good and paternal charity" (*par bonne et paternelle charite*).
106. That is, from the Franciscan monastery in Nozeroy.
107. The House of Orange.

Also, in 1531, monseigneur came with the upper nobility and estate to Gex to celebrate the Feast of the Kings [Epiphany], and he called for the leaders of Bern and Fribourg so they could reach some kind of agreement. But they refused to negotiate. So the good prince went back to his city of Chambéry and forbade anyone in his lands, under great penalty, to bring food or anything else to Geneva, which was a pity and caused great poverty in the town, especially the lack of wheat and wood, because the snow and cold were the severest they had been in twenty-five years. Houses fell to the ground. It was a piteous thing to hear the wails and lamentations of poor beggars. That prohibition on supplies lasted from the Feast of Saint Sebastian [January 20, 1532] until the Feast of Saint Peter's Chair [February 22, 1532], when the prince called it off.

That same February another council was held with Bern and Fribourg, and the Genevans decided not [59] to be subject to monseigneur and to uphold their Eidguenot[108] alliance and have no other affiliations.

A LETTER FROM JACQUES GAUCOURT ABOUT THE ATTACK OF THE GRAND TURK IN HUNGARY

At that time the Grand Turk was bearing down on Christendom with great force. He miraculously suffered a major defeat at the hands of Monseigneur the Cardinal of Hungary in his city of Esztergom,[109] as was made known by the contents of the letter sent to the Christian kingdom of France, which follows.

"My most honored uncle, I commend myself most humbly to your good grace, not forgetting my brother, Monseigneur the Archbishop of Arles,[110] and since [60] you are now at the French court, I am sending you some news so you can show it to the king our lord and to all the princes and lords in the

---

108. See above, note 1.

109. Feld identifies this city, which Jussie calls Congres, as Esztergom (in German, Gran), rather than Köszeg (in German, Güns), as previous editors have presumed. (See Jussie, *Le Levain du calvinisme* [1865], 237.) Although the Turks did lay siege to Köszeg in 1532, the city in question must be Esztergom, says Feld, since Jussie identifies it as the city of residence of the Cardinal of Hungary. (Esztergom was, in fact, the residence not of a cardinal, but of an archbishop. Pavol Várdai was Archbishop of Esztergom from 1526 to 1459.) According to Feld, the information that Jussie provides about Turkish attacks on Hungary in 1532 is a mixture of truth, half-truth, and fantasy. No evidence has been found that the medieval cathedral of Esztergom contained either the grave of Godefroy of Billon or the banner that Jussie describes. The authenticity of the letter she cites is, therefore, highly uncertain. See Feld's introduction to the *Petite chronique*, lx–lxii.

110. The Archbishop of Arles (1521–50) was Jean Ferrier.

court, so they will know about the great miracle of the most sacred Virgin Mary the Mother of God. Here is the news:

"On the Feast of Saint Matthew [February 24], 1532, the Very Reverend Lord Monseigneur the Cardinal of Hungary did me the honor of making me his chief steward, and he was in his city of Esztergom under siege by ninety thousand Turks, which frightened him terribly because he did not have any soldiers with him, only the inhabitants of the city. Nonetheless, my lord set things right, trusting that God and the Holy Virgin Mary would come to his aid. He went to the cathedral church, founded in honor of Our Lady, and visited the holy relics of the church. In particular, he found a banner that Godefroy of Billon had carried in war when he conquered Jerusalem and the holy land, on which were depicted a fine image of Our Lady and a silver shield with three golden crowns; Godefroy's tomb was in the church, and every year, on the Feast of Saint Matthew, the banner and emblem were raised as a sign of victory. The Very Reverend Lord called for a general procession [61], and afterward he gave a sermon charging the people to be truly pious and to ask God for deliverance from their enemies. A little while later he sought and took counsel as to how he might obtain help and aid, and he was advised that he could escape easily through a secret tunnel in the castle that would allow him to go underground until he was at least two leagues from the town. So a group went out, and he was the fifth one out and I was in this group; we carried the banner folded with us, and we went straight to German lands, and in that country my lord assembled at least thirty thousand foot soldiers and at least two hundred armed men, whom he led in orderly fashion. One evening he arrived near his enemies, as secretly as he could. However, the well-armed Turks ambushed my lord and his men at about nine or ten o'clock at night because a spy had told them we were coming. But even though there were lots of Turks, many more than there were of us, they had it worse because of the will of God and the Blessed Virgin Mary. Because as soon as our banner was unfurled, astonishing weather was seen in the sky, and very large hail and a sudden wind astonishingly struck the Turks head-on, and they threw themselves to the ground and began to kill each other. You should know that it is all true and that because of our banner, God and Our Lady caused such a great brightness that it seemed like the light of day. When the skirmish had ended [62], five troops of Turkish foot soldiers surrendered to my lord because of the fine miracles they had seen come from the image of the Blessed Virgin Mary. And so, ninety thousand Turks were completely defeated and surrendered to my lord. The banner is dearer to us than ever. Now a chapel is being built on the battlefield, and it is called Our Lady of Victory.

"Written in Esztergom in Hungary. By your loyal nephew Jacques Gaucourt."

MIRACLE OF THE VIRGIN MARY IN TOURNAI IN PICARDY

The following is another fine miracle of the Virgin Mary that happened in the city of Tournai, in 1532, in April.

All true and good Christians bought with the precious blood of Jesus Christ, keep in reverence the fine miracles of the glorious Virgin Mary, especially one that happened on Easter Tuesday, the twelfth day of April, 1532, one evening after vespers in the city and town of Tournai in Picardy[111] because [63] of a perverted and wicked Christian. His body was almost all covered in filth, and he was a glutton and had drunk too much. When he was on his way back from Ere, near Tournai, and was near the Sainte-Fontaine gate, he started to beat a poor, sinful woman.[112] When she saw she was being assaulted, she began to shout and scream, and she looked up at the statue of the Virgin above the gate and said out loud, "Blessed Virgin Mary, please help me and come to my aid."

At those words, the perverted man turned toward the statue with a rock in his hand and said to the woman, "You are really crazy if you think she will help you because she has no power and is as much a virgin as you, a public whore."

The next day [April 13, 1532] a great crowd of people gathered at the gate to look at the statue, which was covered with blood, on its face and in other places, and the blood flowed miraculously down its forehead from near the crown all the way down to below its throat. Seeing this, messieurs the governors climbed up to the statue and observed that it was miraculous blood. [64]

The next Friday it was taken down and carried to the church of the Madeleine and put into the treasury as a worthy relic, and it was visited by messieurs the canons of the chapter of Our Lady of Tournai, by Augustinians, by Franciscans, by the Abbess of the Prés-aux-Nonnains, and by the captain of the castle and messieurs the governors. They collected the miraculous blood, and Madame the Abbess, in particular, used a lovely cloth made of fine fabric from Holland to touch and wipe and clean the statue. It was returned to her and is regarded as a singular relic. On the fourteenth of the month [of

111. In 1518, Henry VIII of England returned Tournai to France. In 1521, the city surrendered to the emperor's troops and was incorporated into the Netherlands.
112. That is, a prostitute.

April] a general procession was held, and afterward there was a fine sermon exhorting the people to be pious and to pray to God and the Virgin Mary to grant the Emperor Charles V a victory [65] over his enemies; and on Monday [April 18] the statue was shown to a painter so it could be painted and put back in its usual place. A more beautiful and sumptuous shrine than ever will be made. 1532.

LETTER FROM THE GRAND TURK TO POPE CLEMENT VII

The following are the contents of bold and astonishing letters of defiance that the Grand Turk sent to our holy father the pope and to all the other Christian princes and that the emperor sent to the king of France in 1532, in the month of March, explaining what Turkey was doing.[113]

"We,[114] Süleyman, son of Selim, by the grace of the Great God and the intercession of Mohammed and his rightful descendants, prophets of our law, the Grand Emperor of Turkey and Constantinople and the Sultan of Babylon and all the eastern lands where thirty-six powerful kings reign under our law and imperial majesty, send you greetings, Prince of Christians. [66]

"We are writing to warn you about the great military challenge we have already launched against the Christian emperor, the king of Spain and a formidable power on the Mediterranean Sea,[115] to whom we have graciously offered a truce until the twentieth of May. You may be certain that our fear of spilling the blood of so many Christians has moved us to write to you, so that you may warn all the Christian kings. You may believe that we are

---

113. Like the letter from Jacques Gaucourt cited above (see note 109), the authenticity of this letter is highly doubtful, according to Feld. No original or translated copy of it has been found in Rome, Paris, or Vienna, and its style differs considerably from other known diplomatic writings of the Grand Turk. The letter, and Jussie's comments below on the conduct and customs of the Turks, grew out of the many rumors and fears about the Turks circulating throughout Christian Europe during this period. Although the Turks did possess considerable military strength and skill, reports of their power were often greatly exaggerated. The only piece of information given here by Jussie that Feld admits to be more or less correct is her comment that the Turks took their meals sitting on rugs. See Feld's introduction to the *Petite chronique*, lxii–lxiii. For a comprehensive study of European impressions of the Turks, and especially, of the Grand Turk, in the late fifteenth and early sixteenth centuries, as well as a consideration of the sources of these impressions, see Robert Schwoebel, *The Shadow of the Crescent: The Renaissance Image of the Turk, 1453–1517* (New York: Saint Martin's, 1967). More recently, Lucette Valensi has shown that much information about the Ottoman Empire reached Western Europe in the sixteenth century through the reports of Venetian ambassadors. See *The Birth of the Despot: Venice and the Sublime Porte*, trans. Arthur Denner (Ithaca, N.Y.: Cornell University Press, 1993).

114. The Grand Turk uses the royal plural through most of this letter.

115. That is, Charles V.

powerful enough to hold all lands in the world under our imperial crown. And you should know that we believe it to be right, lawful, and proper that, just as a single God reigns in heaven, so should a single emperor reign over the earth, to be feared and obeyed by all. We intend for it to be us because of our military strength. So we ask you to tell all the lands and kingdoms in Christendom to pay us homage. Or else we will wage such a great war on them that, by force, strength, and severity, they will be controlled by our inestimable power. If it is the will of Mohammed and his rightful descendants for you Christians to be subject to our imperial crown, we will ask all kings for their loyalty and homage, and they must be loyal to only one crown, and we will ask for the bells and cymbals in their temples and monasteries to be applied to our war efforts.[116] You should know that we would force no one to renounce the law but would give each person the freedom to choose which god to serve and to worship. [67] To show you that I am feared and obeyed more than anyone else, I am sending to your papal domain two messengers, that is, two great kings from my imperial court, my great and faithful friends, of whom one is the king of Ishorte and the other the king of Fraulte.[117] We have asked the king of Ishorte, in the name of Mohammed, to present my letters to you directly and, as soon as you have heard them, directly and without delay and under penalty of deprivation and separation from the laws of Mohammed and his rightful descendants, to pierce his Turkish heart with all his might so that he will then die.

"Written in our city of Vlorë,[118] in the land of Syria, during our reign, 6,066 years after the creation of the world.[119]"

After the letters were heard, the Turk stabbed himself in the stomach with a dagger and fell dead to the floor, which horrified everyone present. The other Turk said he would rather die than disobey his prince and that such was the law in Turkey. Then his servants led him away and took him to where they were staying, in the belvedere behind Saint Peter's palace in Rome. [68]

116. That is, the metal should be melted down and recast into weapons.

117. According to Feld, the kings of Ishorte (spelled Ishorque on second reference) and Fraulte are unknown elsewhere and are likely an invention. See Feld's edition of the *Petite chronique*, 67, nn. 5 and 6.

118. Also called Valona. A city and port on the coast of Albania, then the site of a Turkish fortress.

119. According to Feld, the year 6066 is an invented date. The year 1532 is the Jewish year 5292, the Byzantine year 7040, and the Muslim year 939. See Feld's edition of the *Petite chronique*, 67, n. 8.

CONDUCT AND CUSTOMS OF THE TURKS

To understand Turkish ways you must know that the Grand Turk has thirty-six kingdoms subject to him and many islands and cities in the sea over there. Like a glutton and a disloyal, insatiable dog, he is always waging war to get more land. In all of his kingdoms he takes a wife, and they are called queens; and they gather their courts all together in one city for the Turk's pleasure; and he has as many concubines as he has in the city and more. They are in groups in different cities.

Also, all the other Turks, whatever their estate, are free to take as many wives as they want. When one wife is pregnant, the husband no longer lives with her but with another one. They say that law comes from Mohammed, who said what God said to Adam and Eve, "Be fruitful and multiply."[120] Sometimes it happens in Turkey that in a single day three [69] or four wives[121] have babies. That is why there are so many men and innumerable soldiers, because the Grand Turk always takes two fifteen-year-old male children from all of his subjects and raises them in great companies in his cities and castles, ten or twelve thousand of them together, and he teaches them the ways of war, and they play with Slavonic swords and bows and firearms, and when he needs them, they are always ready to go.

Also, the Grand Turk has an astonishingly large number of people in his court, and as for his costume, he wears a great golden chain embellished with fine oriental gems around his neck, from which a golden pig hangs, in remembrance of Mohammed, who was strangled by a pig, and the thirty-six kings in his court also wear it. He also has fifty thousand harquebusiers[122] who fire their guns twice a day, that is, before dinner and supper; they have to reload them before they sit down on his rug, and they eat on the floor. He also has eighty thousand halberdiers,[123] five thousand archers, and forty thousand light horses that he uses when he goes from one land to another. It is no surprise that he has such great wealth because when anyone dies all

---

120. "And one of His signs is that he created you from dust, then lo! you are mortals who scatter." *Qur'an Translation*, trans. Mahomodali H. Shakir (Elmhurst, N.Y.: Tahrike Tarsile Qu'ran, 1985), chap. 30, v. 20. "God blessed them, and God said to them 'Be fruitful and multiply, and fill the earth and subdue it; and have dominion over the fish of the sea and over the birds of the air and over every living thing that moves upon the earth" (Gn 1:28); "And you, be fruitful and multiply, abound on the earth and multiply in it" (Gn 9:7).

121. That is, of one man.

122. That is, soldiers with rifles. Manuscript B reduces the figure to thirty thousand.

123. That is, soldiers with halberds, long-handled weapons that ended in a combined spearhead and battleaxe.

the property goes to him, whether the person is of low or high estate, in his [70] court or otherwise.[124] There is plenty of money in his treasury to maintain his standard of living or even increase it.

Also, when someone claims the property of a man who has died, he must give one-tenth of it to the treasury and provide for the dead man's wife and children, until age fifteen for the boys and until marriage for the girls. He is given half of what remains and nothing else. Written and printed the twelfth[125] of June, 1532.

THE HERETICS' PLACARDS ON THE DOORS OF THE CHURCHES IN GENEVA

In June of that year, on a Sunday morning [June 9], some brazen men posted large printed placards on all the church doors in Geneva, stating all the principal claims of the perverse Lutheran sect, but they were soon torn down by good Christians. [71] After saying matins, one of messieurs the canons,[126] a brave and good Catholic[127] who stood up to the heretics, tore down the placards they had posted at Saint Peter's church, which angered those troublemakers. One of them drew his sword and struck him in the arm, and he lost almost all his blood and was sick in bed for a long time; no one thought he would live, and all the honorable people grieved for him. However, with the help of God, for whose honor he had risked his life, he was healed by the surgeon's good care.

The next Tuesday, which was the Feast of Saint Barnabas [June 11], it was proclaimed to the sound of a trumpet that no one should put up any more of those placards, under penalty of three *traits de corde*[128] and banishment from the city for a year.

THE GRAND TURK ENTERS THE KINGDOM OF HUNGARY

The next July, when monseigneur was in Chambéry, he received a letter from the emperor telling him the Grand Turk had attacked the kingdom of

124. Manuscript B omits this explanation for the Grand Turk's wealth.

125. Manuscript B says the fifteenth.

126. Peter Werle (Verly) from Fribourg.

127. Manuscript B adds "and a zealot in the Christian religion" (*et zelateur de la foy chrestienne*).

128. Jussie is likely referring to *strappado*, a common method of torture or punishment in the late medieval and early modern period in which a subject was lifted off the ground by a pulley and rope (usually tied to the subject's wrists, which were bound behind his or her back) and then dropped back down the length of the rope.

Hungary on the eve of the Feast of Saint John the Baptist [June 24]. [72] The noble prince was very upset, and as a good Christian, to invoke God's aid by the intercession of the Virgin Mary and the glorious saints,[129] on the second Sunday of the month, the Feast of Monseigneur Saint Bonaventure [July 14], he called for a great general procession, and he himself attended with bare feet and head, and his son, Monseigneur Louis, Lord and Prince of the Piedmont, was there with his whole estate and the nobles and all the people in order and in great piety. The clerics carried the relics of the glorious saints that were in the church in the city of Chambéry. And so, many gentlemen in his lands, because of his good will, decided to go to the aid of the holy religion. Our Lord granted the noble emperor a victory, and the Turk retreated; the gentlemen returned to their lands. Monseigneur of Allemogne of the noble House of Viry[130] died of the plague on the way. [73]

THE COMET OF 1532

The following August a giant comet appeared in the sky around sunrise at four o'clock in the morning, and its large burning tail could be seen every day until the following November. And I who write this saw it. God knows its meaning.

GUILLAUME FAREL'S SECOND STAY IN GENEVA

The following October, in 1532, a miserable wretched preacher named Master Guillaume [Farel] from the town of Gap in the Dauphiné came to Geneva. The day after he arrived he began to preach secretly in a room where he was staying, and many people who had heard he was there and who were already infected with his heresy came to hear him.

Monseigneur the vicar general, named Monseigneur Aymé de Gingis, the Abbot of Bonmont, was told about this, and he summoned all of messieurs the canons to [74] discuss what to do to stop the heretics. They advised him to send for the preacher [Farel], and the lord's secretary[131] sent for him. They brought him and two of his associates before the lords, and

---

129. Once again, Jussie refers explicitly to both male and female saints: *tous les glorieulx sains et sainctes.*

130. Aymé de Viry, Lord of Allemogne and of Mategnin, brother of Baron Michel de Viry, who will host the nuns at his castle during their journey to Annecy. See below, text surrounding note 361.

131. According to Feld, probably Louis Marchard. See Feld's edition of the *Petite chronique*, 74, n. 15.

monseigneur the official, a learned and eloquent man named Master Guillaume de Vège,[132] asked him who had sent him and why and under whose
authority. The wretched man answered that he was sent by God and that he
had come to proclaim His word. Monseigneur the official said to him, "Why
don't you show us visible signs that you are sent by God, as Moses showed
the pharaoh king visible signs that he was sent by God? As for preaching to
us, you do not have the permission or authority of our very reverend prelate,
Monseigneur of Geneva, and no preacher has ever preached in his diocese
without his authority and good will. What is more, you are not wearing a
habit like men who usually preach the word of God and the holy Gospel to
us. You dress like [75] a soldier and a bandit. And how is it that you are so
bold as to preach? For the holy church has forbidden laypersons to preach
publicly, under penalty of excommunication, as it is contained in the decrees
of our holy mother church.[133] So you are a deceitful and criminal man."

During that trial all the priests of the cathedral church gathered in front
of monseigneur the vicar's house, about eighty of them, and they were all
armed to defend the holy religion and prepared to die for it, wanting to
make this wretched man[134] and his accomplices die miserable deaths if they
came near them. After examining him thoroughly, monseigneur the vicar
told Farel to get out of his house and out of his sight and told him and his
two associates[135] to be out of the city in six hours or else they would be
burned. Then Farel asked for a testimonial letter to take to Bern, saying that
he had done his duty and preached in the city. They told him he would
have no such letter, and [76] he departed and left without a word. But he did
not dare go outside because he could hear the noise the clerics were making
outside the door and he was afraid they would kill him.

When they saw that he had not left, two of the lord canons began to
insult him, saying that since he did not want to go out willingly and in God's
name, he should go out in the name of all the great devils whose minister
and servant he was. One of them kicked him in the shoulders, and the other
hit him in the head and face with his fists. In great confusion they threw
him out with his two associates, accursed preachers of their criminal law. At
that moment messeigneurs the syndics appeared with all the city sentinels

---

132. Guillaume de Vège, an official of the diocese of Geneva (1531–35).

133. See the decrees of Gregory IX, book V, title 7, chap. 12, in Aemilius Friedberg, ed., *Corpus Iuris Canonici* (Leipzig, 1879/1881), 744–87.

134. The writer of manuscript B calls him an "accursed dog" (*mauldict chien*).

135. Feld identifies his companions as Pierre Robert Olivétan and Antoine Saunier. See Feld's edition of the *Petite chronique*, 75, n. 19.

and all their halberdiers;[136] they told messieurs the clerics not to hurt him, saying they had come to see that justice was done. Then they arrested the wretched man and took him away. But those good priests were not satisfied, and when he passed in front of them, one of them tried to stab him. But one of the syndics held him back with his arm. Many people were upset that he had not done it. When he was passing in the streets, men and women shouted that he should be thrown into [77] the Rhone. The next day, on the Feast of Saint Francis [October 4], he and his associates were put in a little boat, very early in the morning so that no one would see. They took refuge in Morat, a city of their allies that was already perverted by the foul preachers of the Antichrist.

ANOTHER FRENCH PREACHER IN GENEVA

Those heretics kept at it, and in the month of December another French preacher [Antoine Fromment] came and preached secretly in a residence until Christmas, when he began to do it openly, since his listeners were multiplying, and he did it in a large room with a round table, so that he could be heard better. Seeing that there were more Lutherans every day, they wanted him to preach on the Feast of Saint Sylvester [December 31] in the church of the Madeleine, after dinner. But the vicars were advised to close the church and [78] to resist forcibly. Then the heretics tried to climb up to the bell tower to take the bell down. But some people inside rang it in alarm, and a crowd gathered to save the church, and there was a great uproar. The poor ladies of Saint Clare, who were having dinner, heard the commotion that was so near them. They got up from the table to appeal to Our Sovereign Lord and make a procession in great piety and tears, truly fearing that they would come for them next because they had already threatened to remove them from the convent and make them get married. Messieurs the syndics and governors appeared promptly and calmed things down, so there was no killing or violence, by the grace of God.

FROMMENT'S SERMON AT THE PLACE DU MOLARD

The next day, the first day of the year 1533, after the regular sermon at Saint [79] Peter's, those Lutherans brought their idol to preach in the large Place du Molard. Monseigneur the vicar[137] heard about it, and he immediately

136. See above, note 123.
137. Aymé de Gingins, Abbot of Bonmont.

sent messieurs the syndics to stop them. He sent monsieur the lieutenant[138] to order them, under great penalty, to leave and take their idol with them. They did not dare oppose him because they were not powerful enough to use force. Then messieurs the governors discussed the matter and decided to have a general council meeting the next morning.

THE COUNCIL OF GENEVA'S EDICT AGAINST THE HERETICAL PREACHERS

The next day [January 2, 1533], after they had told the lord councilors about those heretics' stubbornness, they decided they did not want that sect to reign in their town, that it should be abolished and eradicated absolutely, and that there should no longer be any question of it among the people.

At that, great edicts and orders went out from messieurs the governors and councilors that no preacher could preach anywhere in town, secretly or publicly, without the permission of Monseigneur of Geneva or [80] his vicar, except for Dominicans and Franciscans, and that anyone who hid a preacher at home or supported that heresy would be punished severely. Severe punishment was ordered for all persons, men and women, who ate meat on Friday and other times forbidden by the holy church. And so the commotion among the people was calmed down a bit.

Also, the council levied and imposed taxes and fees for the aid and care of the city, and all the butchers had to contribute one-twelfth of their profits, which they did not agree to, and so on Saturday during the octave of the Feast of Kings [January 11] they all decided not to sell any meat. Anyone who wanted some had to send for it outside the city limits. Then the governors found out, and the next Monday all the butchers' workbenches [81] were chopped into big pieces, which was a great damage and loss, and people said it was because the butchers did not want to be heretics.

TURMOIL AMONG THE GENEVANS

In that year, 1533, on March 28, which was Good Friday, there was another great upheaval among the citizens of Geneva because of that heresy. There was a throng and gathering of people of that sect all morning long. The news spread quickly through the city, and no one knew what they were going to

---

138. At this time, the lieutenant, the main judicial officer of Geneva, was Claude de Chateau-neuf. According to Fromment, however, it was actually Petremant Falquet who prevented him from preaching. Fromment, *Les actes et gestes*, 22–42.

do, but everyone supposed they were going to plunder the churches they had set their hearts on and all the convents and monasteries. And so the good Christians, to prepare, gathered in great numbers in Saint Peter's church to oppose them, along with messieurs the clerics, and they discussed what to do. The syndics, who heard about the gathering, came there with their sentinels to hear the reason for it. The people answered, [82] "We are going to attack those Lutherans who are gathered in the Rue des Allemands,[139] and we do not know why they are there. They are always scaring us. But we will put an end to it and not allow this infection in town anymore, for they are worse than Turks."

As those words were spoken, two wicked guards came to spy on the Christians, and they stopped on the portal steps. One of them could not keep from saying villainous words, at which several people immediately drew their swords to strike him. But the syndics ordered them not to do it. Nonetheless, the guard was knocked down and trampled and hit with a sword and gravely wounded so that he bled profusely. The church was violated, and no bell or divine service was heard there again until monseigneur the suffragan advised it, [83] nor in any other church or convent or monastery; the mother church was coming to an end. However, the convents and monasteries did not forsake divine service. The sisters of Saint Clare recited the canonical office, and the monks said the Mass publicly, although without ringing any bells.

The guard's comrade, seeing his comrade moaning on the ground, ran to tell the heretics everything. But the good Christians were more incited than before, and when they saw him go, many clerics and others, well armed and brave, went out to fight those scoundrels. Some Christians, to rouse the others, rang the large bell in great distress. At that sound, the whole town was armed and in turmoil. Some of them went to Saint Peter's, others to the large Place du Molard.

When the syndics realized they could not keep the people from going out, they had all the church doors closed. Then they had a large bough of a laurel tree brought in and gave a branch to each Christian so that they could distinguish them from the evildoers. Some attached them to their heads [84], others held them in their hands. When they all had this laurel emblem, messieurs the canons all knelt before the main altar in great piety, and the whole company too, commending themselves to God and reciting

139. Now Rue de la Confédération.

tearfully "Vexila regis prodeun"[140] and commending themselves to the glorious Virgin Mary, asking her to intercede for the holy religion and for them, offering her a "Salve regina."[141] The people encouraged each other, saying, "Today represents the day that Our Lord died and shed His blood for us, and so let us not hesitate to shed our own out of love and honor for Him; we will take vengeance on His enemies, who are crucifying Him again more shamefully than the Jews."[142]

They raised such a wail that it was a very lamentable thing to hear, and they were not brave enough to keep from breaking into tears. The bell stopped ringing, and the people lined up for battle. Messieurs the clerics set up troops and named captains. The syndics opened the doors, and the company went out. They went down the Rue du Perron to the large Place du Molard. There [85] was already a large company there, men and women, well armed and as determined as the others, and there were at least 2,500 armed men,[143] not counting women, old people, and children. They unfurled the city banner and raised it. Then the people let out a great yell and got ready to go after those heretics in their streets. When the heretics saw the Christians attacking them so bravely and realized they would have to defend themselves or die villainously, they were terrified and wished they had not started any trouble. Because they knew well that the Christians from Saint-Gervais were coming up behind them, they went to the bridge and closed the gate after them so they could not enter the city. Afterward it was proclaimed to the sound of a trumpet throughout the whole city that all foreigners should either take refuge in their homes or leave the city immediately under penalty of three *traits de corde*.[144] Then the weapons were brought out, and six great cannons were set up facing the lake. The Christians got ready to fire upon the Lutherans, and [86] a very large one was set up facing the Rue de la Pélisserie. The syndics could not stop them, no matter what they asked or ordered them to do. In those troubled times there was so much hostility between the two parties that the child turned against his father and the mother against her daughter.

---

140. "Vexilla regis prodeunt" (Abroad, the royal banners fly), a hymn in honor of the holy cross.

141. "Salve regina, mater misericordiae" (Hail holy queen, mother of mercy), a chant in honor of the Virgin Mary.

142. Manuscript B omits the comparison to Jews.

143. Manuscript B reduces the number to 2,200.

144. Probably the *strappado* (see above, note 128).

One woman, whose father was a Lutheran, saw her Christian husband in arms, and she began to weep grievously. Her husband told her, "Wife, weep as much as you want. For if we are fighting and I see your father, he will be the first one I risk my life to kill or be killed by because that miserable Baudichon[145] is a wicked Christian and the worst of the worst."

Also, the wives of Christians gathered and shouted, "If our husbands fight those infidels, let's wage war on and kill their heretical wives, so that the whole race will be exterminated."

Many of the women who were gathered there carried rocks in their bodices to throw at the Lutherans. Along with the women there were at least seven hundred children between twelve and fifteen years old who were determined to do their duty with their [87] mothers. Some of them carried little rapiers, others daggers, others rocks in their belts, hats, and caps. Messieurs the priests went first to defend their holy bride the church, and there were a good 140 or 160 of them. Messieurs the syndics, seeing so much commotion, were very surprised and afraid that human blood would be shed, so they tried to come up with a solution. Two of them went up to the band of infidels, who had very big cannons. The syndics told them they did not want blood to be shed, or for brothers, native Genevans, and neighbors to kill each other, because it would be a very shameful scandal. The infidels, suspecting they were not powerful enough to stand up to the Christians, rejoiced and called for a truce for the time being. This was bad for the Christians because afterward the infidels caused them great harm and persecution and took control of the town and the Christians were never able to overthrow them again, although at that time they would easily have defeated and overthrown them.

They agreed that the Lutherans would turn over three of their most powerful leaders[146] as hostages, who would be kept in the house of a Christian, and [88] that the Christians would likewise turn three men over to those infidels. The Christians gave them a lord canon named Monsieur François Guet and two good lord merchants,[147] and they were taken to the home of a perverted [Swiss] German named [Jean] Goulaz. The Lutherans were taken to the home of a good Catholic man, Sire Pierre Malbosson, who was a syndic at the time. Then both sides were ordered to go home and not start up any more trouble or arguments, under penalty of hanging, which

145. Baudichon de la Maisonneuve.

146. Fromment identifies these men as Étienne Chapeau Rouge, Michel Balthasar, and Jean Lullin. Fromment, *Les actes et gestes*, 56.

147. Jean Malbosson and Jean de Pesmes.

was done, although it grieved the Christians deeply, and they complained
to each other and said, "We should stir everyone up again now so that we
do not have any more quarrels or troubles."

And truly it would have been better than letting them live. However, in
obedience to the law, they left peacefully without any other complaints. To
keep everyone calm it was proclaimed throughout the city, under penalty
of banishment and whipping, that no one should dare to sing any songs or
ballads that might start an argument, and so things were calmed down. [89]

On that day, as the crowd was gathering, a good Christian merchant
who was passing in front of the gathering of heretics was villainously struck
on the head, and he was carried to his house like a dead man; they had to
pull bones from his head, and he finally died of it. He was deeply mourned
by Christians because he was such an honorable man. The Christian women,
seeing that nasty attack, let out a great cry, and they turned to an apothecary's wife who was a Lutheran like her husband,[148] and they shouted out,
"To start our war, let's throw this bitch[149] into the Rhone." But the cunning
woman quickly locked herself in her house, and they could not get her. But,
out of spite, they threw on the ground and in the street everything they
found in the shop and on the workbench. And they were very sorry they
could not get her or anyone else.[150]

The poor nuns of Saint Clare were in great weeping and piety before
God all day long, begging for mercy, that by the intercession of the Virgin
Mary and all the glorious saints He would grant the good Christians a victory and guide the poor sinners back into the path of salvation. To be even
more [90] humble and to convince God to have mercy on the poor city, the
mother abbess put ashes on each of their heads, one by one. Then they had
a procession in their cloister with the sacred litany, and they called for the
intercession of the whole heavenly court;[151] then they all gathered together
in the shape of a cross in the middle of the choir and cried out for mercy and
did other pious acts that I do not have the space to write. You may believe
piteously that they were greatly afflicted and weeping. Their good fathers
went to battle with many other monks because it was for the religion, but
they did not bear arms. Good Christian women came and told the sisters

---

148. According to Feld, the woman in question was probably Claudine, wife of Aymé Levet.
See Feld's edition of the *Petite chronique*, 89, n. 21. On Claudine Levet, see below, note 341.

149. *Chienne.*

150. See volume editor's introduction, note 40, on similar acts of violence by Catholic women
in other cities.

151. Manuscript B omits the reference to the heavenly court.

that if the heretics won, it was true that they would all, old and young, have to get married, which would be perdition for all of them. There had already been talk of it. However, Our Lord allowed that day to go by without any other harm or bloodshed.

COUNCIL MEETING

On Sunday [March 30, 1533] the council met to decide what to do, and they decided that they would enforce law and order and that there would be no battle. [91] First, they ordered the release of the hostages. Second, under penalty of being hanged and strangled,[152] no one was to speak ill of or dishonor the church or the holy sacraments or sing songs against the sacraments of the altar, as had been done before. Third, no preacher was to preach without the permission of the bishop or his vicar, as it is written above.

Also, no Christian of any estate was to give a heretical preacher lodging, secretly or otherwise, under penalty of death, and anyone who knew of this happening and did not say anything would be declared guilty and suffer the same penalty.

Also, and under the same penalty, no one was to eat meat during Lent or at any other forbidden time, but only when it was allowed by the holy church. And anyone who cooked meat during such times would be punished.

Also, under penalty of banishment from the city, no one was to speak ill of or insult anyone by saying "You are a Lutheran or Mamellus," as had been done before. And other fine rules were drawn up. All the dizaines[153] in the city were told to announce all these things in their own districts and to have everyone raise their hands and swear and promise to [92] live and die in the religion of our ancestors, and if any man opposed them, he was to be identified to the syndics.

The dizaines immediately called all the inhabitants of their districts to a designated location and announced what is said above, and they urged them all to live in peace, friendship, and charity like good Christian brothers, as messieurs the councilors had ordered, and they told them all to raise their hands as a sign of agreement, which they did, shouting that they were glad to do it. In one dizaine there was a man who did not raise his hand or renounce his heresy. The other people, upset, shouted that he should be thrown mercilessly into the Rhone like a disloyal dog. When he saw the danger he was

---

152. Manuscript B omits "and strangled" (*et estrangler*).
153. The *dizaines* were elected administrators of individual districts in the city of Geneva.

in, he did what the others had done. After the canons' vespers, monseigneur the vicar called all the clerics, both priests and monks, to Saint Peter's, and he preached a fine sermon to them there, in Latin and in French. Then he urged them all to live well, serve God, do their duty, and uphold their positions as good clerics. [93]

GENERAL PROCESSION OF THE GENEVANS

On that same Sunday a general procession was held in the city in good order and great piety, giving praise to God, and that day was peaceful without any bloodshed. The Lutherans were there, both men and women, which made everyone happy, because they thought they had all converted. But alas, they were only pretending, as they showed afterward, very soon, bit by bit.

SERMON IN FRONT OF THE DOMINICAN CHURCH INTERRUPTED BY THE HERETICS

The next Sunday, Palm Sunday [April 6, 1533], an honorable monk and very learned man from Auxerre gave a sermon at the Dominican monastery. There was such a crowd that he preached in the large square in front of the church. Suddenly, when no one was watching, a book was thrown hard at the people, which upset everyone; some people shouted loudly, "Close the gates! Close the gates!" [94]

At that exclamation people were very frightened, and they feared treachery. The men unsheathed and drew their swords and daggers and prepared to defend themselves. The poor preacher, thinking those Lutherans were going to kill him and all the people, fainted and fell from the pulpit to the ground. However, nothing else happened, and those who had thrown the book to obstruct the word of God and to disturb people on that holy day[154] quickly fled, and the sermon remained unfinished, which angered everyone.[155] From that moment on, it was very clear that those wretches had returned to their vomit[156] and that the promises they had made on the previous Sunday had only been to save their lives.

---

154. This clause ("to obstruct . . . that holy day") is missing in manuscript B.

155. This sentence is also missing in manuscript B.

156. "Like a dog that returns to its vomit is a fool who reverts to his folly" (Prv 26:11); "It has happened to them according to the true proverb, 'The dog turns back to its own vomit,' and, 'The sow is washed only to wallow in the mud' " (2 Pt 2:22).

HOLY WEEK 1533

All that holy week, people were afraid because you could see the heretics walking around in large bands. There were rumors that they wanted to obstruct the holy sacraments and make sure that no Mass was held on Easter Day. Thus everyone carried weapons, and even priests did not dare go into the streets without weapons. It was in that way that they gave people the sacrament.[157] Messieurs the canons decided that the passion would be preached on Good Friday at Saint [95] Peter's, which had never been done during anyone's lifetime. Men came with their weapons, and there was no trouble.

On Holy Thursday [April 10] those Jews gathered in a garden, at least eighty of them, and women, to have their own Last Supper and to eat the Paschal Lamb. A homicidal and murderous criminal pretending to be Jesus Christ washed the others' feet, and then as a sign of peace and union, one after the other, they all bit off pieces of bread and cheese. The Christians laughed at them.

On Easter Monday [April 14] the good preacher bid the Christians farewell and hurried to take refuge in his land, because they were trying to kill him. There was no preaching from then on, which was very strange, because according to a very old custom, there was preaching in the convents without fail every Sunday and on solemn feast days.

NEW UPHEAVALS AMONG THE GENEVANS; DEATH OF CANON PETER WERLE

Also, on the fourth of May, Jubilate Sunday, those heretics gathered in the large Place du Molard, and no [96] one knew why. There were rumors that they were going to plunder the church. So the Christians gathered on the other side, near the market, waving their banner and shouting, "True and good Christians, gather here and be brave and uphold the holy religion."

There was a great commotion among them. At nine o'clock at night the Christians sounded the large bell in much alarm, which really scared everyone; they got up and grabbed their weapons. It was a piteous thing to hear the commotion and shouting in the streets. Among the rest of them, messieurs the clerics, canons and others, were the first to reach the banner.

One of the canons, a staunch defender of the religion, was Messire Peter Werle, a native of Fribourg who had already been gravely wounded an-

---

157. That is, carrying weapons.

other time. He burned [97] with love for God when he saw the heresy and contempt for the holy sacraments multiplying daily. His heart broke when he saw them hiding behind a chapel near the choir during singing at Saint Peter's and then howling like rabid wolves to obstruct and corrupt divine worship and when he saw them walking in the street in large bands—in front of processions invoking God's aid for the holy religion and the trials of the world and asking Our Lord to lead the heretics back into the path of truth—and saying to each other "Give those braying asses some thistles" and other very spiteful things that no one could write in a year. And so this good knight, Messire Peter Werle, being well armed, and not having the patience to wait for the other lord clerics, was the first one out and ran with fiery courage to the Place du Molard, where he expected to find the group of Christians, and he shouted with fiery fervor, "Good Christians, let's not spare those scoundrels anything!"

But, alas, he was mistaken; he was among his enemies but did not realize it, since it was night. And because of the great commotion and turmoil, the Christians on the other side, by the market, did not see him. His enemies, who hated him the most of all, pretended to be [98] on his side until he was surrounded by them. To betray him even more, they pulled him aside into a small street, and then they attacked him. He defended himself valiantly, but he could go no further because it was so narrow. They took away his weapons, and because he was so well and cleverly armed that they could not touch him, a criminal traitor struck him from underneath, straight through his body, so that he fell dead, a blessed martyr and a sacrifice to God. That Sunday had been the grand occasion of the precious Holy Shroud,[158] and because he was a pious and well educated man and a very fine cantor, monseigneur the vicar had asked him to recite the office all day long, and everyone had said that there was no finer officiant in the world and that no finer office had been said in Geneva for ten years. When that villainous act was done, they left him in the square, and he stayed there until nine o'clock the next day. [99]

When the Christians had gathered, messieurs the priests came across a band of those Lutherans and fought them so hard that those dogs fled.

Another canon, Monseigneur de la Biolee,[159] was gravely wounded, as

---

158. The Holy Shroud, now known as the Shroud of Turin, was an object of particularly high veneration in Savoy, as it was owned by the Duke of Savoy, who kept it in the royal chapel of his castle in Chambéry. Mary B. McKinley describes the fate of the shroud in her notes to Marie Dentière's *Epistle to Marguerite of Navarre*, 84 n.65.

159. Jacques de Biolée.

was one of the syndics. The Christians were in arms all night looking for those dogs, but it was to no avail, because they were all hiding. If the murder had been known, everyone would have been scandalized. But the Christians did not hear about it until the next day [May 5], when his body was found. When it became known, the whole city was in turmoil and distress. The city gates were not opened. Those heretics gathered again with weapons in the house of a man named Baudichon,[160] to damage the churches and convents. Messieurs the syndics proclaimed throughout the city under great penalty that no one of any estate should carry or stockpile weapons. Those dogs were forced to retreat, in spite of themselves. Afterward, Messire Peter's body was visited and carried to be buried at the cathedral church at five [100] o'clock in the evening, and they went to get him from the house near where he had been killed, where they had dressed him in his canon's robe. When they brought him out of that house, the people let out a great wail, lamenting and weeping over the innocent man's death.

He was carried by six priests, accompanied most honorably by monseigneur the vicar, all of messieurs the canons and their whole college, and all the clerics with the crosses of the seven parishes[161] and the convents. The whole town came to pay its respects to the blessed martyr, and after the very solemn office he was buried in front of the image of the crucifix, in whose honor he had died. Many of the miscreants came to see what was happening, and they laughed among themselves, saying, "See how nice he looks in a hypocrite's robe today, and yesterday he was an armed man."

MONSEIGNEUR WERLE'S BODY IS DUG UP AND MOVED TO FRIBOURG

The death of that good Catholic man was announced promptly to his relatives in Fribourg, [101] who were greatly outraged and immediately sent a messenger, along with the martyr's brother-in-law. When they arrived in Geneva, they asked to speak to the council as representatives of messieurs of Fribourg, which was granted them. When they were before the Council of Two Hundred, they told them that messieurs of Fribourg commended themselves to them and that they asked them to dig up Monseigneur Werle because they wanted to have his body in his city with his family, which was

---

160. Baudichon de la Maisonneuve.
161. The seven parishes of Geneva.

granted them. On that same day at three o'clock in the afternoon the grave was opened enough that you could see the dead man's clothes. All the crosses in town were brought there, and all the bells were rung, and messieurs the clerics of the collegial church all came, canons and altarists and priests, and the monks, Domincans and Franciscans and the ones from Madame Saint Clare, just like at the burial.

At five o'clock in the evening the body was raised out of the ground to be placed in a box. A wondrous thing occurred, worthy of the remembrance and great approbation [102] of our holy religion: because that body had been murdered to preserve the religion, God the Creator made a visible sign to confound the heretics who had murdered him, some of whom were present. He was raised straight up out of the grave in his canon's robe and immediately began to bleed, and the blood that flowed was as clear and fresh as if he were alive. The body that had been buried in the ground for five days, during hot weather, was as fresh, rosy, and whole as on the first day, and it did not stink, but smelled very good. It was witnessed by more than eight hundred people who were present and who saw and confirmed it. You may believe that that fine, clear blood flowing from the body was a call to avenge God and the world.

He was put in a box and carried honorably by eight priests accompanied by the whole noble college of Saint Peter's and all of messieurs the clerics, the Benedictine monks, the Dominicans, the Augustins, the Franciscans, and the ones from Saint Clare, messieurs the syndics, the leaders and councilors of the city, burghers, merchants, and people of every estate. It was a piteous thing to hear people lamenting over that body. All the bells were rung solemnly. They accompanied him to the shore of the lake, where he was put on a boat and taken by his people to Fribourg.

When the people in Fribourg saw him, the clerics came up and carried him to messieurs his brothers' house, and they lifted him up onto a table. It was said that they kept him there for three or four days [103] to be visited, and that no one, low or high, was turned away. He was never seen to alter or change, and his body always remained whole. It was said that such a great lamentation as was made over his death had not been made in that canton for a long time, and especially by messieurs his brothers and family, who were all of high and powerful estate. He was buried with his family. He was dug up on Friday, the sixth day after his death [May 9]. May God allow us to share in his merits, and by his great merits and intercession may he convert those poor infidels, for he is without a doubt in glorious communion with the blessed saints.

ACTIONS OF THE HERETICS IN GENEVA
AGAINST THE CHURCH

After that murder those dogs did not stop disturbing and afflicting the church, pillaging, attacking, and killing and doing other evil deeds. It got so bad that clerics did not dare go out in public without arms and weapons under their long robes. What Our Lord said to his apostles in the twenty-second chapter of Saint Luke came to pass: "Let he who has no sword sell his cloak and buy one,"[162] etc. If messieurs the clerics had not been bold [104] and of great courage during that time, those ravenous wolves[163] would have completely exterminated and abolished the holy church. But their accursed enterprise did not have its intended effect, thanks to the grace of God Our Sovereign Creator, who has never failed His bride the holy church.

BISHOP PIERRE DE LA BAUME'S LAST STAY IN GENEVA

On the first day of the following July, Monseigneur of Geneva, who had not been in town for five years, arrived to deal with his enemies. The Christians were overjoyed, and the heretics were very angry.

The day after his arrival a general procession was ordered and proclaimed [July 2]. [105] It was done piously, and then a general council meeting was called. The burghers and citizens gathered in front of Saint Peter's, and when everyone was there, the lord and prelate arrived with his nobles and with messieurs the syndics in order and in silence. Monseigneur the bailiff of Dôle, speaking for the lord, gave a very fine speech to the people, for he was a very learned and eloquent man. When he was done, Monseigneur of Geneva spoke and addressed them in a fine, clear voice, in language that was intelligible to everyone, and he asked them, first of all, if they regarded him as their prince and lord. They said they did. And so, as prelate, out of duty and for the salvation of their souls, he gave them a pious exhortation and warning. They should first show love and fear of [106] God by observing His commandments and obeying the holy church, the bride of Jesus Christ, as Christians, and from then on, they should live in peace and show love and charity for each other, as good citizens, friends,

---

162. "He said to them, 'But now, the one who has a purse must take it, and likewise a bag. And the one who has no sword must sell his cloak and buy one'" (Lk 22:36).

163. "Beware of false prophets, who come to you in sheep's clothing but inwardly are ravenous wolves" (Mt 7:15); "I know that after I have gone, savage wolves will come in among you, not sparing the flock" (Acts 20:29).

and neighbors. He said it so humbly and piously that everyone wept. It was done without any uproar or disturbance, for which God Our Lord be praised.

On July 5, ten leaders of the heresy[164] were arrested and put in prison, including a gentleman who was the Genevans' ally, Monseigneur of Thozain.[165] As soon as he was notified, the most high Monseigneur Philippe of Savoy, Count of the Genevois, called for his troops and seized all his lands and his domain, as did the most excellent monseigneur the viscount,[166] who was in his domain. Because he was a heretic, that poor perverted man was stripped of all of his property. When he was freed, he returned to Bern with his allies. Those heretics kept after Monseigneur of Geneva; they tried to kill him several times and to attack him at home at [107] night. When he realized the danger he was in and saw he could do nothing to stop it, he left Geneva and took refuge in his Tower of Meix, which greatly upset all of the Christians. The prisoners were freed.

EXECUTION OF THE CANON WERLE'S MURDERER

The people of Fribourg continued in their pursuit of justice; they had promised they would not give up until the canon's murderers were put to death. And it was done. The man who had treacherously run his sword through him was executed on August 16; his head was cut off and his body placed on the gibbet[167] like a criminal's. Even though he was a Lutheran, they preached to him until he returned and died in the faith. Praise be to God the Creator. [108]

MEETING OF POPE CLEMENT VII AND FRANCIS I, KING OF FRANCE, IN MARSEILLES

In the following month of September, the Holy Father Pope Clement VII came to Marseilles, a low country, and met the king of France, Francis I, of the House of Angoulême and, on his mother's side, of the most illustrious

---

164. Fromment lists twelve men and one woman taken captive: "Amy Perrin, Domeyne D'Arlod, Pierre Vandelly, Iehan Pecollat, Iehan Velliard brodeur, Ayme Leuet, Philbert de Compey Seig^r de Touren, Claude Paste, Anthonin Derbey, Anrry Doulen, Iehan Rouzettez, Iacques Fichet, Claude Geneue, citoiens et bourjoix, et la femme de Iehan Chautemps." Fromment, *Les actes et gestes*, 61.

165. Philibert de Compeys, Lord of Thorens.

166. François of Luxembourg, Viscount of Martigues and Governor of Savoy.

167. After execution, criminals' bodies were commonly hung from a vertical post called a gibbet.

House of Savoy. The king acted in complete honor and as a good Christian; he realized the holy father was the representative of Our Savior Jesus Christ and knelt down on the ground and kissed his feet, and the holy father kissed him on the forehead. Then the king presented his three sons to him: monseigneur the dauphin, named Francis;[168] Monseigneur of Orléans, named Henry;[169] and Monseigneur of Angoulême, named Charles.[170] Then the queen[171] paid her respects to him with [109] the king's two daughters,[172] and they negotiated the marriage of Monseigneur of Orléans, the king's second son, to the holy father's niece. People thought it would calm down those heresies. But it was not yet time.

Philippe of Savoy, Duke of Nemours and Count of the Genevois, accompanied the king. He died of a continual fever[173] in Marseilles. It was a great loss for the land and greatly mourned. He was taken to be buried in the collegial church of his city of Annecy, in front of Notre Dame de Liesse. He had married the most excellent Mademoiselle de Dunois of Longueville,[174] by whom he left two children, a son and a daughter. May God allow them to reach the peak of all perfection.

THE DOMINICAN GUY FURBITY PREACHES AT ADVENT IN GENEVA

In that same year, 1533, an honorable preacher of the [110] Reformed Dominican order and the Monastery of Montmélian near Chambéry, Friar Guy Furbity, a grand master in holy theology, preached at Advent. He preached very fervently, without any fear or hypocrisy, against all vice, and he especially spoke out against the Lutheran heresy, which is why the heretics watched him like a cat watches a mouse. On the first Sunday and Monday

---

168. Francis (1517–36), eldest son of Francis I, became Duke of Brittany in 1524 but died before becoming king.

169. Henry (1519–59), second son of Francis I, succeeded his father on the French throne as Henry II in 1547. As Jussie mentions below, he married Catherine de Medicis (1519–89), great-niece of Pope Clement VII.

170. Charles (1521–45), third son of Francis I, became Duke of Angoulême in 1522, Duke of Orléans in 1540, and Duke of Bourbon in 1543.

171. Eleanor (1498–1558), Spanish infanta and eldest sister of Emperor Charles V, became the second wife of Francis I in 1530. All five children listed here were from the first wife of Francis I, Claude (1499–1524), daughter of Louis XII.

172. Madeleine of France (1520–37), who later married King James V of Scotland, and Marguerite of France (1523–74), who later married Duke Emmanuel Philibert of Savoy.

173. As opposed to a quartan fever (see below, notes 342 and 343 and related text).

174. Charlotte of Orléans (1512–49), daughter of Louis I of Orléans, Duke of Longueville.

they gave him no trouble. On Tuesday a wicked young man[175] stood up after the preaching and shouted, "Messieurs, Messieurs, listen to what I tell you." And when the people were silent, he said in a loud voice, "Messieurs, I would risk my life and expose myself to be burned to maintain that this man has said nothing but lies and words of the Antichrist."

Then the people stood up and shouted, "Burn him! Burn him!" and they tried to capture him. But he fled, and they could not catch him. However, the women followed him and threw stones at him. One of his comrades, who was just like him, said he would maintain upon his life what his comrade had said.[176] He was immediately arrested [111] and put in prison. There were at least a hundred Lutherans at that sermon, but no one said a word except for those two who spoke for them all. After dinner messieurs the syndics and their regular councilors had a meeting, and they ordered those two Mohammedists to be banished perpetually from the town, and they told them to be out in twenty-four hours and never to return.

THE RETURN OF FOUR HERETICAL PREACHERS TO THE CITY

During the third week of Advent those heretics brought four preachers[177] into the city, and on the fourth Sunday [December 31, 1533], after the sermon and vespers had been said at Saint Peter's, some wicked heretics were discovered among the Christians, and they swore and blasphemed against God and said their idols were going to preach in the church along with the papist[178] preachers. The Christians responded boldly [112] that they would do no such thing and that they would rather die. Those heretics got ready to fight, but the wise Christians said that it was not a good time and that they would show them they observed the holy Gospel better than those who called themselves "Evangelicals"[179] did and that they would not fight, out of respect for the holy Sunday, unless they were forced to do so to defend the holy religion. "But so that you will not think we are cowards, tomorrow in

175. Feld identifies this *jeusne meschant garsson* as Antoine Fromment. See Feld's edition of the *Petite chronique*, 110, n. 2

176. Feld identifies this man as Alexandre Canus (also called Dumoulin), a former Dominican monk. See Feld's edition of the *Petite chronique*, 110, n. 3.

177. Guillaume Farel, Pierre Viret, Antoine Fromment, and Alexandre Canus.

178. By calling priests "papists," Jussie is appropriating Reformed terminology—or using free indirect speech.

179. See volume editor's introduction, pp. 17–18.

the light of day you will find us in the main square, and we will not be afraid to risk our lives to defend the holy church."

PREPARATIONS FOR CIVIL WAR BETWEEN CATHOLICS AND EVANGELICALS IN GENEVA

On Monday morning [December 22, 1533], true to their word, about eight or nine hundred gathered at the house of Monseigneur of Geneva, and they got ready there and took up arms to resist those miscreants with honorable courage; they were all reputable people who were well equipped. When they were ready, they discussed how best to handle the matter. They ordered about two hundred men to stay at Saint Peter's [113], to bring up the rear when those heretics advanced. They all left at noon, in fine form and eager and burning with the love of God, which made them very fine to see, and it was a very pious and very piteous thing to see those fine people risk their lives to preserve the holy religion.

That fine company of clerics and monks and people of every estate was led by the captain of the priests and by a nobleman who was valiant and very skilled with weapons, Monseigneur the Squire of Pesmes,[180] a man of great bravery, as his valorous acts showed many times, and who later suffered great harm and martyrdom for the religion.

When they reached the Place du Molard, the whole town was in an uproar and Christians rushed there with fiery courage; women came in great droves carrying rocks, and children were equally determined, as it is recorded above about the first gathering in the month of March. I who write this saw with my own eyes those days full of misfortune; I bore my part of those afflictions with my company of twenty-four who could not carry weapons of iron but carried weapons [114] of hope and the shield of faith.[181] I promise that I write nothing I do not know to be true, and still I do not write a tenth of it, but only a very small part of the main events so that they will be remembered, so that in the future those who suffer for the love of God in this world will know that our ancestors suffered as much as we do, and as people after us will, and always, to varying degrees, in the example of Our Lord and Redeemer, who suffered the first and the most.[182]

---

180. Perceval de Pesmes, the prince-bishop's squire and a Genevan standard-bearer.

181. "With all of these, take the shield of faith, with which you will be able to quench all the flaming arrows of the evil one" (Eph 6:16).

182. Manuscript B alters this passage slightly, especially the ending, which reads "in the example of Our Lord and Redeemer who suffered first, and of the blessed saints" (*a l'exemple de nostre seigneur et redempteur qui a souffert le premier, et de ses benoists saincts*).

The miscreant infidels took up weapons and gathered on the other side in the Rue des Allemands. But they were still weak and dared not attack. The Christians did not want to start any trouble. Again, the syndics did not authorize fighting but, to prevent bloodshed, announced in the city and sent word to both parties, with the council's approval, that everyone should retreat without harming anyone else, under penalty of death. The Christians responded that they were already too upset by all the rioting that was going on unpunished and that something had to be done. When the syndics heard the response, they went there in person. When the Christians saw them coming, messieurs their captains went up to them [115] to pay their respects and to present their just and honorable reasons for not following their orders to retreat. The trumpets were immediately sounded again, three times, and then it was proclaimed loudly that Monseigneur of Geneva and messieurs the syndics and governors ordered everyone to retreat and not to bear any more weapons in the city, under penalty of death without mercy. The captains rejected those orders on behalf of all their followers, saying firmly that they truly wished to obey their prince and the law but that they would not retreat until the miscreants were cleared out and disarmed because they had already betrayed them many times and did not keep their promises. Hearing that, the syndics went up to the band of miscreants and asked them to retreat and to live in peace, which they promised to do. The syndics returned to the Christians and reported the other side's response to them, saying the heretics had been the first to obey the law and asking the Christians likewise to obey and be pacified and live in good concord and friendship as good neighbors, brothers, and friends. But the Christians did not retreat until six o'clock at night, when all the enemies had retreated and disarmed. They spent a very cold day, for there had not been so much wind and ice in ten years. [116]

CHRISTMAS 1533

After that the two sides were somewhat pacified. But those criminals soon started pillaging the churches and trying to arrange it so that on Our Lord's birthday [December 25] no Mass or other office would be celebrated in any church. But God gave the Christians so much courage that they made the heretics tremble, and despite their plans, such an excellent and solemn Divine Office as was celebrated on that day at Saint Peter's and in all of the churches and convents and monasteries had never been seen in anyone's lifetime. Many people confessed and received communion in parishes and mendicant monasteries in great piety. After dinner the father preacher preached so fervently that people were inspired and amazed, and he did it the next day [December 26] too. And he[183] said, with good cause, that he would not preach on the Feast of Saint John [December 27], which upset everyone. But to avoid any more trouble, they agreed. Since those heretics were threatening him so much, messieurs the canons had him stay in the house of Monseigneur of Geneva. [117] And he still preached in the great cathedral church. On Christmas Eve [December 24], some heretics who had already won the syndics over with favors put Saint Peter's under the guard of four sentinels so that he could not leave or go anywhere without them, which greatly upset the poor Christians, even though no one knew why they did it.

On the Feast of Saint Thomas of Canterbury [December 29] the reverend father preached, and he spoke powerfully about those dogs, saying that all those who followed those sects were lustful, gluttonous, lewd, murderous thieves who loved nothing but their own sensuality and who lived like animals without recognizing God or their superiors, but lived in damnable liberty, and other things against them, at which the Christians rejoiced. But those dogs were filled with great anger and malice against him, and they did not dare show it. [118]

ARREST OF GUY FURBITY

After the sermon, the Squire of Pesmes, the good people's captain, went with several of the leaders of his band to find the reverend father, and he thanked him for having spoken such fine words against those errors, and he told him not to fear, that they would keep him out of their hands. The reverend master replied, "Monsieur Captain, I am only doing my duty, for we are each expected to do our own work. I beg you and all good and faithful Christians to use your swords skillfully, and as for me, I will use the spirit and my voice to defend the truth my whole life long."

On New Year's Day he gave his sermon with great fervor and piety, and he offered his fine courage to all people of every estate. Then he bid the people farewell so honorably and piously that everyone wept, and he thanked them for their good company and attention and told them to persevere in their piety and to remain firm against those heretics; he said that they should do their best to keep them from getting the upper hand, for bad things could come of it. The people thanked him as well. After blessing them, [119] he bid them farewell and swore upon his life that he would stand by everything he had preached, every bit of it and in every place and before the University

---

183. The subject of the verb "said" is unclear.

of Paris, of which he was a graduate and a grand master in sacred theology. And then he left and retired to his room.

But those guards would not let him leave the city, and, to satisfy the Lutherans' appetite, he was immediately put in prison and greatly tortured and abused to make him recant and say he had spoken disrespectfully of messieurs of Bern. He was put in a crude cell with a floor of bare earth and was guarded by heretics who tortured him greatly, injured him, and constantly tried to convert him. This caused the Christians great sorrow and displeasure, especially the ladies and the burgher women, and they offered many vows, prayers, and pious acts for his release. They often came in great droves to the Convent of Saint Clare to have a Mass to Our Lady recited for him, and after Mass the sisters would recite the "Salve regina"[184] in great piety and the good Christians would all pray for him. But Our Lord had chosen him to suffer and to be an example to the world of firm constancy and a mirror of patience. He did not recant, but always kept his word, saying he had spoken nothing but the truth and citing the Holy Scripture as proof. They brought him to dispute[185] with the satanical Farel many times, [120] but he never accepted, saying he would in no way use his divine knowledge before such a vile and criminal man and that he would not lower himself to listen to him. It infuriated that wretched Farel to be thought so vile, and it pained the heretics very much not to be able to win over the reverend father. They kept him cruelly in his cell, although he was a delicate man from a good house.

But Our Lord did him this favor: the wife of the soldier[186] who was guarding him was a Christian, and, out of great concern and humanity, she did what she could for him, and the burgher women sent him jam and other goods, which she slipped to him secretly. But unfortunately she was accused and revealed to the heretics, who reprimanded her husband severely. He beat her and cruelly mistreated her. But, even so, she never wavered in goodness and piety. And because the sisters of Saint Clare had great pity for that holy man, with the help of that good woman, who was a second Saint Anastasia,[187] they wrote him letters of [121] consolation as best they could, and they gave him candles secretly and ink and paper. Then he wrote back and told

---

184. See above, note 141.

185. Evangelicals often challenged Catholic clergy to public debates called disputations.

186. Jussie spells this term *saudant*, as close to "sultan" as to "soldier." The orthographical blurring perhaps carries a suggestion that he is an infidel.

187. During the persecutions under the Emperor Diocletian (284–305), the Roman martyr Anastasia and her maid visited incarcerated Christians and brought them supplies. The Feast of Saint Anastasia is December 25.

the sisters he was consoled, and he exhorted them to good constancy and patience because he knew well that their time of persecution had come. It may piteously be believed that God had revealed it to him. For I have no doubt but that God comforted him greatly and that he was often visited by angels, although I have no direct knowledge of it. But I do affirm that, purely for the love of God and to uphold the truth and preserve the holy religion, he was deprived of all human consolation and suffered great physical pain.

FURBITY, REFUSING TO REVOKE HIS WORDS AGAINST THE LORDS OF BERN, IS PUT BACK INTO PRISON

Also, those heretics kept at him, trying to get him to preach on Septuagesima Sunday;[188] they had ordered him to beg messieurs of Bern for mercy in front of all the people and to say that he had spoken wrongly and disrespectfully [122] toward them when he called them heretics. He refused to do so, but he did agree to preach and to review all the main points he had preached during all of Advent. But they did not let him speak very long because as soon as he got into the pulpit and made the sign of the cross and led an "Ave Maria,"[189] he was scolded by a Bernese man who said that if he was not going to say anything else, he should keep quiet, because he was not supposed to say such things. They very villainously grabbed him and pulled him from the pulpit and treated him harshly, so that he almost died there and then. Afterward they tore down the pulpit.

People were so scandalized and terrified by that commotion that all the Christians left the church, and no one dared to say a word; the good father remained alone in his enemies' hands, in the example of Jesus Christ who remained alone in the garden in the Jews' hands,[190] forsaken by all His friends. A certain pious and trustworthy person told me that there was never such an understanding of the passion and capture of Our Lord in the garden as was reawakened when this holy man was handed over.

He was locked away in that crude cell, and they kept him there inhumanely for seven months, and then at the honorable people's request he was let out and put in a room, but it was very small. Several prominent lords and [123] ladies asked for his release, but it did no good. Many ladies and

---

188. February 15, 1534. Septuagesima Sunday is the third Sunday before Lent.

189. See above, note 29.

190. "Then all the disciples deserted him and fled" (Mt 26:56); "All of them deserted him and fled" (Mk 14:50); "The hour is coming, indeed it has come, when you will be scattered, each one to his home, and you will leave me alone. Yet I am not alone because the Father is with me" (Jn 16:32).

burgher women of the city came in person and offered fine gifts for his release and made pleas to messieurs of Bern. But it did no good because an
infidel named Michel Balthasar,[191] who was a syndic at the time, condemned
him to die in prison if he did not renounce truth and maintain error—which,
with God's help, he did not do, but was solid as a rock and maintained the
truth of the Holy Scripture. He is still suffering today.[192] May Blessed Jesus
give him comfort, consolation, and patience.

On the Monday of Pentecost of this present year,[193] the syndics gave
the articles of errors to the soldier's wife,[194] directing her to give them to him
and to tell him to [124] prepare to dispute with three or four preachers and
devilish doctors. For when they had proposed the disputation, messieurs the
clerics had refused to accept unless the poor captive was released to them,
and they chose him to represent them, which is why these instructions were
given to him.

The poor soldier's wife, who out of fear of her husband had not dared
to speak to the reverend father for a long time, passed him the articles on a
small sickle. When he saw that list of errors and did not know why it had
been given to him, he thought the good woman who was taking care of
him[195] had been perverted and had passed it to him as a trick, and he passed
it back. When she realized he would not accept it, she sent her daughter to
tell him that messieurs the syndics had sent it to him and that she asked him
to receive it for his own good. But he, suspecting treachery, did not take it,
which upset her, for she knew well that he would be punished and she did
not want him to be accused of rebellion. So she furtively threw it down to
him through a small window, and he picked it up and ripped it and then
stomped on it. [125]

DISPUTATION OF THE HERETICAL PREACHERS AND FURBITY

On that Monday of Pentecost [May 17, 1535], after dinner, at about eleven
o'clock, the four syndics brought with them the satanical Guillaume Farel,

191. Michel Sept, also called Balthasar or Batezard, had been a syndic since February 8, 1534.
Jussie generally spells his name "Baptisard" or "Batissart" in her chronicle.

192. Guy Furbity was not released until April 5, 1536.

193. May 17, 1535. This comment and the reference to Furbity's ongoing imprisonment sug-
gest that Jussie composed this part of the chronicle, at least, in 1535—perhaps shortly after her
convent's resettlement in Annecy.

194. The *souldanne*. See above, note 186. The editor of the 1682 edition of the text changes
the term to the more neutral "jail keeper" (*Geoliere*).

195. *sa bonne honestesse.*

Pierre Viret of Orbe, and a leading doctor of Paris, Master Pierre Caroli,[196] who had formerly been the reverend father's teacher, and several others of their sect, and they had the father taken out of his cell and brought before them in a room. He was thin, weak, and debilitated, so it was a pity to see him, and not without cause, because he had been in prison for seventeen months already and he had been sick and feverish for a long time. When he saw his theology teacher and realized he was perverted, he fainted and fell to the floor. But they revived him, and Caroli said to him, "What, Friar Guy, do you want to die in your stubbornness and heresy? Up until [126] now, we were in error, and at present we have seen the truth of the Gospel. Do you not wish to recognize your error and turn back to God?"

The reverend father answered, "God would not want me to quarrel with my teacher, except to defend the religion. I wish to die in the truth of the Holy Scripture as I learned it from you. If my health were a little better and I had gradual books[197] to study, I would not shrink from defending the religion. If I have to dispute against that poor idiot Farel, I want his master the devil's dwelling to be taken from him first, that is, for all the hair to be shaved and shorn from his body, and I will be shaved first too, and we must dispute in a public place with unbiased judges. I will give my life if I do not defeat the five devils he keeps as counselors."

But they would hear none of it. They tormented him until four o'clock in the afternoon, until his heart faltered because he was so weak, and when they saw he was defeating them, they sent him back down to his cell with nothing to drink or eat, which was a very cruel thing, and they caused him so many other great evils and injuries and trials that it is impossible to write even half of them. I, who am writing this, know it to be true because I heard it from the soldier's wife, who is a close friend of mine. He is still a prisoner. May Our Lord make him persevere in strength and patience, and may He allow us to share in his merits. Amen. [127]

THE HERETICS WIN A MAJORITY; EXECUTION OF A CATHOLIC

In the year 1534 the venerable guardian father [François Coutellier] of the Franciscans in Chambéry preached at Lent. On the first Sunday, which was the first day of March, after the reverend father's sermon, the Lutherans gath-

---

196. Theologian from the Sorbonne who took part in the Disuptation of Rive and the Disputation of Lausanne.

197. Gradual books contain parts of the Mass that are sung or recited.

ered at the Rive Monastery[198] and went to the bell and rang it for about an hour, and then, whether the Christians liked it or not, they took over the preaching there, and they have not missed a day since then, including all of the feast days and Sundays.[199] [128] This really upset the Christians. But they were already getting discouraged because more and more people were being perverted every day, and none of the Christians dared to say a word against it because they would be put to death. A case in point: one day a perverted heretic was mocking the holy church and the divine sacraments and saying very shameful words. A true Christian there could not stand it but drew his sword and stabbed him, and he died immediately. Then the Christian was hunted down and captured in the church next to Saint Peter's steeple and was executed on the Feast of Saint Agatha[200] around noon. He was told that if he wanted to be an Evangelical, that is, a Lutheran, no harm would be done to him. But he answered that he would not be an agent of iniquity just to save his brief life. They brought Farel to preach to him and to trick him, but he refused to listen. But he begged that before his death he be allowed to see the reverend master who was in prison. At the honorable people's plea, it was granted to him, and he was taken to the prison. When they saw each other, they wept tenderly. Then that good Catholic confessed and declared that he was being sentenced to the gibbet for the love of Jesus Christ, and he commended himself to the reverend father's holy prayers. The father kissed him and said, [129] "Sire Claude, go joyfully to receive your martyrdom and fear nothing because the kingdom of heaven is open and the angels await you."

Then he was taken back to the place of his beheading. When he was in front of the Convent of Saint Clare, he lifted his eyes to the heavens and then said to his sister, who was following him in tears, "Sister, go tell the ladies that I commend my soul to them, and do not weep for me, because I am going away joyfully."

The sisters, who were getting ready to sit down for dinner, were told immediately. Out of surprise and sorrow several of them were frozen and numb; they dined on anguish.

When he was at the place of his martyrdom, he cried out for mercy on

---

198. The Franciscan Rive Monastery was founded in Geneva in 1268. See Revilliod's 1853 edition of Jussie's chronicle, xi.

199. To the end of this sentence in manuscript A is added *conbien que je nen tiengne point deux foys*. Manuscript B omits the clause, and Jussie's 1611 editor simply writes "and twice on Sundays" (*& Dimanches deux fois*). *Le levain du calvinisme* (1611), 81.

200. February 5, 1534. Jussie is referring here to Claude Pennet, the bishop's head jail keeper, who had stabbed Nicolas Berger, a poor hatter, on February 3, 1534.

the world and commended all good Christians to God, and he commended his wife, who was about to give birth, to the honor of God, and also his small children, and then in great fervor and steady patience he bid his executioner farewell. His head was chopped off, and his body was put on the gibbet like a thief's. People said that a white dove was often seen on his head and that there were other visible signs. After he had been on the gibbet for three days, his face was spotless and fresh and his mouth was as red as if he were alive. After a while his family and [130] other good Christians took his body off the gibbet and put him solemnly in a tomb at Notre Dame de Grâce. His name was Sire Claude Pennet.

He had a very young brother [Pierre Pennet] who upheld the holy religion no less ardently, who had already been wounded and slashed behind his knee so that he limped severely for the rest of his life. They tried to do to him what they had done to his brother. But on the fiscal prosecutor's [Nycodus de Prato] advice, he took refuge in a poor beggar woman's home, and no one knew about it except for the sisters of Saint Clare, who prepared his food and sent it to him secretly. Then he was advised to get out of the city, and so, one night after matins, he walked barefoot through the streets to the convent, and there was a lot of frost. After matins he bid them farewell and commended his brother's soul to them, weeping bitterly. Then, in the morning, when the gates were opened, he went out in disguise, and the convent's lay brothers carried his clothing to him secretly later. And so he was saved by the grace that God never withholds from His friends. [131]

BEHEADING OF THE SECRETARY PORTIER

Likewise on the tenth of March Monseigneur the Secretary Portier[201] was beheaded at the place where they behead martyrs and criminals because he had carried letters from Monseigneur of Geneva that said that if people found Lutherans anywhere, they could capture, kill, or hang them from a tree without any hesitation or fear of reprisal. For that reason he was martyred by the miscreants at two o'clock in the afternoon. No court had ever sentenced a criminal in Geneva in the afternoon, so everyone was scandalized, and he was mourned deeply because he was an honorable man. Like the other man he came to a holy end and left a wife and children. Those dogs did not allow him to be taken off the gibbet, but his holy body remained,[202] as I understand

---

201. Jean Portier, the prince-bishop's secretary and notary.
202. Or, "but his body remained fresh" (*il demorat se corps sains*).

it, among the murderers and sinners. It was said that fine, visible signs were seen on him. But I do not know if it is true, so I will not write it. [132]

EXECUTION OF A YOUNG LUTHERAN BANDIT

On that day[203] a young guard, a thief and bandit of the Lutheran sect, was executed. The Franciscans preached to him to convert him so that he would die repentant and in the religion, but on the way he was taken out of their hands and given to Farel and his associate to preach to him, and he died in that heresy and damnable path.

Another miraculous thing: after that murder, on the fifteenth day of March, which was Letare Sunday,[204] a woman who had been on the gibbet for about a year already, who had died in the religion of the holy mother church, miraculously turned to that Lutheran man who had been put on the gibbet the previous Thursday and who was near her, opened her mouth wide, and bit him on the chin. Because it was an amazing thing, the news spread quickly through the town. Many people ran there to see it and to find out if it was true. The Lutherans tried to separate them with their pikes because the [133] Christians were making fun of them, but she kept turning back. On that day, more than four thousand people from all estates saw the event and true thing.

THE LENTEN PREACHER'S REQUEST TO THE COUNCIL OF GENEVA

On the following Monday [March 16, 1534], one of messieurs the syndics ordered the father preacher to appear before the council in the city hall. He did not go, but two good Christians went in his place. The council wanted him to preach according to their wishes and not according to the spirit of God, but because he was afraid they would put him in prison as they had done to the holy father [Furbity] the previous Advent, he preached only what they allowed. And so on Tuesday, he made them a request consisting of three articles: the first was that, if it pleased messieurs, he would preach about [134] repentance and sacramental confession; second, about the Holy Sacrament of the altar; and third, about pardons and indulgences. The syndics and twenty-five principal councilors answered him that he should simply preach as he usually did but refrain from saying anything that was not contained in

---

203. Actually, on the following day, Wednesday, March 11, 1534.
204. The fourth Sunday of Lent.

the Holy Scripture, and they promised to defend him from everyone and to everyone. Thus he did not dare to talk about the holy sacraments or about perfection and virtues, except very indirectly. Otherwise he would never have reached the end of Lent without risking his life like the first Dominican [Furbity].

AROUND EASTER 1534

On the Friday [March 27] before Palm Sunday, in the Franciscan refectory, one of the monks was hit hard in the face by his brother, a Lutheran, for arguing about the Holy Sacrament. On that same day that accursed Farel started to baptize children in their accursed manner. A great many people watched, and even Christians came to witness their delusion. [135]

The holy week passed in great fear and anxiety. Nonetheless, praise be to God, there was no scandal and divine service was celebrated in all the churches.

BEGINNING OF MARRIAGES BY FAREL
ACCORDING TO THE NEW FORM

On Quasimodo Sunday,[205] that wretched Farel started to marry men and women together according to their way and tradition, with no rites or piety, but simply by ordering them to come together and multiply. He spoke some shameful words that I will not write, because it is horrible for a chaste heart to think of them.

HEMME FAULSON'S VISIT TO THE
CONVENT OF SAINT CLARE

On Misericordia Sunday,[206] a rich burgher woman,[207] a perverted Lutheran whose sister was a nun at the convent of Madame Saint Clare, came to talk to the sisters. Because the sisters were not yet [136] certain that she was completely perverted, she was taken to the grille. She greeted the sisters very respectfully. Then she asked them to let her speak to her aunt [Claudine Lignotte] and to her sister [Blaisine Varembert], which they did. After a few respectful words she could not hold back her venom but poured it out on the poor nuns' hearts, saying that the world had been in error and idolatry

---

205. The first Sunday after Easter, also called Low Sunday, April 12, 1534.
206. The second Sunday after Easter, also called Divine Mercy Sunday, April 19, 1534.
207. Hemme Faulson, née Varembert, the wife of Joseph Faulson.

until now and that our ancestors had lived wrongly and had been deceived because God's commandments had not been proclaimed in truth. Immediately the mother vicaress [Pernette de Montluel], who was there in place of the mother abbess [Louise Rambo], who was sick then, said to her, "Lady, we do not wish to hear such talk. If you want to speak with us about Our Lord and piety, as you have done in the past, we will keep you good company, but if you go on like this, we will turn deaf ears to you.[208] Your perversion is a mortal wound in our souls because we see clearly that you have drunk that accursed Farel's poison, and your soul weighs heavily on us."

Again she began to say horrible words about the Holy Sacrament, that it was nothing but a wafer[209] and she would never believe in it. Then mother vicaress and her [137] companions chided her piously, telling her she was deceived, and in a few kind words they asked her not to believe those messages of the Antichrist, but to live respectably like her late father and mother, who had been very honorable people. Her aunt and sister also spoke to her, respectfully and in few words, about the Holy Scripture, for they did not wish to hear such errors. She said other words of error. At that, mother vicaress and her company stood up and closed the doors[210] to her, telling her that their prelate had forbidden them to listen to those errors. She stayed there for a long time, even though her words fell on deaf ears, and she said that she really thought the sisters obeyed the devil's ministers more than God and other insults. But she got no response, which made her very angry; after that, she kept trying to turn the heretics against them and to remove her sister from the convent.

EVENTS IN APRIL–MAY 1534

On Jubilate Sunday,[211] a girl was married to a Lutheran according to their tradition. Neither the girl's mother nor any of her family attended the wedding. [138]

---

208. "We will make you wooden faces" (*vos ferons visaige de boix*).

209. *que ce nestoit que une nyble.* Jussie uses the term *nyble* four times in her chronicle; in each case, a Reformer uses it to refer derisively to the bread of the Eucharist (and, thus, as an indication of his or her rejection of the doctrine of transubstantiation). According to Godefroy, the term *nyble* is a variant of *niule* ("cloud") and was used, by metaphor, to refer to crumbs or thin sheets of unleavened bread that were decorated with religious symbols and sold in some churches on feast days in the thirteenth century. (See Frédéric Godefroy, *Dictionnaire de l'ancienne langue française et de tous ses dialectes du IXe au XVe siècle.* Geneva: Slatkine, 1982), 5: 501. I will translate *nyble* as "wafer." See also Feld, "Jeanne de Jussie," 324.

210. The doors on the nuns' side of the grille.

211. The third Sunday after Easter, April 26, 1534.

Also, on the first of May, a Genevan man named Louis Chanevard went into the Franciscans' church after the sermon, and he poked the eyes of the image of Saint Anthony of Padua with the point of his sword several times, in the monks' presence. After he left, he went to the market to buy what he needed at home and then he dined, untroubled and cheerful. A wondrous example of divine judgment: as soon as he got up from the table, he immediately lost his voice, and he died at four o'clock in the afternoon. He was carried off and buried like an animal, without any rites.

On the Feast of the Holy Cross [May 5], which was a Sunday, a Franciscan monk who had been in the monastery for six years took off his habit in front of everyone after the sermon and very spitefully stomped on it, at which all the heretics greatly rejoiced. He took up the trade of weaving to earn a living.

That week [May 5–12] a good Catholic woman had a baby. Her heretical husband had it baptized by the wicked Farel, which made the poor lady faint and then die of grief. She was greatly mourned. [139]

On the eve of Pentecost [May 23], at ten o'clock at night those heretical dogs cut the heads off six statues in front of the Franciscans' gate. Then they carried them to the well in front of Saint Clare and threw them in. It was piteous and very shocking to see the headless bodies.

On the Feast of Pentecost [May 24], a secular priest, a fine man and a most excellent cantor, who was one of the twelve priests ordained by the cathedral church of Saint Peter and who was named Messire Louis Bernard, attended the Lutheran sermon, and he shouted in a loud voice that he wanted to be one of them. Then he removed his long robe and put on a Spanish cape.[212] Then all the people of that sect, men, women, and children, welcomed him with great joy [140] and reverence. Afterward the preacher announced his marriage to a young Lutheran widow. The next Tuesday [May 26] they were married, which greatly scandalized all the Christians. He had a benefice of two hundred florins and more. On that night they pulled up two fine angels at the cemetery of the Madeleine and threw them in the well at Saint Clare.

PROCESSION OF THE FEAST OF CORPUS CHRISTI IN 1534

On the Feast of Corpus Christi [June 4] the Christians courageously held the usual procession through the city. Several Lutheran woman wearing velvet

---

212. A short coat without a collar. Jussie is making the point that he is changing into secular attire.

hoods[213] sat at their windows so that everyone could see them working with distaffs and needles. They did the same thing on all the feast days, more than on other days, in plain view from the streets, which caused the Christians much turmoil. It was said that on the days after Easter and Pentecost many of them washed and did their laundry. Some good people went and threw their laundry into the Rhone, and the women did not have an easy time of it, because they had to work hard to get it back and to keep from losing it. When the procession was passing by, someone [141] pulled the distaff from a fat Lutheran woman's side and hit her on the head with it and threw her work into the mud and trampled it. Then that person went back into the procession before she knew what had happened. She thought she would die from the pain of such an insult.

Also, two days before the Feast of Saint John the Baptist,[214] at night, the Lutherans tore down and destroyed a very handsome statue of Jesus and Monseigneur Saint Christopher in front of the church of the Madeleine, which had been there longer than anyone had been alive.

FRIAR MICHEL DES GARINES

And the next Sunday [June 28] a friar minor who was priest of a monastery in Orléans came to Geneva and publicly removed his habit. Then, because it was God's will, he regretted it and came to the Convent of Saint Clare and revealed his sins to the father confessor and to the sisters, asking for their help to guide him and to bring him back into the bosom of our mother the holy church. The sisters had pity on him, and the confessor told a good lord of the canons about it, as well as monseigneur the city treasurer,[215] Monseigneur the secretary Magistri,[216] and three or four of the best Catholics who were very honorable people.[217] They came secretly [142] to the con-

---

213. *chapirons de vellour.* Women often wore decorative hoods, which ranged from simple to elaborate. Velvet hoods were a sign of high social status. About the lady's hood, John Calvin wrote, "It is fancied by many people, and even by women of estate, who think it makes them look fetching. From which it is easy to judge that there are respectable French women wearing velvet hoods, which makes them honorable whores." (Il est favorisé de beaucoup de gens, et mesmes d'aucunes femmes d'estat, lesquelles le tiennent pour leur grand mignon. Dont il est facile de juger qu'il y a de bonnes galloises coiffées de chapperons de veloux, pour estre putains honnorables.) *Epistre contre un cordelier,* 7: 345, cited in Huguet, *Dictionnaire,* 2.195.

214. June 22, 1534. The Feast of Saint John the Baptist is on June 24.

215. Étienne Pecollat, treasurer (1532–35).

216. According to Feld, Jussie is probably referring to the notary Pierre Magistri. See Feld's edition of the *Petite chronique,* 141, n. 16.

217. Manuscript B says "true zealots in the holy religion" (*vrays zelateurs de la saincte foy*).

vent, and he acknowledged his guilt humbly before them; each of them did his duty to correct him very well and to reprimand him benevolently. Then, last of all, the good father confessor gave him a very good lecture. Then, following Jesus Christ's example, they received him into the bosom of the holy church, and on the order and authority of the prelates, they gave him a general absolution. And he was found to be of good will and contrite. Early the next morning, the father confessor helped him leave Geneva quietly and took him to Annecy to the reverend father's care. The reverend father took him to Lyons, where the friar put his habit back on, and then he went to Rome, and the following Lent he preached in Montréal,[218] and from there he wrote a letter to the father confessor and the sisters, thanking them for their kindness in helping him in his salvation. I do not know what became of him after that. He was named Friar Michel des Garines. Those dogs were very angry to have lost him, and they did not know what had become of him. There was a lot of talk in the city, and if they had known how he had escaped, the father confessor and the sisters would have been punished without a doubt. [143]

ICONOCLASTIC ACTIONS IN JULY 1534

Afterward, on the Feast of Saint Anne [July 26], which was a Sunday, ringing the bells for Holy Mass was forbidden, so as not to obstruct the contemptible preaching, and after that accursed sermon they tore down many fine images and completely destroyed the altar of the chapel of the Queen of Cyprus;[219] and they smashed the statue of Our Lady that was tall and wonderfully handsome and sumptuous, carved in alabaster. They took the ciborium that contained the Holy Sacrament and carried it off, and no one knew what they did with it. They also destroyed the four pillars in front of the main altar. Then a monk took away the remains of the images and uncovered all the altars. It was a brutal thing to see such poverty in the house of God. [144]

On the penultimate day of July, the Genevans saw a company of men near the city. So it was immediately announced that everyone should take up arms, Christians and heretics together. That whole week [July 31–August 8]

---

218. Near Nantua.

219. Anne of Cyprus, Duchess of Savoy, the eldest daughter of King Janus of Cyprus, Jerusalem and Armenia, married Duke Louis of Savoy (1402–65). She founded the Chapel of Our Lady of Bethlehem built in the Franciscan monastery of Rive and was buried in it after her death in 1462. The chapel was built 1457–60.

the city gates were kept closed and there were many watchmen. All the churches were told not to ring bells, day or night, not even the city clock, until they received orders. And so everyone in Geneva lived in continual fear and melancholy, especially the honorable people, but mainly the poor ladies of Saint Clare, because the commotion always happened right outside their convent, and when they heard the noise, they always thought that people were coming to take them out or do them some great harm. You can believe that their rest was little and uncertain. [145]

A YOUNG SISTER SPENDS THE NIGHT IN THE CHURCH

One night a young nun happened to fall asleep during her prayers, and the mother vicaress inadvertently locked her in the church, and all the others retired together to the dormitory as usual. In the still of the night, between ten and eleven o'clock, the poor young sister awoke and saw[220] the souls of the dead walking around in the church, and she was scared and ran to the door, thinking she could get out. When she found the door locked, she did not dare shout for fear of breaking her vow of silence, but, utterly terrified, she beat on the door. Immediately, all the sisters, who were in prayers and at rest, were roused, all terribly frightened. She beat on the door two or three more times as hard as she could. So they all got out of bed terrified and trembling, and several of them remained frozen, as if they were completely overcome and bewildered, thinking that those heretics had already broken into the convent and had reached the church and that they had come to carry out their accursed intentions, for they had often threatened to plunder and violate them all some night. They did not know what to do, thinking that help could come from nowhere. They did not know if they should all stay in the cloister and await God's will or go out to see what it could be. The mother abbess said, [146] "My dear sisters and children, I beg and ask you to be firm and constant and to fight virilely[221] for the love of God and to remain together with God's blessing, which I give you as best I can. As for me, I am going to see what it is, and those who wish may come with me. But first of all, I want to know if all the sheep are in the fold."

Then with a steady spirit she visited all the beds and looked at them and called for each of the sisters one by one. She discovered that one was

220. Manuscript B adds "comme il luy sembloit," that is, *"thought* she saw"

221. On "virility" as a positive value for women in the early modern era, see Barbara Newman, *From Virile Woman to WomanChrist* (Philadelphia: University of Pennsylvania Press, 1995).

missing, which caused great anguish. No one knew a thing, and no one could guess where she was or imagine what had happened, and it never occurred to them that she might be the one making the noise. In the meantime she beat on the door again even harder.

"In the name of Our Lord," said the mother abbess, "Let us leave here and go to the church, because it is better for us to be before God than in the dormitory."

She opened the door as best she could, and they all went directly to the church, and they found that poor girl at the door. When she saw the community so shaken and frightened, she considered her mistake and her fear and fell paralyzed at the sisters' feet. They had great pity on her.

Several of them got very sick afterward, and they often had similar frights, and their fears were not unfounded, because they were greatly threatened. [147]

A DOMINICAN LEAVES HIS ORDER

On that last Sunday of July, after the bell was rung to gather their people for the sermon, a Dominican monk removed his monk's robe in front of that multitude, and at that moment he climbed up into the pulpit. Then, like a desperate man, he began to shout to God and to the world for mercy and to wail and say that in the past he had lived wrongly and had greatly deceived people by preaching about pardons and praising the Mass and holy sacraments and ceremonies of the church, and that they were vile empty things and he renounced them. Then he began to insult the holy church and the life of devotion and celibacy with words that are not fit to be written down. Then he delivered a heretical sermon. Then after his sermon he married a woman whom everyone said had a very bad reputation.

DEMOLITION OF THE MONASTERY OF SAINT VICTOR

During the first week of the next month of August [2–8] the monastery of Saint Victor was completely pillaged. Fifty florins were given to poor wage earners who [148] helped them open the church to destroy it completely, along with the priory and monastery, which was done. The monks took refuge, but I do not know where. It was turned into profaned ground. It was said that, for a while, when you walked by there you could hear the souls of the departed wailing and lamenting audibly day and night and that it was a serene and very piteous thing, and it was not without cause, because many holy people were buried there. It was the oldest church in Geneva and one of the seven parishes, along with the priory of Saint Benedict.

IMPRISONMENT AND BEHEADING OF JACQUES MALBOSSON

And on the eve of the Assumption of Our Lady, at night, the heretics captured [149] Sire Jacques Malbosson, a very honorable man and a good and true Catholic, and he was put in prison because of it.[222] He never got out except to meet his death. On that night several good Christians departed and left the city. That poor Lord Jacques was kept cruelly in prison, even though he had plenty of money at home to pay for his release[223] since he was a wealthy merchant. After he was greatly tortured with ropes[224] he was beheaded on the seventeenth of July, 1535, at Molard, in the city, and his body was cruelly quartered and carried to the gibbet, and his head was raised over Molard facing the lake so that everyone could see it. His wife could not leave her house without seeing it. [150] She did not dare take it down.

When the poor lady, who was very fine and beautiful, was running after her husband, whom they were dragging by the neck, she was in utter disarray and frantic and wailing piteously, and she begged for mercy for her loyal companion. But they pushed her away rudely and called her a drunk and a crazy madwoman,[225] which was a piercing sword to the poor, suffering man. When he reached the place of his martyrdom, he took the liberty of speaking and said, "Messieurs, I go to my death here purely for the love of my God, because I never committed any offense deserving of death, and if I had wanted to be an Evangelical, I would not be killed. But I declare that I am dying in my worthy ancestors' religion and just as they did, except that I have not been given the holy sacraments. But I confess them to be true, and I receive them mentally.[226] I have always offered up my body and my property, as my ancestors did, to defend the city and its sovereignty. I confess that I did everything I could to bring Monseigneur of Geneva, my

---

222. That is, because he was a good Catholic.

223. Manuscript B omits this clause.

224. See above, note 128.

225. Manuscript B omits this sentence.

226. Manuscript clarifies this sentence as follows: "But I confess them to be true, and if I cannot have them sacramentally and really, I declare that I desire and receive them mentally" (*mais je les confesse vray, et si je ne les puis avoir sacramentellement et reallement, je proteste, que je les desire et avoir mentelle*).

prince and prelate, into the city, so that with his help the heresies could be driven out of the city, and for this I am condemned. I accept it willingly for the love of my God who was ignominiously crucified for me, and I freely pardon you for my death. I cry out for mercy for everyone, although I never did any harm to those people who send me to my death, for they were my brothers, friends, and neighbors. I ask my Christian brothers to remember my wife and to commend me to [151] her and to tell her I commend my children to her and to ask her to give a teston[227] to my confessor and to satisfy my servants and anyone else to whom I owe money."

Then a great heretic[228] stepped forward and said, "You owe me some money."

He answered, "I don't recall owing you a thing, but so that my soul will be unburdened, I order it to be given to you. I commend myself to my brothers and beg them to remember my wife and my children. I commend all good Christians to God and commend my soul to them."

Then he was beheaded and quartered, and they did with him what is written above. Everyone was upset and frightened that they had dared to kill such a person, a native Genevan, without any good cause, but only because he fought virilely for the holy religion. Everyone mourned him, even the wretched people who had sent him to his death, and the syndic who had judged him wept so bitterly over him you could have washed your hands underneath his chin with his tears.[229] [152]

After a short while, on his head, which was raised above the Place du Molard, a most beautiful dove, white as snow,[230] was seen, and it came down from the heavens in the beauty of daybreak and flew around his head seven times. Then it landed on top, beat its wings in joy,[231] and then abruptly flew back up into the sky, and his face remained as fine and rosy and fresh as if he were alive, and he was the handsomest son of Geneva and not more than thirty years old.[232] Several honorable people noticed it when they came at dawn to watch over him, and they saw it was true for several days. Then all at once that most handsome and fresh head shrank and all of the flesh and hair vanished and there was nothing left but white mortified bone. No

227. A silver coin.

228. Possibly Jean Goulaz, according to Feld. See his edition of the *Petite chronique*, 151, n. 4.

229. Manuscript B shortens the description of the weeping syndic.

230. Manuscript B omits this comparison, saying only that the dove was white.

231. Manuscript B omits "in joy" (*en maniere de joie*).

232. Manuscript B adds "The news of this marvel spread quickly through the city" (*Incontinent ceste merveille fut publie par la ville*).

one ever knew what had happened to it so suddenly, so they were all very amazed.

EXCOMMUNICATION OF THE GENEVANS BY THE BISHOP

On the first Sunday of August [August 2, 1534] a great excommunication was announced in the whole bishopric, on the authority of Monseigneur of Geneva, who forbade anyone in his diocese to bring anything into Geneva or to communicate with the Genevans, which made the heretics' fury go from bad to worse. They threatened [153] that by Christmas at the latest, all the churches would be emptied[233] and the whole city would be united in religion. During all of Advent the only sermons in Geneva were given by these wretches, which had never happened in anyone's lifetime[234] and was very strange to the Christians.

CHRISTMAS 1534

On Christmas Day, to keep the heretics from coming to matins, the syndics went to the churches and placed some armed watchmen at the doors until divine service was completely finished. The Lutherans did not observe any rites, and they dressed in their simplest clothing as if it were an ordinary day, and they did not bake any white bread, because that is what the Christians did. They said in mockery, "The papists[235] are having their feast. They will eat so much white bread that they will die of it."

On that holy day their preacher announced in his sermon that on the next Sunday [154] they should all gather together[236] at a designated location to celebrate their Lord's Supper. Very many people came. Their accursed preacher told them to be strong and remain firm and constant in their new law because they were on the rightful path of truth. After his sermon he married the bastard Jean de Genève's servant girl.

PLEA BY THE SISTERS OF SAINT CLARE TO THE SYNDICS

On the Feast of Monseigneur Saint Stephen the sisters of Saint Clare sent a plea to messieurs the syndics, commending themselves, as always, to their

---

233. Presumably of their images and icons.
234. Manuscript B omits this clause.
235. Manuscript B changes "papists" (*papiste* [sic]) to "Christians" (*chrestiens*).
236. Jussie specifies both men and women here: *tous et toutes ensenbles*.

protection and good grace, saying they were very frightened by those troubles, and asking them to allow them to ring bells for matins and the other canonical hours. It was granted to them, as long as they only rang a little bit. From then on, they rang bells for matins, until it was forbidden again.

NEW YEAR'S DAY 1535

On New Year's Day the Lutherans worked all day and even opened their stores, although the syndics had forbidden it. [155]

EVENTS OF THE YEAR 1535

The following is a part of what happened in the year 1535.

First, on Brand Sunday, February 13,[237] an accursed apostate Franciscan monk, still wearing the habit of the sacred religion, began to preach in the parish of Saint Germain[238] in the heresiarchal fashion, which upset the good people. But nothing could be done because the priest was of that sect.

Then, on the nineteenth of that month, on a Saturday, the guardian of Rive[239] posted notices in the city announcing that throughout Lent, after dinner, he would preach the usual Gospel in the grand refectory of the monastery if messieurs of the city would allow it. He preached the [156] first week, and many people came, men and women, Christians and Lutherans. He did not make the sign of the cross at the beginning of his sermon or at the end, which scandalized the Christians, and they never came back.

POISONING OF PIERRE VIRET

A preacher, Pierre Viret from Orbe, happened to fall sick, and a man and his wife were accused of poisoning him. The man was cleared, but his wife[240] was convicted by the court long afterward, and it was said that she was perverted and died in that law.

---

237. The first Sunday in Lent. In fact, it was February 14, 1535.

238. This church still stands in the old town of Geneva, near the cathedral.

239. Jacques Bernard (d. 1559).

240. Antonie Vax from Bourg-en-Bresse, arrested on March 11, 1535. She was apparently interrogated and tortured, but denied any guilt. On March 31, in her second interrogation, apparently without torture, she confessed to the crime. She was condemned to death on April 13 and executed on July 31. See Jean Barnaud, *Pierre Viret: Sa vie et son oeuvre* (Saint-Amans: G. Carayol, 1911; reprint Nieuwkoop: B. de Graaf, 1973), 89–101.

SUPPLEMENT TO THE EVENTS OF THE YEAR 1534

The following is a short chapter about what happened in the year 1534, which the writer forgot, but which is nonetheless worth remembering and piteous and very true. She herself experienced a part of it with her companions. [157]

In the penultimate week of September [20–26], the Genevans began to tear down and destroy the faubourgs of the city, sparing neither poor nor rich, and it was a piteous thing to hear the poor people lament. They started to dig a garden around the walls of the Poor Clares' garden in order to fortify the city walls. They forced good people, low and high, to carry earth, on both holidays and workdays. Then they tried to take over the poor ladies' garden, to break through the wall and cloister. And, indeed, on the Feast of Monseigneur Saint Jerome [September 30], at four o'clock in the morning, the sisters were told to take their things out of the garden, because it was all true; messieurs [the syndics] had given orders to break through, which caused them much sorrow, and not without cause, because they had no recourse and could ask no one to defend them inasmuch as the governors and superiors had given the orders. When they wrote their complaint, they received no other response, except that they were so busy with city business that they could not listen to their appeal. So they had no recourse but to God alone by the intercession of his Virgin Mary and the blessed saints. [158]

That same day after dinner the captain from Bern arrived, a man named [Jacques] Tribollet, a prominent Lutheran whom the Bernese had ordered to govern the town according to his own will and pleasure. He came to the convent to speak to the mother portress, and he asked to come inside because messieurs had sent him to inspect the convent to see where would be the most suitable place to break through so that they could come and go as they pleased for the service and aid of the city.

The mother portress sent for the mother abbess and her vicaress who, after greeting him, explained their way of life to him and how they were prisoners secluded for the love of God and how no one could come in with them, and they begged him not to break into their holy cloister or to come in with them. But he refused to listen to them and said furiously that if they did not obey the orders of messieurs of Bern as lords and superiors of the city, they would break in and make them sorry for it. Then the poor ladies, fearing worse danger, opened the doors, and he came in as furious as a lion with a company of his sect.

The poor sisters, all as one, took refuge in the church, prostrate, their heads bowed down to the ground, and they prayed [159] to God with a great abundance of tears and in anguish. When he passed by the church, he stopped at the door and looked at the sisters without making any move to enter, and he felt such pity for them that he began to console them and asked the mother abbess to have them rise. So she and her vicaress stood up and did their best to commend that poor, anguished company to him, and they ordered the sisters to greet him and to ask him for mercy and to be allowed to serve God in their unbroken cloister. God allowed his heart to be wholly transformed by pity, and he did not know what to say, except to reassure them and to promise that he would never do them any harm again, and he offered to do all he could to guard and protect them against anyone who tried to harm them. He went away completely edified without causing any more trouble.

One of his comrades, a citizen of Geneva named Claude Testus, washed his hands in the holy water and spat in it. When they were outside and people asked him how the ladies were and what they had done, that wicked guard boasted that he had uncovered one nun's face and kissed her. But he was lying falsely because he never touched any nun in there and no one did them any harm that day. [160]

BURIAL OF A CATHOLIC BURGHER WOMAN IN THE HERETICAL FASHION

That week [September 27–October 3] a good burgher woman, a good and faithful Catholic, died. Her husband, a wicked Lutheran, buried her in the heretics' tomb and according to their traditions, despite her family's wishes. So everyone was very upset, because they put bodies in the plain, bare earth and without any rites, and no one is there except the people who carry the body, unless they come to mock the honor[241] that Christians show them. When they put them in the ground they say only, "Sleep until the one God calls for you."[242]

DEATH AND BURIAL OF A LUTHERAN APOTHECARY

The next Friday a Lutheran apothecary died suddenly. His wife was a good Christian, and when she saw him near death, she did her duty to urge him to turn back to God and make his confession. But he would not listen, and he asked and begged her to call for the accursed Farel. She said that she

241. That is, the rites for the dead.
242. Manuscript B omits this sentence.

would not do it and that if he came, she would leave the house because she would have nothing to do with such company, and so he died. Because he had [161] died in his error, his father, who was a Christian, had him thrown out of his house and carried to the cemetery of the Madeleine so that his accomplices could do as they wished with him because he did not regard him as his son and his wife likewise regarded him as nothing more than a dog. The heretics took him and buried him in their fashion. Then they left. The little Christian children who had watched how they did it said to each other, "Those dogs did not put any holy water on their brother. Let's give him what he deserves to soothe his soul."[243] All together they poured their urine on his grave.

OTHER DEMOLITIONS OF CHURCHES

On the Feast of the Dedication of Saint Peter[244] they destroyed the church of the temple outside the city gates,[245] which was fine and pious. [162]

On the Feast of Saint Denis [October 9, 1534] the parish church of Saint Leodegar outside the city was broken into, and in the month of October it was entirely torn down and destroyed and all the altars were ruined and chopped into pieces. Some people bought them to use as washtubs in their houses. They pulled down and chopped the heads off all the statues and took away everything they found in the church. A perverted native of Geneva named Jean Goulaz took the sacred host of God's precious body to feed to his horse, which was pulling a wagon. But immediately the horse, by God's will, blew on it with its nostrils and drew back as if it were afraid. That wretched man ran to where he had seen it fall to pick it up. But it floated above the ground as if to show that there was no worthy place for it to land, and that disloyal criminal dog[246] chased after it. But all of a sudden it vanished before his eyes and before all those present, which was a large company, as I, who write, was told by an honorable man, who declared it to be as true as the "Pater Noster"[247] on his faith as a good Christian, and many related it in this way.

243. Manuscript B omits "to soothe his soul" (*pour resfrigere de son ame*).

244. October 18, 1534. The Feast of the Dedication of the Basilicas of the Apostles Peter and Paul is actually on November 18.

245. The temple of Saint John of Jerusalem was located in the Faubourg du Temple, today in Eaux-Vives.

246. Manuscript B says only "that disloyal criminal" (*ce meschans des loyal*).

247. Manuscript B says only that the man said it was "true" (*veritable*). The "Pater Noster" is the Lord's Prayer ("Our Father").

On the Sunday of the octave of the Feast of Saint Francis [October 16], a young heretical man [163] who was on the steps during the sermon fell and hit his head hard, and he never spoke again. When they carried him away, the good Christians, low and high, shouted, "May the same thing happen to everyone in that sect."

THE HERETICS INTERRUPT THE VESPERS OF THE
SISTERS OF SAINT CLARE

On the Feast of Saint Simon and Saint Jude [October 28], they continued tearing down churches and houses in the faubourgs. Then in the evening, when the sisters of Saint Clare were saying vespers and the doors had inadvertently been left open after some burgher women had come to visit the sisters, a company of those dogs came into the church. Then they turned toward the sisters, who were reciting vespers. All together lifted their heads and began to shout, howl, and bawl at the top of their lungs like enraged wolves, a more hideous sound than was ever heard in the pit of hell, or so it seemed, and they did it to obstruct the divine service. But Our Lord strengthened the sisters' heart so that without appearing to notice them, with an ardent heart they all raised their voices so high that the intruders could not [164] drown them out, even though they continued from the first psalm all through the chapter. Then, seeing that they could not go on, they carried out their malicious intentions on a wooden cross, which they smashed into pieces and threw into the well in front of the convent. They took a statue of Saint Ursula,[248] in whose breast was a reliquary for offerings, and they threw it down the steps and onto the pavement in the street to destroy it, and they threw it into the well too, which greatly upset the sisters. Their father confessor and one of his associates were in an enclosed chapel saying their vespers, and they saw everything and recognized a good many of those people, who were from the city, and the others were German.[249] They did not dare come out or make any noise, because they would certainly have been injured.[250]

---

248. The legend of Saint Ursula and the ten thousand virgins who accompanied her at sea and were then martyred at Cologne was popularized by Jacques de Voragine's *La légende dorée* in the thirteenth century.

249. That is, German speakers, probably from Bern.

250. The day after this incident, Jussie drafted an appeal to the syndics, which is preserved at the *Archives d'État* in Geneva and cited by Ganter, *Les Clarisses*, 83–84.

THE DIET OF THONON

That November a diet was held at Thonon[251] to discuss issues of [165] peace and prosperity in the land, and it was all at monseigneur's expense. A true prince of peace, he did not want to spill human blood. He attended in person with the high and excellent nobles of his lands, including monseigneur the viscount,[252] his most noble nephew, Monseigneur the Marshal of Savoy, Count [René] of Challand, the Count of La Chambre,[253] and the Count of Gruyère,[254] messieurs the bishops, Monseigneur of Geneva [Pierre de la Baume] in person, Monseigneur the Bishop of Tarentaise, of Belley,[255] and many of the leading nobles of the land. Ambassadors came from all of the allied cantons at monseigneur's expense, and it did no good because the heretics would not see reason or renounce their heresy. So, without any agreement, everyone left, which upset everyone, and it made those heretics even prouder and more arrogant than before. They started disfiguring images again right away. During the first week of December[256] they tore down and removed all the crosses around Geneva; there were two in particular that were very handsome and made of sumptuous stone, one in front [166] of Notre Dame de Grace and the other one near the bishop's, which were a great loss. All the rest of that year there were great trials and troubles.

EVENTS OF SPRING 1535; STAUNCHNESS OF CATHOLIC WOMEN

The following March, on the Saturday before Palm Sunday [March 20] in 1535, the Genevans hanged a good Christian villager, and they did not let him confess to a priest. But a tailor was sent to him and preached to him for a long time and had him say his "Pater Noster"[257] in French, the way they do it. But in spite of them he cried out to God and the people for mercy, and he asked all good Christians to say a "Pater" and an "Ave Maria"[258] for his

---

251. A diet is a gathering of princes or estates to discuss political matters. The Diet of Thonon lasted from November 27 to December 16, 1534.
252. François of Luxembourg, Viscount of Martigues.
253. Name unknown according to Feld, *Petite chronique*, 165, n. 22.
254. Name unknown according to Feld, *Petite chronique*, 165, n. 23.
255. Claude d'Estavayer, who died soon afterward, on December 28, 1534. See above, note 62.
256. November 11–December 5, 1534.
257. See above, note 247.
258. See above, note 29.

salvation, and he died in the religion. The next morning, on Palm Sunday, those heretics all celebrated their Lord's Supper together at the monastery.[259] Married men brought their wives. But many heretical men in Geneva had good Christian wives who, to defend the holy religion, suffered worse than martyrs because [167] since they did not renounce their religion, they were very severely beaten, tricked, and tortured. Yet women were always found to be much more steadfast and constant in the religion than men, and young girls and women were especially virile during those Lutheran errors. One father tried to force his young daughter to go with him to that Lord's Supper. Knowing by divine inspiration that she was not obligated to obey what was not for her salvation, she refused to go even though he threatened and beat her. So he banished her from his house and renounced her as his daughter. She became a servant.

Three young women likewise refused to go even though their husbands beat and tortured them. So the three husbands, like felons, at the other heretics' insistence, put those three women in prison in a fortified room locked with two keys and said, "Papist ladies, you refused to obey and come to our solemn Easter Lord's Supper. So you will stay there locked up without comfort from anyone until the papists' rites are finished, and you will not eat the wafer that you think is the body of God." [168]

A wondrous thing was brought about by the goodness of Our Lord who always helps His friends when they are in extreme need: those three true champions of the religion had spent that whole holy week in great sorrow and agony—mainly because they could not act as good Catholics, as God wished—and on Holy Wednesday [March 24], when they saw that their husbands had gone to the sermon, with steadfast and firm conviction they sneaked out, one after the other, through a window, and all three went to receive Our Lord in great piety, and then they went back. Those dogs never knew a thing.

Likewise, another young wife of a rich merchant refused to go to the sermon or to that Lord's Supper. So the other heretics, men and women, made fun of him, saying "Hah, you poor fellow,[260] you are governed by a woman and subject to her. She must be a whore, for if she were an honorable woman, would she not be with you?"

And the man was upset by that, so he grabbed his wife by her hair and tried to pull her by force, and she, who had faith in God, did her best to resist, commending herself to God with all her heart. All of a sudden a bed caught

---

259. Manuscript B says "at the Monastery of R" (*au convent des r*).

260. Manuscript A reads *povre cuffez*, which manuscript B changes to *povre homme*.

on fire and he had to leave his wife to put out the fire, which nonetheless caused a lot of damage in his house. He was not yet satisfied, [169] but swore before God that on Easter Day she would not eat the wafer but would come to their Lord's Supper. She paid no attention but commended herself to God with all her heart. When Easter Day [March 28] arrived, he brought six strong men with him to carry her by force, but as they were taking her out of the house, he suddenly felt such a great burning in his stomach that he thought he was dying, and he said, "Alas, my friends, listen to me, for I am dying." They had to leave the woman and carry the man back into the house. An honorable man, his close neighbor, told and assured me that in one day he lost more than five hundred florins in wares.

On Holy Thursday [March 25] and Easter Day [March 28] they also had other Lord's Suppers. On Holy Thursday, Friday, and Saturday[261] they rang the bell for their sermons, and longer than usual, because the bells were not supposed to be rung on those days according to the rules and customs of the holy church.

On Easter Day, since they thought the men at the garrison in Peney[262] would be busy with the divine sacrament and they could defeat them easily, at least three hundred armed men left Geneva to attack those Christians. But they met with such a strong defense that they left without doing a thing. [170] When the men in Peney saw that, they built a large fire out of straw on the castle towers as if to say that if they came any closer, they would be burned. But there were no other injuries on either side.

On Holy Thursday, after the sermon at four o'clock in the afternoon, the preacher married a Lutheran man to a servant woman. The whole thing was astonishing.

Beginning on that holy Easter, the Genevans often went out into monseigneur's lands at night to catch the men at the garrison of Peney unaware.

During the first week of April they captured a lord canon named Monseigneur Gonin Dorsiere in his house, and he was put in prison with his priest, all because of the religion.[263] His sister, who was married to a very rich apothecary, had a baby. Her heretical husband[264] wanted to have it [171] baptized by the satanical Farel, and he called him to his house. When that

---

261. March 25, 26, and 27, 1535. Manuscript B says only Friday and Saturday (*Le vendredy et samedy sainct*).

262. A group of partisans of the prince bishop had left Geneva and taken refuge in the Castle of Peney at this time. See Gaberel, vol. 1, pt. 2, pp. 28–31.

263. Gonin Dorsiere, a canon of Saint Peter's Cathedral, and his prior, Jean Gardat, were suspected of involvement in the attempted poisoning of Pierre Viret by Antonie Vax.

264. Probably Michel Varoz, according to Feld, *Petite chronique*, 170, n. 15.

blessed girl, who was only fourteen or fifteen years old, saw her first offspring given to those dogs, firm in her religion and in her love of God, she got out of her childbed to go pull her child from the arms of that wretched man, and she immediately fell in a faint, from sorrow and the labor of childbirth. Her husband had pity on her and had her carried back to bed and was obliged to leave her child with her. She called the priest to her house, and he baptized the child in front of her.

Also, on the eve [April 24] of the Feast of Saint George, some people went out at night from Geneva into the countryside, and they captured a good priest in a village named Bernex[265] and took him to prison. They pulled him and his limbs so much that he died from the rope,[266] which everyone thought was excessive cruelty even if he had been a Turk.[267]

On the next Saturday they went out to the village of Cologny[268] and to the home of Lord André Guat. They got him out of bed at nine or ten o'clock at night and took him away. The poor lady his wife ran after them shouting piteously. But since they enjoyed afflicting honorable people, they took him all the way to the city gates. Then they bid him farewell. He got very sick from it. [172]

FAREL AND VIRET TAKE OVER THE FRANCISCAN MONASTERY OF RIVE; INSULTS MADE TO THE SISTERS OF SAINT CLARE

In the month of April, the wretched preacher Guillaume Farel, along with Pierre Viret from Orbe, took up residence in the Franciscan monastery in the chambers of the reverend father the suffragan.[269]

Since he was near the convent of the poor sisters of Saint Clare, he caused them a lot of trouble with his followers, commending them to his listeners from the pulpit, saying they were poor blind women who had strayed in their religion and that for their salvation they should be set free from prison and that everyone should throw stones at them because it was all debauchery and hypocrisy, because they want people to think they maintain their virginity, which God has not commanded because it is not possible to maintain it. They feed those frauds and Franciscans with good partridges and fat capons so that they will sleep with them at night, and messieurs of the

265. Southwest of Geneva.
266. Probably the *strappado*. See above, note 128.
267. Manuscript B omits the comparison to a Turk.
268. Northeast of Geneva, on Lake Geneva.
269. Pierre Farfein, assistant bishop of Geneva.

city should not allow it but should put them out of the convent [173] and make them all marry according to God's commandment. At other times he said they were causing divisions in the city, preventing him from converting people because they renounced everything he did, that the city would never be unified in religion until they were out of the convent, and other criminal and immoral words about them and about the monks, which I dare not write.

And he said so many such things that the heretics began to give them [the sisters] a lot of trouble, with both words and actions, and disloyal men got up on the city walls right next to the sisters' garden, and all day long they played with their harquebuses and sang indecent songs. The sisters could not go into their garden without the men seeing them and shouting insulting, indecent words or injuries at them. So they did not go in unless several of them went together with their faces covered. Finally, when the men saw that they did not respond or react to them in any way, they started to throw stones at them and tried to hit and bruise them, and so several of them were struck, and if God had not intervened, they would have knocked their brains out. They had to close the gate and not go there anymore to work, garden, or gather herbs, which caused them great poverty. [174]

ANNOUNCEMENT OF THE DISPUTATION OF RIVE BY FRIAR JACQUES BERNARD; THE GENEVANS BESIEGE THE CASTLE OF PENEY

On the last Friday of April, on behalf of messieurs of the city, the Franciscans' guardian, Friar Jacques Bernard, carried declarations containing five heretical articles to all the churches, convents, and monasteries of the city, and he took them personally to the chapter of messieurs of Saint Peter's Cathedral Church, and he carried them to people of all estates, to clergy and lay people, and even into monseigneur's lands and to gentlemen's houses, and he presented them and instructed people of [175] all estates to come to the monastery in Geneva on the Sunday after Trinity Sunday[270] to dispute the articles, which he would defend to the death, at which everyone was very surprised and in great perplexity about what to do because they were commanded by the strict orders of messieurs of the city. The matter was immediately referred to Monseigneur of Geneva. Wisely, he immediately announced the very dangerous threat of excommunication throughout his diocese, forbidding all faithful Christians to attend such disputations and

270. Trinity Sunday is the first Sunday after Pentecost.

saying they should leave them to their errors, at which they were all enraged and threatened to pillage churches and monasteries and even in monseigneur's lands.

They plotted secretly among themselves to attack the Castle of Peney
on the night of the Ascension of Our Lord [May 6, 1535], which they did,
thinking they would capture them [176] unaware on the holy occasion. The
Christians in Geneva did not know anything about that business until the
night before the Ascension of Our Lord, when suddenly, at eleven o'clock at
night, a great proclamation was made throughout the city that, under great
penalty, no foreigners should move about or leave their houses no matter
what they heard, which surprised and frightened many poor merchants who
were planning to go to the fair. Then they went from door to door telling all
Christians to prepare their weapons and go to a designated location and be
ready to follow messieurs' orders, which shocked them all. However, they
had to obey, and they were not allowed to ring any bells or clocks.

The poor sisters, who knew nothing of this, rang their bell at midnight
as usual for matins, which angered many people; they immediately and im-
petuously sent guards, and they beat on the main door of the convent so
hard that it resounded throughout the convent. The poor sisters, who were
in the church, trembled with fear. The mother portresses, very terrified, went
down and called for the lay brothers to find out what it was. But the brothers
had no less fear than the sisters. Nevertheless, the lay brothers went to find
out what it was. Then the visitors told them that the nuns were ringing the
bells too much and that by the [177] great devil they should not ring them
anymore until they had permission.

Afterward, that gathering of armed men sent guards to each gate to
protect the city. Then about twelve hundred of them went out, all armed,
with six large cannons, and they put the Christians in front to receive the
first blows. After they had left, they reached the castle at about three o'clock
in the morning. There they prepared their cannons to attack the castle. The
people on the inside, who did not know anything about that treachery, were
still in bed. But when they heard the noise, they immediately got up and,
without making any sound or giving any sign, they prepared their own artillery, and they kept so quiet that there seemed to be no one in the castle,
at which that band rejoiced and, indeed, thought it had already taken over
the castle. Their gunner loaded the largest cannon and lit it to fire it at the
castle.

But, as it was God's will, that great weapon turned against them and split
down the middle, gravely wounding the gunner and another man. However,
it did break the door of the castle. Then the people inside showed them-

selves quite clearly and then put up another door stronger than the first one. Then the attackers realized that the castle was not without men and a strong defense, which surprised them very much. They immediately tried to fire another cannon, but God [178] did not let a ball come out of it, and that second attempt was a failure. They fired a third time, trying to hit the castle. They hit a bale of wool that they themselves had brought to use as a barricade in front of them. They fired another one, and the cannonball broke. It was said that they were so frightened that at least a hundred men who were near the gunners fell down on their backs. All their gunpowder was burned up.

Then those in the castle, seeing their persistence, began to fire cannons and harquebuses from the castle so freely that it seemed to be raining, and so accurately that not a single one failed to kill or gravely wound someone. Therefore, many of them died there and others retreated and died on the way back. When they realized that they were losing and could not see the castle because of the attacks and the smoke from the cannons, they threw themselves to the ground and hastily returned to Geneva. To mock and insult them even more, the people in the castle climbed up to the battlements and took big glasses of wine with them and then danced in pairs around the battlements, shouting in loud voices, "Oh, you Genevan dogs, go listen to your parish Mass on this solemn day of our redemption, or if you want to drink at the Castle of Peney, come closer, for we have what you need." [179]

At this they began to lose patience, as they recognized their great dishonor and shame, and they would have given a thousand écus, in addition to what they had lost, not to have attempted such a foolish enterprise.

At ten o'clock in the morning they returned to Geneva very upset because everyone was mocking them and several of them were seriously wounded. Even worse, it was said that there had been no more than sixteen men in the castle, who had frightened an army of more than thirteen hundred so badly and done so much damage, and that nothing could have harmed that small company because God was protecting them. When everyone had left and gone away, the people in the castle came down to get the remaining balls and artillery, and in trees on the main road they hanged the dead bodies they found by their feet. They found one man who was not dead yet but spoke to them and told them all about the Genevans' plan. They urged him to turn back and recognize his creator and the sacraments of the holy church. But he would not do it, and he died in his heresy and was hanged with his comrades. The people in the castle praised God for granting them such a fine victory, with so few people, over those dogs, whom everyone everywhere blamed and criticized very much. [180]

THE HERETICS TAKE DOWN THE BELLS FROM THE CHURCHES IN GENEVA

On the next Wednesday [May 12] those dogs removed the bell from Notre Dame de Grace and threw it down from the steeple to destroy it. It was said that several of them struck it as hard as they could with stones and hammers, but they could not damage it. Afterward they went to see the bells at the monastery of Palais and at the parish of Saint-Gervais because they wanted to melt them down and make weapons to use against monseigneur and the Christians. Every day they caused some new scandal. [181]

THE SISTERS OF SAINT CLARE REFUSE TO ATTEND THE DISPUTATION OF RIVE

The following is what happened at the previously announced disputation. When the date drew near, the syndics personally ordered the father confessor [Jean Gacy] of the sisters of Saint Clare to be present without fail at the Franciscan monastery on Sunday for the disputation. Then on the Friday of the octave of the Feast of Corpus Christi, at five o'clock in the evening, when the sisters were gathered in the refectory for a sermon, the syndics and several of the leading heretics came to the turning window[271] [182] and told the mother portress[272] that they were messieurs the syndics and had come to tell the ladies that they were all required to attend the disputation the next Sunday. The mother portress immediately had this piteous news announced to the sisters and called for the mother abbess and her vicaress to speak to them and respond. They came together. The sisters who remained in the refectory to keep each other company drank an abundance of the wine of anguish, and they recited compline lamentably in tears.

The mother abbess and the vicaress greeted them humbly. They told them that messieurs had ordered them all to be at the disputation without fail. They answered humbly, "Messieurs, you will have to forgive us because we cannot obey. For our whole lives, we have been obedient to your lordship and your commands when it was permissible. But we cannot submit to this

---

271. The *tornet*, also spelled *tornoit*, was a window next to the main entrance to the cloister through which visitors to the convent could speak to the portress and ask permission to speak to other nuns. If permission was granted, visitors would be directed to go to the church and climb a staircase from the nave up to the level of the nuns' choir where they would find the *treille* or *treillie*, through which they could speak to the nuns.

272. Guillaume de Villette, from Gaillard.

command because we have taken a vow of perpetual holy seclusion, and we wish to observe it." [183]

The syndics replied, "We don't care a bit for your ceremonies, and you must follow messieurs' orders. All honorable people are summoned to this disputation so that the truth of the Gospel can be shown and proven to them because we must reach a unity of religion."

"What?" said the mother abbess and the vicaress. "It is not women's place to dispute, because study is not prescribed for women. Surely you do not think that they should dispute since even illiterate men, according to the decrees of the holy church, are forbidden to make claims about the Holy Scripture[273] and no woman has ever been called to witness in a disputation, so we will not be the first, and it would be no honor to you to try to force us."[274]

The syndics replied, "Arguing does you no good, and you will come with your good fathers."

Mother vicaress replied, "Messieurs, we beg you not to obstruct divine service. Hearing your foolish questions, we do not believe you are messieurs the syndics, for we think messieurs are too wise [184] even to dream of causing us any trouble. But you are wicked guards who do nothing but harass the servants of God."

The syndic said, "Lady Vicaress, do not make fun of us. Open your doors; we will come in, and you will see who we are. You have five or six young ladies in there who have lived in the city and will recognize us right away, for we are honorable people, governors and councilors of the city, and with good intentions."

Mother vicaress said, "You cannot come in right now to speak with those for whom you ask because they are at compline, or divine service; furthermore, it is time for us to retire, so we bid you good evening."

"Lady Vicaress, they are not all of your opinion, for there are some nuns in there whom you restrain with force, by your traditions and your control, who would immediately surrender to the truth of the Gospel if it was preached to them; and so that no one will have the excuse of ignorance, messieurs have ordered everyone to come to this disputation, and they want you all to be there."

---

273. See above, note 133.

274. The abbess and vicaress are playing freely with the question of women—particularly religious women—and authority. For a related discussion, see Charmarie Jenkins Blaisdell, "Religion, Gender, and Class: Nuns and Authority in Early Modern France," in *Changing Identities in Early Modern France*, ed. Michael Wolfe (Durham, N.C.: Duke University Press, 1999): 147–68.

"Messieurs," said the ladies, "be gracious, for we were all brought here by the grace of the Holy Spirit, and not by force, to do penance and pray for the world, and not to be idle, and we are not hypocrites, as you say, but pure virgins."

The syndics replied, "You are truly very much deceived, because God did not make as many rules as men have invented to deceive the world, and, in the name of religion, they are ministers of the great devil. You [185] expect us to believe that you are chaste, which is not possible in nature. You are all corrupt women."

"What?" said mother vicaress. "You, who call yourselves Evangelicals, do you find in the Gospel that you should speak ill of others? The devil may well take what is his, but he will have no part of us."

The syndic said, "You name the devil, you who pretend to be so holy."

"I am following your example, and you name him as a joke, and I do it out of spite."

The syndic said, "Lady Vicaress, be quiet and let others who are not of your opinion speak."

Mother vicaress said, "I will be glad to. Sisters," she said, "tell messieurs your intentions."

So the three portresses, the bursar, the two cooks, the nurse, and several of the aged mothers who were there to hear what happened all cried out together in a clear voice, "We say the same thing she does and want to die and live in our holy vocation."

They were all astonished to hear such a cry, and they said to each other, "Listen, Messieurs, what a clamor those women are making in there and what a racket."

Mother vicaress replied, "Messieurs, this is nothing. You will hear much worse if you take us to your synagogue, because when we are all together, we will cause such a disturbance that we will have the upper hand." [186]

The syndics declared, "You are terribly stubborn. But you will come."

Mother vicaress replied, "We will not."

"We will take you there," they said, "and, what is more, you will never return to your den, because we will each take one of you home with us, and we will take you to hear preaching every day, because you must change your wicked lives and live according to God. We lived immorally in the past. I," said the syndic, "was a thief and a bandit and lived in great luxury, not knowing the truth of the Gospel until now."

Mother vicaress replied, "Those acts are all wicked and contrary to divine commandments. It is very good for you to mend your ways because you have lived badly. But my companions and I, thanks be to Our Lord, have never committed any murders or other acts that require us to take up another life, and so we will not change in any way but will continue in holy service." She spoke to them so forcefully with the mother abbess and the portress that they were all astonished.

"Lady Vicaress," said the syndic, "you are most arrogant. But if you make us angry, we will make you regret it."

"Messieurs," she said, "you can punish only my body. This is what I desire for the love of my God, and neither I nor my companions will deny the holy religion, for Our Lord wants people to confess Him in front of men.[275] And if I say anything that displeases you, I wish [187] to suffer alone for it; and so that you may know better who I am and so that others will not suffer in my place, I tell you my name, which is Sister Pernette de Montluel or de Châteaufort."

When the syndics realized that they were wasting their breath and no one was paying much attention to them, they left and said furiously as they departed, "We order you again, on messieurs' behalf, to come to the Franciscan monastery with your good fathers without fail for the disputation next Sunday, and to be on time. Do not make us come get you."

And with that they left. When they had gone, the reverend mother abbess, the vicaress, and the portresses went up to the church with the others. Then they lifted the curtain on the grille to worship the Holy Sacrament, which was lying on the altar, as it is the good custom. Then all together with their voices raised, prostrate to the ground and calling themselves poor sinful women, they cried out for mercy; it was enough to break a piteous heart. They asked for aid and comfort from God and for advice from the blessed Holy Spirit about how to leave and escape those sorrows and perils. Then the mother abbess, the mother vicaress, and the portresses went back down to the turning window to ask for the good advice and counsel of their father confessor and some respectable Catholic burghers. They were all very upset; there was no human remedy to that commandment, for they had all received it. [188] There was nothing to do but go back and commend themselves to God.

Those poor sisters spent that night in vigil, discipline, prayer, and piteous affliction. On Saturday morning [May 29] at four o'clock they gave the good fathers and lay brothers permission to depart and to leave the city.

---

275. "Everyone therefore who acknowledges me before others, I also will acknowledge before my Father in heaven; but whoever denies me before others, I also will deny before my Father in heaven" (Mt 10:32–33); "And I tell you, everyone who acknowledges me before others, the Son of Man also will acknowledge before the angels of God; but whoever denies me before others will be denied before the angels of God" (Lk 12:8–9).

One of the good fathers and two lay brothers left. The father confessor planned to leave in the evening. There was so much anguish all day long that the sisters did not dare look at each other or they would lose heart, and not without cause, because they were in the teeth of ravenous wolves and there was no way to escape unless God worked a visible miracle. They knew well that it was true that many people sought to devour them wickedly and seduce them all and turn them from holy service.

THE CONFESSOR'S FAREWELL

After dinner their father confessor went up to the grille to bid them all farewell because he was going to take refuge outside the city. That tearful and sorrowful farewell cannot be described, and no one on either side could say a word. After a good while the mother abbess and the mother vicaress took heart and said, [189] "Father, your daughters here, seeing the danger you are in, all agree and ask you to leave, for your presence cannot help us, and it is better for us to perish alone than for you to perish with us because you can certainly get away and pray to God for us. We all ask you humbly for mercy if we ever caused you displeasure or were irreverent, and we thank you for all your service and good companionship."

Then the good father wept bitterly, and he asked the ladies likewise for mercy, saying, "Alas, mother and very dear daughters, how hard this departure is for me. Anguish is all around us. If I leave you in such peril and danger, I will be shameful and disloyal and my heart will break. If I stay, I will not be able to escape and I will be taken to the disputation. The people will excommunicate me and suspect me of heresy, and so I cannot avoid anguish and peril and do not know what to do."

The sisters told him again, "For the love of God, dear father, save yourself."

And so he gave them his blessing and absolution. Those who were able told him good-bye. "Alas, Father, how hard this day is. You are leaving us, and we will never see you here again. The day of dispersion has come. As we await, we bid you a last farewell." [190]

And so he went down, deeply afflicted, and he walked alone through the nave of the church, seeming completely outside of himself and unsure of what to do. While he was in that agony, as it was God's will, two good peasant men from the village arrived, and they asked him why he was grieving, and he told them everything. At that, they reassured him and told him it would be safest and most respectable not to abandon the poor nuns in such a plight and that it would be a great shame in the eyes of God and the people, and they asked him not to be afraid, for they would stay at the convent with him the whole next day to see what happened. At that, he took heart and decided not to go away. So that day was spent very piteously and in great sorrow.

THE CONFESSOR IS TAKEN TO THE DISPUTATION

The next day, the designated Sunday [May 30], the good father said Mass in front of the sisters. When the Mass was finished, four sergeants took him to the monastery for the disputation. The two peasants stayed at the convent to see what would happen to the ladies. They were convinced that they would come for them as they had declared and promised the previous Friday. [191] But Our Lord made them forget, and no one harmed them that day, although they waited in great sorrow and continuous prayers.

NARRATION OF THE DISPUTATION OF RIVE

At about three o'clock in the afternoon the father confessor returned, and, before drinking or eating, he went up to the grille and told the sisters about the first session of the disputation, how at the beginning that accursed Jacques Bernard had put the rules and statutes of the church up for debate, despite the habit he wore. How a pious Dominican monk, Master [Jean] Chapuis, had disputed vigorously and defeated him.

The next day they returned as before, proposed other foolish questions, and were defeated by the Dominican. They continued that whole week, and God intervened so that everyone present saw their accursed and deceptive pretense clearly. Then those dogs saw that God was granting a victory for His holy religion, so when the Dominican tried to answer a question, they all began to [192] spit and make noise, and those dogs howled so much that no one could hear him, which greatly upset the Christians; fearing that the good father would be attacked at night, they agreed that he should go away and that no more Christians should go to dispute. This enraged those false heretics, so they continued the disputation among themselves; it went on every day until the Feast of Saint John [June 24], greatly injuring the holy Catholic religion and cultivating and sowing very dangerous and damnable errors.

They completely condemned the Holy Mass as worthless and the divine sacraments as filthy and abominable things and all the other sacraments of the holy church.

Also, they called the Virgin Mary an immoral woman, with no power or merit before God, and they also said that all the saints[276] in paradise were worth no more than men in this world, and less.

Also, they said that there was no purgatory and that no one should pray for the departed after their death because they would be judged at the end of the world and sent to paradise or to hell eternally.

And more other terrible heresies than it is possible to write, and as for me, I am horrified to think of and relate them. [193]

JACQUES BERNARD'S WEDDING

After that accursed conclusion, the Franciscan Jacques Bernard, the guardian of the monastery of Rive, a priest and a preacher, scorned his order insultingly and put on a secular habit, on the twentieth day of July, and soon afterward he married a beautiful young girl, the daughter of a wealthy printer and bookseller.[277]

THE HERETICS OBSTRUCT DIVINE SERVICE IN THE CHURCHES OF GENEVA

On the Feast of the Madeleine [July 22], when the bells were ringing solemnly for the Mass in her church and the whole parish and other good Christians in town were gathered there to hear the Holy Mass in great piety, that miserable preacher Farel brought his whole congregation. They came in their ordinary clothing to the church of the blessed Madeleine to obstruct her feast, and when they got inside they closed the church and stood at the door to force people to hear that sermon. This greatly distressed [194] and troubled everyone; the women cried out loudly and made such a ruckus that they left the church despite their plans. All divine service was stopped. But after those dogs left, the Christian people came back to the church, and the priests said Mass more solemnly than ever and in great piety. Those dogs did the same thing at vespers, and they took possession of that holy church and preached there every day afterward, and then in the church of Saint-Gervais. They did the same thing at the Dominican monastery on the Feast of their father Saint Dominic, and they obstructed divine service in all the churches. They gave the poor sisters of Madame Saint Clare an especially hard time. They begged their good Catholic friends for good advice and support. But no one could do a thing except weep with them in pity.

276. Again, Jussie refers explicitly to both male and female saints: *tous les sains et sainctes*.
277. Georgia, the daughter of Wigand Köln.

GUILLAUME FAREL TRIES TO PREACH AT THE
CONVENT OF SAINT CLARE

On Sunday during the octave of the Visitation of Our Lady at ten o'clock in the morning, when the poor sisters were having dinner, the syndics came [195] to the convent with the wretched preacher Guillaume Farel and Pierre Viret and a miserable Franciscan who looked more like a great devil than a human, together with a dozen of the leaders of the town, all heretics. They asked to come inside for our own good and consolation, saying they were our fathers and good friends. The mother portress told mother abbess and mother vicaress, who told the community to ask Our Lord to inspire them to respond in His honor and praise because they were convinced there was treachery and trickery.

The sisters left the table and went to the church, and the mother abbess and mother vicaress went to the turning window and said, "Messieurs, you will have to forgive us because it is not our calling to open our doors. But if you would like to go up to the grille, we will greet you there willingly."

The syndic replied, "We are lords of justice and want to come in. But do not be afraid, for we will treat you honorably."

Mother vicaress replied, "Messieurs, my heart tells me that you have brought your devilish preachers, whom we do not wish to hear."

The syndic said, "Lady Vicaress, you are always giving us a hard time. We are good people and do not use trickery and have come to comfort you. So open the doors, because you may not and must not refuse us." [196]

"Messieurs," said mother vicaress, "please state your reason for wanting to come in here. Treat us graciously and allow us to serve God without any more obstacles."

The syndic said, "By the shroud of God we will come in. If you don't open up, we will break down your doors, and you will be sorry."

Mother vicaress said, "If you are coming to do evil, you might as well break them. But I think you are wise men who do not want to cause such a scandal."

The syndic said, "Lady Vicaress, we told you we have come for your own good, and only three or four of your good friends want to come in."

Hearing this, mother abbess and some of the sisters said, "We had better open the doors so they do not cause us any more trouble."

To avoid their wrath, they opened the doors. They promised that they had not brought a preacher with them and that only three or four people would come in. But at least fifteen came in with the father confessor, who had fearfully advised them to open the door with another good father, his associate. Then they went straight to the chapter room.

Then the syndics said, "Mother Abbess, call all your sisters here, and without argument or delay, or else we ourselves will look for them in the convent." [197]

Mother vicaress said, "Ah, Messieurs, you have betrayed us. I do not wish to hear your sermon of perdition."

She made all possible excuses. But out of holy obedience the father confessor and the mother abbess called for all the sisters, young and old, healthy and sick.

When they were all gathered, with that accursed Farel in front of the young nuns and those Evangelicals on both sides of them to flatter and deceive them, silence was ordered and Farel announced his theme, "Exurgens maria abiit in montana,"[278] and he said that the Virgin Mary had not led a life of solitude, but was quick to give help and aid to her aged cousin. Thus, he insultingly dishonored holy seclusion and the convent and the state of holy chastity and virginity, which pierced the poor sisters' hearts.

When mother vicaress saw those seducers talking to and flattering the young sisters, she stood up among the older nuns and said, "Monsieur Syndic, since your men are not keeping silent, I will not either. I will be the one to speak to my sisters here." She went among the young nuns and up to those gallants and said, "If your preacher is so holy, why don't you revere and obey him? You are wicked seducers, but you will get nothing here."

This angered them, and they said, "What a devil of a woman this is! Lady Vicaress, are you possessed by the devil? Or, if you are crazy, get back in your place." [198]

"I will not," she said, "until those men are taken away from my sisters."

The wretched preacher was so angry, or so terrified by the will of God, that he did not know what to say; his voice shook and he could not maintain his composure. The two other preachers were no less affected, and they did not say a word. The agitated syndics furiously ordered mother vicaress to be sent away. She said, "You do me a great favor, for I desire nothing but to be away from you all, and I do not want to hear your accursed traditions."

Then several of them grabbed her and took her out of the chapter room. All the sisters got up to follow her out, but the door was closed. So they began to weep and to cry out for mercy. But silence was again ordered by the confessor, who was more frightened than they were, and by the mother

---

278. "Exsurgens autem Maria in diebus illis abiit in montana cum festinatione in civitatem Iudae, et intravit in domum Zachariae et salutavit Elisabeth" (In those days Mary set out and went with haste to a Judean town in the hill country, where she entered the house of Zechariah and greeted Elizabeth; Lk 1:39–40).

abbess, who was with them. The poor mother, who was very old and sick, obeyed their orders and told the sisters to remain. One poor sister who was afraid of their infection ran to the dormitory and closed the door, but they made her come back and even called for the very sick nuns. That preacher began speaking his deceitful words again, about the goodness of marriage and freedom and other very abusive and damnable things. When he spoke of fleshly corruption, the sisters cried out, "It's lies!" And they all spat on him in scorn, especially the young sisters who were in front of him, and they said "We cannot listen to these errors anymore." [199]

At this he was greatly outraged, and he said, "And you, Father Confessor, who keep these poor blind women in this damnable captivity, why don't you make them be quiet and listen to the word of God? But they cannot hear it because they are not from God,[279] but all have corrupt hearts, pretending to live chastely in seclusion and tricking everyone. However, we know well that many of these poor young girls would come willingly to the truth of the Gospel and the great goodness of marriage if you and the old women did not keep them in such restraint and subjection."

At this the utterly terrified confessor and his associate and the mother abbess[280] commanded silence again, saying Saint Paul commands women to keep silent, etc.[281]

But mother vicaress, who was outside, did not keep silent but went up to the wall right next to the preacher and hit it hard with her two fists and shouted, "Oh, you wretched and wicked coward, you speak your false words in vain. You will gain nothing here. I beg you, sisters, not to listen to anything he says."

This disturbed them even more than before, and she made such a noise with her hands and her loud shouting that he forgot what he was saying. The syndics swore they would put her in prison. But she was steadfast in her strong will and not afraid to die for the honor of God.

Some of the sisters had stuffed their ears with wax so they would not hear him. [200]

When he saw that they were not paying any attention to him, the preacher stopped, and from the look of him, he wished he had never come inside and thought he could not get out soon enough. I who write this, being

---

279. "Whoever is from God hears the words of God. The reason you do not hear them is that you are not from God" (Jn 8:47).

280. Manuscript B removes the abbess from this list.

281. "Women should be silent in the churches. For they are not permitted to speak, but should be subordinate, as the law also says" (1 Cor 14:34).

present and observing his attitude carefully with the firm conviction not to sway from the love of my God and of my vocation, firmly believe that the devils that guided him could not endure the company of the true brides of Jesus and their virtuous constancy and the sign of the holy cross, which they made continuously in spite of him. The syndics and the others wanted to talk to the sisters and to dispute; however, the door of the chapter room was opened, and mother vicaress was called back in at mother abbess's request. And she kept contradicting them and would not say much to them.

Some of the young nuns had tried to hide in the church, so four or five of those merchants went to get them, and they were mainly seeking the two from the city and the ones who had gone to school in their city, whom they knew. I, among them, was recognized by one of them, and he tried to lift up my veil forcibly and see my face; when I did not let him, he was angry and said that he would not do any other harm at that moment, "But I will soon see you freely in the street."

These were words that pierced my soul and my poor companions' souls. The criminal preacher Viret said the same thing to the poor sister from Orbe,[282] whom he kept trying [201] to deceive. They especially wanted to speak secretly with the ones from Geneva, but mother vicaress kept them away. The poor apostate nun [Blaisine Varembert] spoke uprightly at that time. The aged mothers answered them firmly from the Holy Scripture. The poor sisters were tried sorrowfully that day from ten o'clock in the morning until five o'clock in the evening, and many of them did not drink or eat anything except great abundances of tears. When they saw that it was doing no good and that they were gaining nothing but great insults, they went outside, and that criminal Farel ran to be the first one out; he washed his hands impatiently to cool himself because he felt like he was burning with rage. When he was going down the steps, that criminal Franciscan, who was all covered with splotches and hideous to see, could not go down but stayed behind. One sister went after him and hit his shoulders with both her fists and said, "Wretched apostate, hurry up and get out of my sight."

But he did not react and never said a word. I think his tongue was bound and tied.

And when they went out, the syndics said, "We will come back often to proclaim the word of God to you."

Mother vicaress said, "Don't come back for any reason, for we will never open the doors." [202]

They tried to return many times after that. But Farel never came, nor

282. Claude de Pierrefleur from Orbe.

did any other preacher, because they said it was a waste of time to preach to those hypocrites. "Instead, put them out of their den and make them come to the public sermon."

HEMME FAULSON TRIES TO REMOVE HER SISTER, BLAISINE VAREMBERT, FROM THE CONVENT

When they left, there were at least three hundred people in front of the convent waiting to see if any nuns would come out with them, and they thought there was no way they would not be perverted, and several wicked persons planned to take nuns home and marry them. Even an apostate Franciscan had sworn to marry one. Our poor apostate's sister, who planned to take her sister away, was waiting there; she had gotten up from her childbed to remove and pervert her, for she had given birth only a week ago. Her heretical husband had carried his own child in his bosom to be baptized without anyone else.[283] When that miserable woman realized her sister was not coming out, she went up to the grille with some other burgher women, pretending she wanted to speak with the sisters in good friendship to find out what those preachers had done to them. Then she asked to speak to her sister. The mother abbess with several of the discreets[284] and others spoke to them piously. Then, with a false [203] serpentine tongue, preaching with sweet words and thinking she could do more than the preachers had, she started to talk about the Gospel, and she said, "Poor ladies, you are very stubborn and blind. Don't you understand that God said His burden is tender and sweet,[285] and He said, 'Come to me, all who have labored and are weary, and I will give you rest,'[286] and didn't He say that you imprison and torture yourselves by doing penance as you do?"

Then she spoke words about the Holy Sacrament that I would be horrified to write, words that were deceitful and completely the opposite of salvation.

---

283. That is, he had not observed the church's traditional baptismal rites.

284. The Rule of Saint Clare (chap. 4, no. 17) provides for eight discreets to be elected as advisors to the abbess. According to the rule (chap. 5, no. 7), nuns may not speak to visitors at the grille unless they are accompanied by at least three of these discreets, selected by the abbess or vicaress ("Quelles ne prennent pas la liberté de se rendre à la grille sans la compagnie de trois soeurs au moins, choisies parmi les huit discrètes par l'abbesse ou sa vicaire"). See Vorreux, *Sainte Claire d'Assise*, 114–15.

285. "For my yoke is easy, and my burden is light" (Mt 11:30).

286. "Come to me, all you that are weary and are carrying heavy burdens, and I will give you rest" (Mt 11:28).

The mother abbess knew the Holy Scripture well and gave a spirited response, and so did that poor apostate. However, she showed her sister much friendship and intimacy, which made the sisters very suspicious. Some of the sisters asked mother vicaress to end their discussion. She went right up and took mother abbess by the arm and said, "Mother, seeing that these good ladies have changed to a law that is opposed to salvation and to us, you should not listen to them." Then she said to that lady, "Daughter, if you wish to discuss Our Lord and proper subjects here, as in the past, we will speak willingly to you. [204] But we do not wish to hear about those innovations of law, because our prelates have forbidden it."

Then, without saying good-bye, she closed the door,[287] and they were left facing wood, which greatly disturbed them. They shouted at them for at least a half hour, saying, "Hah! You false frauds scorn the word of God and obey your frauds and great ministers of the devil."

Then that miserable woman said, "Hah! My sisters and friends, you see how they treat my poor sister and how they keep her in so much subjection that the poor girl does not dare say what is in her heart, even though she would willingly listen to us," and other words that should not be spoken.

THE HERETICS HARASS THE SISTERS OF SAINT CLARE

And after that day not a single day passed without someone of their sect coming to spy on and try the poor nuns, and they often said dishonorable and detestable words. But the mother portress [Guillaume de Villette] was sensible and discreet and did not talk long to them before closing the turning window; and if a response was necessary, she would call for the mother abbess and the mother vicaress and the sisters would pray. Our Lord always allowed them to respond appropriately, and they defeated them. It is true that they often threatened [205] mother vicaress with imprisonment as a criminal, and we expected them to do it some day. But some of them were afraid and said, "She is from an important family, and it could cause an uprising against the city. The Duke of Savoy supports them, too, because they pray only for him, and so it would be a mistake to arrest that stupid woman."

Many honorable people came to warn them that they were threatening to take the young ones and marry them, particularly the poor perverted woman, whose sister made daily pleas to the city and to the council. And so, many Catholic burgher women and even some of her relatives came to weep with them and to urge them to be steadfast and to be very patient and

---

287. The wooden door on the nuns' side of the grille.

persevere because it was all true: they were planning to take us from the convent and separate us from each other very soon.

THE SISTERS PROMISE EACH OTHER LOYALTY

The poor sisters, advised by Our Lord, all gathered one day in the chapter room as the small bell rang, and they invoked the aid of Our Lord, of the blessed Holy Spirit and of the sacred Virgin Mary and the whole holy company in such an abundance of tears that they could not hear each other, and the young sisters were asked if they wanted to persevere or to escape somehow [206], if God would inspire them. Some good ladies had offered to take them out secretly and safely, in disguise. All of them, prostrate on the ground, speaking loudly and with an effusion of tears, said to the old ones, "O our most beloved mothers, have pity on us, and help your poor children in this sorrowful danger. Anguish is all around us, for if we are parted and taken from your company, we cannot be certain not to fall into their hands, and if we remain, we cannot escape bodily peril except by divine assistance. And so we ask you to pray for us, and to do all you can to help us, because we are willing to die for God. If they take us by force, do not be afraid to do your best to get us away from them, for we would rather be chopped into pieces than give in to them. And we promise to do our best to be faithful."

When the poor aged women heard this, they wept inconsolably, and some of them collapsed. They all made promises to each other and pledged their loyalty, except for the poor misguided one who was pensive and then laughed and paid no attention to them. They mentioned her aunts and brother-in-law[288] and asked what she thought she would do, and they told her that if she was not as willing[289] as the others and if she wanted, they could help her escape because her two aunts in the city who were well [207] regarded and true Catholics had asked them to help her escape and to get her out of the city and to safety in the home of monseigneur the judge of Gex [François Barrat], who had married her sister, and that from there he would take her very respectably to a convent in Vevey[290] and that she really should agree because it was all true, that she would be captured by the ravenous, perverted wolves.[291] She said that she would have nothing to do with her aunts or her brother-in-law and that she knew well what to do. At

---

288. That is, her family members who were not allied with the Reform.
289. To die for God.
290. The Convent of Saint Clare in Vevey.
291. See above, note 163.

that, the poor mothers saw her wicked intentions clearly and they did what they could to correct her, and as gently as possible. The young ones said to her, "O our most beloved companion, have pity on your poor soul and heed the good mothers' advice, for you are in great peril and, because of you, we all are."

She answered, laughing, "You are really afraid, and you want to get rid of me. But you will not do it this way. Think for yourselves." [208]

THE SISTERS' ATTEMPTS TO RETAIN BLAISINE VAREMBERT

When they saw this, the sisters sent for her aunts, and they told them everything she had said. Then they wept bitterly and called her to come speak with them. But she refused to come until she was told that it was her heretical sister. Then she went immediately and joyfully. Her poor aunts spoke to her as gently and wisely as possible, and they promised never to fail her. But she paid no attention. Then one of them said to her with great affliction, "Hah, Sister Blaisine, I see your foolish opinion clearly, and I see you will bring dishonor on your cousins my daughters and that we will all be greatly blamed because of you." Sister Blaisine left, laughing and without bidding them farewell.

Which afflicted the poor ladies with unbelievable anguish, and mother vicaress said to them, "My ladies and our good mothers, you see the danger we are in because of this girl, and you will be our witnesses to the fact that we have found and proposed all possible means to save her. She sees her companions' good and steadfast constancy clearly, and she knows well that very good nuns are in grave danger because of her."

"Truly, you speak the truth," said those ladies, "For we know well that the wicked people have a great desire to possess certain ones, and they will take them violently if Our Lord does not intervene with His Grace." [209]

At those words the sisters were even more despondent than before, and there was so much anguish that sometimes they did not recognize each other, and they said, "Oh God, what advice will you give us? Have you removed us from the world for our own peril?[292] If we hide the young ones, they will martyr the poor aged ones out of spite, and if they find the young ones, they will take them away violently and we would not know what to do at such a painful separation and tribulation."

They also said, "Oh, our most beloved mothers of the convent, do you

---

292. Manuscript B says "Have you removed us from the world to allow us to fall into a bigger mire?" (*Nous avez vous tiré du monde pour nous permettre tomber en plus grand bourbier?*)

not know the pitiable anguish and sorrowful danger your poor sisters are in? At least help us with your prayers."

SECRET MESSAGE FROM THE SISTERS TO THE DUKE OF SAVOY

And so the sisters lived in fear, tears, and sorrow, and there was no way to let anyone know because they did not dare write a letter since the city had sent eighty armed men to the house of Monseigneur of Coudrée[293] right in front of the convent; and they kept watch day and night so that no nun, nor any goods or furnishings, could leave the convent; and no small child or anyone else could pass by without being searched and asked to declare [210] their intentions, why they were coming and going; and if anyone was bringing alms to the sisters out of pity, they would confiscate them and prevent good creatures from giving them consolation; and in that way they were deprived of all comfort and human counsel.

Nonetheless, discreetly and with Our Lord's help, they sent word of their danger and misfortune to monseigneur the duke, who had great love and pity for them, as did madame. They sent word to the judge of Gex to prepare his monastery in Annecy for us, and they told us not to fear, that he would give it to us to save us from those dogs and that we should not worry about anything except how to get away, that he would give us furnishings and anything else we needed, which was a great comfort and consolation to us. But, alas, there was no way for us to leave without danger because there were guards all around the convent and at all the city gates and no one could come in or go out without their consent, and we were afraid that if we left, we would be captured and separated violently as, indeed, some of the wicked people intended, so the best thing to do was to wait together for the divine will of Our Lord who never leaves His friends without consolation. [211]

INTERRUPTION OF DIVINE SERVICE BY THE HERETICS AT SAINT PETER'S CATHEDRAL

On the Feast of the Octave of Saint Peter ad Vincula,[294] on a Sunday, those heretics showed great disrespect at Saint Peter's Church by interrupting messieurs the canons' divine service, and they hit them and tore

293. Pierre d'Allinges.
294. August 8, 1535. See above, note 23.

their surplices[295] and did many great injustices and criminal acts, and they brought their damnable leader to preach. The next day [August 9] they took all the furnishings and treasures, worth more than ten thousand écus, and defaced the images and fine, priceless, excellently crafted portraits, and they left no symbol of piety untouched. From that day on no service was celebrated in the whole town, except at the Convent of Saint Clare, where the poor sisters still observed the canonical hours, but with the doors closed. The good fathers said Mass every day, and many people came there secretly, which put the sisters in grave danger. On the eve of the Feast of Saint Clare [August 11] it was ordered, under great penalty, that the bells no longer be rung or [212] any other office or Mass celebrated, which was a sword pierced through their poor souls. They all still said the office, but quietly in the middle of the choir and sometimes in the refectory.

THE LAST MASS AT SAINT CLARE

On the Feast of the Assumption of Our Lady [August 15] after matins, the brothers said the Holy Mass, and then the father confessor gave all the sisters communion for the last time. It was carried to the poor sick ones in great agony and tears, and then they commended their father confessor to God, for he was going to leave, to escape and get out of the city, along with his associates,[296] who feared they would be captured and mistreated, and they left the city. The poor sisters were left alone in their suffering, without counsel or comfort from any human creature except a single poor lay brother [Nicholas des Arnox] who was very gravely ill and could not travel far. So they were in pitiable bitterness and expected nothing but sorrow and peril, and there was nothing but weeping and lamentation in that poor congregation. [213]

VIOLENT ENTRY OF THE GENEVANS INTO THE CONVENT OF SAINT CLARE

The following is the violence that was done in the convent and to the poor nuns, a pitiable thing.[297]

On the Feast of Monseigneur Saint Bartholomew the Apostle [August

---

295. Loose, white, wide-sleeved garments worn over clerical robes.

296. Manuscript B does not mention the confessor's associates.

297. This sentence is preceded by the following fragment in manuscript A: "On the Feast of Monseigneur Saint Bartholomew the Apostle, all of a sudden" (*Le jour de monseigneur saint barthellemy appostre, tout subitement*).

24] great companies came, all with arms and weapons and all kinds of swords and dreadful instruments, and they knocked very peacefully on the main door of the convent. The poor lay brother went to see what they wanted. A wicked murderer deceitfully called himself a friend of the convent and said, "Open to me without fear, for I am a very good friend and come to bring comfort to the sisters."

The poor lay brother opened the door with good intentions, and that multitude came inside immediately.[298] The poor lay brother stood frozen with fear. They ran immediately through the convent and the brothers' rooms,[299] destroying and smashing everything they found, images, books, and breviaries; they did worse things than they had done in any other church, and because the images had been taken away and hidden, they threatened to put the poor lay brother's hands in chains if he did not show them where they were. [214] The poor, frightened brother showed them to the room where everything was hidden. Like enraged wolves, they destroyed those fine images with great axes and hammers, especially going after the blessed crucifix, which was wonderfully handsome, and the image of Our Lady; they left no object intact. Then they used a ladder to climb up to a large, amazingly beautiful crucifix, and, a piteous thing to see, they worked very hard and struggled with great axes and torches and all kinds of instruments, and more than fifty of them went at it. But they were never able to damage it or to get it down, which greatly annoyed them.

When the poor sisters heard this commotion, they were very sorrowful and afraid, and they all retreated to the church and asked for Our Lord's aid and assistance. Those evil satanists, after doing their spiteful deeds, went right to the sisters' turning window, and Pierre Vandel and Baudichon,[300] captains of that pestiferous company,[301] struck it with a great iron bar that they carried to break all locks and with a great axe that they used to break through doors, and they knocked down the turning window, which was handsome and made of good strong walnut. When the portress saw the turning window collapse and break into pieces, she barred the door to them and braced it with her back to keep them from opening it. But one of them hit it so hard with his axe that the axe sank in and nearly went into the portress's back. But

---

298. For a consideration of the significance of Reformed intrusions into convent space, see Carrie F. Klaus, "Architecture and Sexual Identity: Jeanne de Jussie's Narrative of the Reformation of Geneva," *Feminist Studies* 29.2 (2003): 279–97.

299. Manuscript B says "in the good fathers' rooms" (*es chambres des beaux peres*).

300. Pierre Vandel, Baudichon de la Maisonneuve, and Aymé Perrin were named as leaders in the iconoclastic acts at Notre Dame des Graces. See Feld's edition of the *Petite chronique*, 214, n. 2.

301. Manuscript B says "captains of that satanical company" (*capitainne de celle sathanique compagnie*).

God the [215] Creator miraculously moved her away, and she left the room with the turning window and closed the door, which was double and strong, and another door that was after the first door, all of which were well built and strong. Then she ran to the church, and all the nuns as one, healthy and sick, gathered in a heap prostrate on the ground in the middle of the choir, covering their faces, in pitiable sorrow and incomparable sighs, awaiting bodily death or peril to the soul and without hope or human comfort.

As soon as the intruders had broken the turning window and the three doors, they spread throughout the convent in great herds, for more than 150 had come in, all with a fanatical desire to do evil, and they left no image or object of devotion untouched in the dormitory, the infirmary, or any place in the convent. When they came to the choir where the poor sisters were waiting, they smashed the fine statues right in front of their eyes, sending shards flying above them, which hurt when they hit them. When they saw this, the poor sisters, with an ardent heart,[302] beginning with mother vicaress and then all in a single, clear, loud voice, cried out for mercy without ceasing, and the terrible cry could be heard faraway; the whole convent resonated with the violence, and they were very astonished, and they too cried out loudly, "Stop that noise, by the great devil."

But mother vicaress said, "We will cry out to Our Blessed God until we receive help and grace from Him. But you who do devilish works, on whose authority do you do [216] such violence? Messieurs the syndics and governors are not here. We ask them for an explanation and to see that justice is done and to tell us what brings you to torture us like this for no reason." This surprised some of them a bit. The others, like ravenous wolves,[303] did not stop devouring every object of piety they found.

They also smashed the sisters' chairs and pulpits, which were handsome and made of good walnut. Also the lectern and the book that was on it, and I believe that such piteous cries and lamentations as the poor sisters made had never been heard before, and several of them, in anguish, swooned and were speechless.

SISTER BLAISINE IS LED OUT OF THE CONVENT

The poor apostate was with the sisters then, and the mother abbess kept her close by her to give her courage, and when the sisters cried out for mercy,

---

302. In this passage, Jussie spells both *choeur* "choir" and *coeur* "heart" as *cueur*—perhaps an intentional orthographical blurring suggesting the identical nature of these most sacred spaces?

303. See above, note 163.

she cried out instead, "Paveant illi et non pavant ego,"[304] which very much surprised those who were near her. Since mother vicaress kept asking for the syndics and to know their full [217] intentions and what they were going to do with us, for the time being they did nothing to any of the sisters. But they all gathered together again and departed, leaving the convent wide open so that anyone could come in.

When He saw that the poor sisters were so weary and afflicted and did not know what to do, Our Lord, who never forgets His friends in their extreme need, inspired two prominent Catholic burgher ladies, the wife of the apothecary Lord Aymé de la Rive, Lady Guillaume, and the wife of a rich merchant,[305] Lady Leonarde Vindrette, to comfort them. They came in boldly, and when the sisters saw them, they cried out for mercy again, thinking those dogs had come back. But the poor, weeping ladies said, "Fear not, for we are your friends and have good intentions." Then the poor sisters all stood up in front of them, with piteous sighs and lamentations, and they said nothing for a long time but used gestures to explain the disrespect and violence that had been done. [218]

The poor ladies said, "Truly, dearest ladies, it displeases us greatly, and if we could have, we would certainly have stopped them. But you know that it is not right to use force. The wicked have power over the servants of God, and the good have no refuge but steady patience. Now take comfort in Our Lord and tell us privately if anyone touched you."

"No," said mother vicaress, "I believe that God did not let them."

"Then be brave," they said, "because this is only the beginning of the sorrows. All you young ones, have courage and trust in Our Lord, for you have a battle ahead of you."

As they were leaving, the miserable captain of malice returned and came in with several of his most infected followers and a crowd of fanatics. This revived the poor sisters' anguish unbelievably, and they said, "O true mothers and friends, why have these miserable people come back? As you see, they have already destroyed everything they could, so what more do they want from us?"

"Turn to Our Lord," said these ladies, "and He will not forsake you. As for us, we will do what we can to help you. And you, Sister Blaisine, be brave, because your sister is bringing this company to get you." [219]

At that, the mother abbess took Sister Blaisine by the hand and said,

---

304. "Paveant illi et non paveam ego" (Let them be dismayed, but do not let me be dismayed (Jer 17:18).

305. Pierre Vindret, a shoe seller.

"My child, if you resist, we will all stand by you until death. I, at least, will stay with you in the midst of the flock, and if they come for you, you will be at your poor mother's bosom."

Mother vicaress was hiding one young nun at her legs, under her habit, and she entrusted her to one of those pious ladies, who slipped her under her own dress and stood there frozen with fear. The poor sisters cried out for mercy just as before in voices that were pitiably hoarse, which moved those people greatly; they could not hear each other, and they dared not touch the sisters since they stood so close together that they could not distinguish the young ones from the old ones. The Catholic lady did her best to reason with them, saying, "Alas, Messieurs, what do you want from these poor ladies, who hurt no one? Dame Hemme, stop trying to remove your sister! Stop, for nothing good will come of it!"

She answered, "We will not force her, or anyone else, if it is not of her own will. But I know well that she would like to be out and that the poor girl lives in great regret and restraint, and Our Lord has given everyone free will to choose between good and evil. When we speak to her, you will see her wishes clearly and you will see how these frauds use force to restrain her and others too." [220]

Then she began to search for her and to shout, saying, "Sister Blaisine, show yourself and speak to us. Sister, have no fear, for I seek and ask for only your good and consolation."

But the miserable girl did not dare answer. The sisters' cries and laments made such a din that no one could hear anyone else.

Then Vandel said, "Be quiet, by the great devil, and keep silent!"

And they cried out for mercy even louder.

The miserable girl's sister said, "Messieurs, leave them to their shouting and their fury. We are looking only for my sister, and so that we may identify her, let us unveil them one by one, whether they like it or not."

They were about to do it, but mother vicaress, who was the first one, stood up straight and said very bravely, "Messieurs, if you touch our bodies, be careful what you do, for I swear to God that if any man hurts me in any way, either I or he will die here and now."

And they were surprised by this and looked at each other without saying a word. But they gestured to the women to go up to the sisters.

Which they did, and they asked them, one at a time, "Are you Sister Blaisine?"

They answered, "No, and I would not wish to be. Go look for her some-place else."

But they finally found her in the middle of the group, near mother abbess, who said to her, [221] "Sister Blaisine, my child, we have protected you until now. I pray you, do not leave the flock, but show yourself to be a true champion of Our Lord, for I cannot help you in this battle. You have free will to choose between good and evil. May Our Lord be in your heart and thoughts."

And at that, the miserable sister shouted, "Messieurs, we have found my sister! But these frauds are preventing her from telling us what she thinks. Come, let us speak to her."

Then she took her and embraced her and pulled her away from the others, drawing her aside to talk to her.

Mother vicaress and several others followed them, saying, "Ah, Sister Blaisine, do not give in! Be a valiant servant[306] of Our Lord, and do not speak to them!"

But the wicked people said, "Go away and let us speak to her, and if she does not want to leave of her own accord, we will not hurt her. Go away, for you could be the cause of greater harm and killing."

At those words, the good Catholic ladies begged the sisters to keep quiet to avoid greater harm. They themselves did all they could to calm those heretics. They spoke privately to Blaisine, and I do not know what they said, but in the end she was taken away without any resistance. [222]

Those good ladies said, "Ah, Messieurs, what are you doing? Nothing good will come of it!"

Then the leaders said, "Lady Guillaume and all of you, you should know that she is kept here against her wishes. We have known her wishes for a long time and will show you letters in her own handwriting by which we know her intentions, and for this reason her sister has called for us and asked us to do this, because we are required to help each other recognize the truth of the holy Gospel. For a long time now, the poor girl has known it and been inspired by it. But she did not dare show it, and so we are not taking her by force, but of her own will." As they said that, two of them gave her their arms and led her away.

Then the sisters raised a great piteous wail, and they cried out, "Ah, Sister Blaisine, do you allow yourself to be deceived? Alas, Mother, she is going away, and you are losing one of your sheep."

And mother vicaress ran forward and several of the sisters, and they said, "Sister Blaisine, turn around, and if you want, we are willing to die to bring you back."

They tried to pull her away forcibly with their hands, but without a word, she moved closer to the wicked people. They took a great shard of wood from the chairs and almost struck mother vicaress's head as she

---

306. A *chevalliere*, or female knight.

was trying to pull her away forcibly. A young sister [223] grabbed that piece of wood and brought it down on one man's shoulders. But he survived the blow and would have hit the sister if one of the ladies had not pulled her away. Mother vicaress and several others would have been killed, because they were trying to pull that miserable girl away with great force. The mother portress[307] was knocked to the ground and trampled villainously. Using force, they lifted the poor miserable girl and pulled her out through the turning window, which they had broken, and took her to a poor cobbler's house to remove her nun's habit.

Those poor Christian ladies had endured such an ordeal that they could stand it no more. Our Lord had done well to send them, for if it had not been for their good sense, there would have been much injury and death. After the departure of that whole perverse company, which had done them such harm, those poor ladies, who had endured so much, looked at each other with great abundances of tears and burned with such agony that one of them, who was pregnant, collapsed, for she had been in the thick of things the whole time and had fought mightily to save the sisters and, even more boldly, had gone up to the heretics and said, "Messieurs, do not think of me, but of the child I am carrying," and so they had been ashamed to strike her harshly. But she was so exhausted that she could hardly breathe anymore, but lay there half-dead. The other woman quickly loosened her dress and her cloak to relieve the child that could be seen moving [224] in her stomach. They thought she was going to deliver then and there and would probably not recover, which was a new wound piercing the poor sisters' poor souls; and since no creature in the world could give them comfort or hope, they burst into tears before God and said, "Ah, good God, do not forsake your poor handmaidens who suffer such agony and sorrow for love of You. Ah, glorious father Saint Francis, Madame Saint Clare, do not leave us in peril in your convent! Alas, if our good mothers and sisters in the convent knew the peril and the pit of sorrow we are in they would break down and weep to beg you to show us mercy and all pious creatures would have pity on us. Ah, most gentle Virgin Mary, save your poor handmaidens and give us help and comfort, because all human consolation has failed us!"[308]

THE SYNDICS VISIT THE CONVENT

The sisters spoke these and other words of piteous sorrow without ceasing, and mother vicaress kept asking for the syndics. They came when that whole

307. The mother vicaress, according to manuscript B.
308. The writer of manuscript B shortens this plea considerably.

criminal business was finished, and they found those two good ladies still there resting and comforting the sisters. The poor sisters prostrated themselves before them, begging for justice and protection, and mother vicaress took the mother abbess by the arm and said, [225] "Mother, ask for the sheep who was taken violently from your bosom," and she said to them, "Hah, Messieurs, you have stooped to treat us with great violence and disrespect, you, whom we regard as fathers and protectors; you have acted treacherously, and the great disrespect of breaking our seclusion and damaging all the convent's treasures was not enough, so you have violently ravished one of our sisters."

The syndics replied, "Truly, fine ladies, it displeases us greatly to see you so afflicted and grieving, and it was not done with our consent. But those Genevans do not obey us, and messieurs of Bern have ordered us all to be unified in faith and in the truth of the Gospel. But you are not unified, for you live in seclusion and in great hypocrisy here. Be patient with your sister, because she was not taken away by violence but of her own will, for her sister had made many pleas to the city and had shown that she was kept in seclusion against her will. We will do the same for any others who wish to welcome the righteous light of truth as she did."

Mother vicaress replied, "As for us, we think it was done with great violence and disrespect, and we beg you, for the honor of God, never to return for such a reason; I really believe there is not one of my companions who would not prefer to die than be taken away. So we ask you very humbly [226] to preserve and keep us as we are, and in holy seclusion, or else to grant us safe conduct to leave your city all together, without violence or crime to our bodies."

"What?" said the syndics. "Where will you go? The city will certainly allow you to stay here in your house, as long as you are prisoners no more and are free to come and go as you wish; and we will help those who want to marry, and the others may do as they wish. But you must change your clothing and say no more offices or masses. Do not think you will be allowed to leave the city whenever you wish!" These were very painful words to the sisters' ears.

Then mother vicaress said, "Alas, Messieurs, for the love of God, have pity on your poor daughters! You see how defenseless we are without locks. If those evildoers come to hurt us at night, who will stop them? Please give us some kind of protection."

"Very well," said the syndic. "We will take care of you and protect you. But these papist women here, why have you come in?"

They immediately fell to their knees and said, "Messieurs, forgive us, for we came in here after the multitude."

"Leave immediately," said the syndics, "for you will do more harm than good." [227]

Which those poor ladies did at once, and without saying good-bye, because they did not have the heart to do it, and the poor sisters were abandoned and deprived of all comfort and consolation and plunged into a pit of utter discomfort and affliction.

THE CONVENT IS GUARDED BY TWO SERGEANTS

Two city sergeants[309] were sent to the convent, to the cloister, to protect the sisters and the convent, or so they said. But you can believe they were doing it more to keep the furnishings from being stolen than to reassure the sisters. Those archers kept watch in front of the convent day and night, and there were sometimes eighty or a hundred or a 120 of them at the house of Monseigneur of Coudrée.[310] The poor sisters were without doors or locks for six whole days, protected solely by and trusting Our Lord. During the day they stayed in the church; at night their rest was full of fear and inestimable sorrow, and they ate the bread of anguish and drank abundances of tears. To tell the whole of it, there was no hope or means of comfort because they could not communicate their sorrow to anyone, and even if they could have made it known, it would not have changed a thing because none of the nobles or good Catholics would enter the city because of the risk of bodily harm. And so there was nothing to do but await God's grace. [228]

BLAISINE VAREMBERT ASKS THE CONVENT TO RETURN HER DOWRY; THE SISTERS' UNCERTAIN SITUATION BEFORE THEIR DEPARTURE FROM GENEVA

The next day, on Wednesday [August 25], the poor, perverted Blaisine and her miserable sister brought a petition to the syndics and the city council, asking them to make the convent pay for her dowry: two hundred écus, a dress and a cloak, chains [jewelry], necklaces, and embroidery, which she claimed her father [Dominique Varembert] had given to the convent. The claim was not true, for the sisters all knew that not a single maille had been given. They also asked for a portion of all of the convent's furnishings. They also asked for four or five of her companions, claiming they shared her wicked intentions and were planning to leave like she had and had scaled

---

309. See above, note 76.
310. Across from the convent. See above, note 293 and related text.

the walls several times to try to get out and that because they feared the older ones, who kept them in subjection, they dared not say what was in their hearts. These were all false lies, as I, who am writing this, testify for myself, whom she named first, and for the others, my beloved companions, who are very righteous and of great piety in the holy convent; we were never [229] her companions in wicked intentions and were careful not to become acquainted with the venom of her thought. But in this way she caused the poor sisters all the damage and unhappiness she could and she spoke shamelessly and with great lies and falseness to conceal her hypocrisy.

But Our Lord, who never abandons His friends in dire situations and who wants the truth to be known, allowed all the malicious things she said to be proven wrong, as I will show later, as truly as I can, how it happened and was determined. The syndics and the council spent that whole Wednesday listening to the apostate and her sister and to their demands, so they did not harass the sisters that day. But the sisters were there with open doors, [230] as stated, under the protection of those two sergeants, who were nonetheless good Christians and showed great pity for the sisters and stayed by the turning window in the portress's place to keep anyone from going in or out.

The poor sisters did not know what to do or what would happen to them, and they expected to be separated and to perish sorrowfully; they languished rather than lived, and death would have been very welcome to them. Because the good mother abbess was quite old and because great fear and sorrow had made her very sick, she and all the sisters begged the venerable mother vicaress, who was so steady and constant and unafraid, to risk her life to preserve the honor of God and the sisters, to take charge of them, and to answer for them, and they said they would all agree to what she did and said.

NEGOTIATIONS BETWEEN THE SISTERS AND THE GENEVAN AUTHORITIES REGARDING THE GOODS CLAIMED BY BLAISINE VAREMBERT

When Thursday came, after their Judaic council, the syndics came to the convent [231] with a great Pharisee, a councilor from Bern[311] who was dressed in velvet and damask, and with Claude Bernard[312] and several others and Blaisine's sister [Hemme Faulson], and, as usual, the sisters ran to the

---

311. Anton Bischoff, an ambassador from Bern to Geneva from September 9, 1534.

312. Council member who also held a variety of civic offices in Geneva; brother of the Franciscans Jacques and Louis Bernard, the latter a canon.

church and mother vicaress kept mother abbess close to her. Those pharisaic rabbis presented the miserable woman's petition and asked for the things written above for her dowry.

"What?" said mother vicaress. "Blaisine knows well that we never received a maille from her father for a dowry, and Lady Hemme, her sister here, also knows it well."

The shameless woman replied, "Yes, you do have it, because my father gave it to you when my sister came in here, when the poor girl, because of your flattery and because she did not know the truth of living well, surrendered herself; and since God alone has enlightened her with true knowledge, she needs her possessions so that she may live, and, in addition, she asks for her share of everything that belongs to the convent, which she served well for fourteen years and where she spent her time."

"What?" said mother vicaress. "The convent's property belongs neither to her nor to us, but to the convent. The good, departed nuns left it to us so that we could leave it [232] to others. It is not property acquired by usury or by our work and labor, but comes from alms given by good people for divine service."

The lieutenant replied, "Lady Vicaress, why don't you let madame the abbess speak?"

"I would be glad to," she said, "But the poor mother's body is too weak."

"Messieurs," said mother abbess, "my sisters and I agree with and support what she does, and she knows the truth of these things better than I do because she was portress for more than fifteen years, including when Dominique Varembert brought his daughter here, and anything that entered the convent passed through her hands."

"Let's get to the point," they said. "You must give back the two hundred écus you received from her."

"Monseigneur Lieutenant," said mother vicaress, "since she and her sister claim we received them, make them bring written proof, for her father would never have done such a thing without putting it in writing."

At this they looked at each other without a word. Then the lieutenant said, "Lady Hemme, lady vicaress speaks reasonably. Can you show written proof?" [233]

The lying woman responded that she could not because her father's legal documents had been taken to Chambéry.

Then a miserable syndic, Michel Balthasar,[313] lied and said, "Lady Vicaress, how dare you speak against the truth? Let me tell you the truth: once

313. See above, note 191.

when I was coming from Lyons with Dominique Varembert he showed me a purse containing two hundred golden écus, and he said to me, 'Lord Michel, this is for my daughter Blaisine, and it will be given with her no matter what path she takes.'"

"He may well have shown them to you at that time," said mother vicaress, "but the truth is that he did not give them to us."

The syndic swore on God's precious blood, "You call me a liar and act as if you are crazy, and if I didn't think it would be wrong to fight a woman, I would make you regret it."

"I do not want to cause you any injury or displeasure," said mother vicaress, "but in good faith I declare it to be the truth. It is true that Varembert had a chapel built here.[314] If he intended it as a dowry, she can have the stones back. We did not put them in the treasury. He also put decorations on the altar in his chapel. We will be glad to give them to her." [234]

"You are full of malice," said the syndic and the lieutenant, "but you will, indeed, pay her what she asks. You have hidden your treasures and furnishings, but you will be accountable for everything."

"What?" said mother vicaress. "What treasures do you ask of us, we who live in poverty? How would we amass them?"

"We know well," they said, "that you have hidden valuable goods in several houses and that you even have a fine dagger in one house."

"What?" said mother vicaress. "What good do you think a dagger would do us? We do not have murderous swords."

"Lady Vicaress," said the lieutenant, "don't act so surprised. We know well that you are trying to trick us."

"Be gracious, for trickery has never been found among faithful people, and we have never thought to use it, and I am surprised if you think we have a dagger. What would we use it for? To wage war on houseflies? I do not think you know what you are saying."

"By God," said the lieutenant, "Lady Vicaress, you are very stubborn. I will prove to you that we know all about you and your malice: you thought it was safe in a package in a certain house, but everything is at the city hall, and here is the dagger I am talking about." [235]

"Oh, Good Lord," said mother vicaress. "You were talking to me about a dagger, but this is the bishop's relic. But since you have it and think it is so valuable, keep it as the dowry you seek, for I tell you in good faith that I thought you were asking me for a dagger."

---

314. Dominique Varembert had probably built the chapel as a tomb for his family. See Feld's edition of the *Petite chronique*, 233, n. 11.

And, indeed, she and all the sisters thought he was asking for a dagger, which is why mother vicaress said they never waged war except on fleas and houseflies. Then the syndics started to lose patience because they thought she was making fun of them, and she answered good-naturedly that she had thought they were talking about a dagger, but that this was a bishop's dagger, not made of gold and not worth three sous. But out of reverence for the holy bishop to whom it had belonged, it had been given to a good burgher woman for safekeeping. I think that the devil had revealed everything to them, and they had immediately sent and carried to the city hall everything that had been taken from the sisters; they treated the sisters badly[315] and did not allow them to keep enough to meet their basic, meager needs. In the end it was declared that they would take two hundred écus worth of furnishings and utensils from the convent. [236]

ARGUMENT ABOUT THE CONVENT BETWEEN THE COUNCILOR FROM BERN AND THE VICARESS

Then the councilor from Bern [Anton Bischoff] wanted to hear how they lived in the convent, and he said, "All those things are nothing but hypocrisy, and we must reach a unity of religion."

"That is well said," said mother vicaress. "As for us, we do not want any innovation but want to live and die like our ancestors."

"That is well said," they said, "but they did not have anyone to show them the truth and were not enlightened like we are."

"Truly, Messieurs, you are blind and not enlightened."

"But you, poor simple women who, in the guise of chastity, which is impossible in nature, are completely corrupted in your thoughts, where do you find that God ordered such a life?"

"He did not order it," said mother abbess and mother vicaress, "but showed us by His example."

"And how is it that neither God nor His mother lived in seclusion, but went into the world preaching and teaching and did not wear a habit as you do? Why do you wear these clothes that are so simple in style and color?" [237]

"Because we like them," said mother vicaress. "And you, why are you dressed so pompously in that robe?"

He answered, "It is not out of pride, but because I like it."

---

315. Manuscript B adds "and angered the poor people who comforted them" (*et facheoient les povres gens, quil leurs faisoient consolation*).

"I do the same thing," said mother vicaress, "because I like this color better than any other, and the style, just as you like yours. And since everyone is free, you keep yours and leave us ours, because we are not forced to do any of the things we do, but each one is here out of her own will, without any compulsion or force. If you will not let us live in your city as our dear, departed mothers lived, let us leave together without danger."

"But where will you go?" they said.

"Wherever God leads us," said mother vicaress.

"We will escort and return each of you to your family if you do not want to stay with us and live as we do. But the women from the city must stay here, as well as the ones who went to school here. And so we wish to speak to Sister Colette [Masuere] and to Sister [Jeanne] de Jussie, who have relatives in this company."

"You may, indeed, speak with them," said mother vicaress, "but do not raise a hand to do with them what you did with the other one [Blaisine Varembert], because we will defend them with our lives, for they do not share the other one's intentions." [238]

MARIE DENTIÈRE TRIES TO MAKE THE YOUNG SISTERS LEAVE THE CONVENT

In that company was a nun, a false, wrinkled abbess with a devilish tongue, who had a husband and children, named Marie Dentière of Picardy, who meddled in preaching and perverting pious people.[316] She came among the sisters looking for Sister Colette Masuere, and she went up to them one by one and asked, "Are you Sister Colette? Daughter, we wish to speak with you."

The first one she addressed was that very woman. But Sister Colette pushed her aside and said, "I am not the one you want. Get behind me and seek her elsewhere!"

Then she went from one to another, and each one insulted her and said, "Get away, you repudiating nun with a venomous tongue!"

But because she wanted to pervert one of them, she paid no attention to any insults or injuries, and she said, "Oh, you poor creatures, if you knew what a good thing it is to be next to a handsome husband and how pleasing to God! Alas, I was for a long time in this darkness and hypocrisy where you are. But God alone showed me the delusions of my wretched life, and I saw

316. See volume editor's introduction, note 11, on Marie Dentière.

the true light of truth and realized I had been living in sorrow the whole time because in these convents there is nothing but hypocrisy, mental corruption, and idleness. And so, without hesitating, I took five hundred ducats from the treasury [239] and left that miserable life, and, thanks to God alone, I already have five fine children and I lead a good and healthy life."

Those false and deceitful words horrified the sisters greatly, and they spat on her in scorn. She replied, saying, "Hah, you false hypocrites, you spurn the word of the one God because you are not from Him.[317] We know well what life you lead. Your sister, enlightened by God, told us all about your devilish and dissolute life, and the poor girl could not stand it."

OTHER ATTEMPTS TO PERSUADE THE YOUNG SISTERS TO LEAVE THE CONVENT

By saying those abominable things, the miserable woman thought she would convince the sisters, and the others thought they would be able to get more of them out.[318] The wretched preacher Viret asked for Sister Claude de Pier-refleur from Orbe,[319] saying he was charged with returning her to her family. They had, indeed, sent for her. When he saw that they were all keeping so close together that he could not see any of their faces, he said to mother abbess, [240] "Bring Sister Colette here, and do not be afraid that we will do her any harm. We only want to know her wishes. Mother Abbess, have her come and show herself here, and the Sister de Jussie too; have her speak to her relative. You cannot refuse her that, and if you do not do it, you will be sorry."

The good mother abbess, trusting their lying words, ordered the sisters to speak to them. They asked Sister Colette, who was standing next to her and to mother vicaress, if she did not want to do like her companion, Blaisine, and return to her family. "We know well that you are mistreated here because you are from the city and want to preserve it, whereas the nuns only support the Duke of Savoy; and since they are all gentlewomen, you will never be happy here. We know how Blaisine and you were tricked."

The poor girl, trembling with fear, replied, "No harm was ever done to me in the holy convent, and I am cherished here as much as the reverend mother abbess, and I have never been beaten or mistreated here, and I still wish to continue divine service in their holy company."

317. See above, note 279.

318. That is, the other Reformers were trying to remove more women from the convent.

319. She became abbess in Annecy after Jussie's death in 1561.

They replied, "And do you ask to leave the city as they do? Poor girl, they will abandon you on the way or make you a servant, for they [241] will have to return to their families, and then, poor girl, what will you do? We will not let you leave, but will return you to your sisters,[320] and do not be afraid, for we will make you a good match."

And as they said that, two wicked guards, Jean Pecollat and Aymé Perrin, grabbed her and pulled her away forcibly. The poor girl threw herself at mother abbess's bosom and cried out, "Oh, good mothers and sisters, I surrender myself to your mercy."

The mother abbess held her and recited the psalm "Judicame, deux, et dicerne,"[321] and one of the wicked men struck her harshly and bruised her whole arm and said, "That false old lady has cast a spell on her."

Mother vicaress and a strong, young sister pulled her away from them immediately and said, "Messieurs, for the love of God, leave us, for you will not take any of us away, even if we all die here and now."

And so they left Sister Colette utterly faint with fear. [242]

DISCUSSION BETWEEN CLAUDE BERNARD AND SISTER JEANNE DE JUSSIE

In the meantime, the wicked Claude Bernard was lecturing Sister Jeanne de Jussie, who was very gravely ill, and he told her that the city council had sent him to tell her that, if she wanted, they would make her a decent match, a marriage like Blaisine's, and he named several possibilities to her. He said that the city would never fail her and that because she had been their schoolgirl and was their close neighbor, she was as dear to them as the Genevan girls; and furthermore, he told her that her uncle, Lord [Guillaume] Pillicier, had asked him to remove her from the convent.

Sister Jeanne replied, "Lord Guillaume Pillicier was formerly my uncle, when he was an honorable man. But since he has chosen a new law, I would be ashamed to call him my uncle. And my aunt's marrying his brother does not make him a close enough relative to be so concerned about me. He did not bring me to this holy company, nor will he take me from it, and messieurs of the city should not be so concerned about me either. I am not from your city, and I would not wish to be. I owe obedience to my mother and my brothers. [243] But I have renounced everything for God of my own accord,

---

320. That is, her natural sisters (not her sisters in the convent).

321. "Judica me, deus, et discerne causam meam de gente non sancta" (Vindicate me, O God, and defend my cause against an ungodly people; Ps 43:1).

and I would do it again because I do not want a husband, but only to be the bride of my God, to whom I have pledged and continue to pledge my faith and all my heart's desires, and neither all the possessions in the world, nor all the tortures, would change my mind."

Then that miserable man again spoke words of flattery and gentle warnings and then words so dissolute and abominable that I am horrified to recall them and do not dare write them. And he said again that she and the others were utterly corrupted.

She said to him, "You have chosen a fine way of living, you who speak of nothing but corruption and make it your God. Get away from me, for you infuriate me and smother my heart with your stinking breath; it does as much good for you to preach to me as to beat yellow bile to make butter. Neither my companions nor I know what corruption is."

At that, the men who had left Sister Colette arrived, and they said, "Sire Claude, how goes it? Have you missed your prey as we have?"

He replied, "I have found my relative to be stubborn, but God will enlighten her. She will think about the goods and the great honor that messieurs offer her, and she will give me a better answer tomorrow." [244]

Sister Jeanne replied, "You get the same thing from me today as tomorrow and as a thousand years from now, and I will never change my mind. As for being your relative, in the past I would have cherished it. But because of your corrupt law, I renounce it. My aunt's marriage to your wife's uncle does not make you my relative."

THE HERETICS LEAVE THE CONVENT

Who would want to recite the loathsome and abusive things that were done to all of them that day? A huge ream of paper would not be enough. That wicked man stood before his comrades and bared his teeth in anger like a starving wolf that cannot find its prey, and they looked at each other in annoyance because night was drawing near. Some of them said they should go away, and they all left the church. As it was God's will, when they were leaving they saw a large pike that the sisters kept to clean the ceiling of the church. Those men all jumped back in fright and said, "Hah! How is it that you have murderous weapons? Why have you put them here?" The sisters, who had thought nothing of it, did not know what they were talking about. And again the lieutenant said, "Hah! You bigoted ladies are plotting something!" [245]

They all turned around in fear, and some of them ran down the steps two and four at a time, afraid that the sisters would strike them, just because they had seen that pike on the ground. Some of them said, "Let the devil take anyone who comes back here and trusts them, for there is no malice and cunning like a woman's."

This did not upset the sisters. The whole day was spent in those sorrowful proceedings, in agony and inestimable grief, and it is not possible to write a quarter of the words and threats and trials.

THE SYNDICS RETURN WITH BLAISINE VAREMBERT AND HEMME FAULSON

On Friday, to make the sorrows worse, the poor miserable perverted woman [Blaisine Varembert] came back with her wretched sister [Hemme Faulson] and the syndics and governors of the city, and she wore a fashionable dress and looked more drunken and dissolute than a common prostitute. They did not come inside but went up to the grille, and the sisters were summoned there. But only monseigneur the lieutenant [Domenne Darlod] and the syndics spoke. The miserable woman[322] hid [246] on the steps and listened to them.

The lieutenant spoke first and said, "Listen here, fine ladies, Lady Blaisine commends herself to you and still wants us to make things right by her. Have you decided to give her what she is asking for? Furthermore, she has filed a serious complaint with us, saying that you beat her and kept her prisoner and put chains on her hands and fetters on her feet and for no reason. Therefore, we want to know why you tortured her so much. Those are acts of murderers and thieves."

To which mother abbess replied, "How could we have put her in irons and chains? For we have none, and we have no prison, so you should not believe her."

He replied, "We believe her more than you because she is telling the truth, and we want to know why you used such cruel punishment."

Mother vicaress spoke up and said, "Monseigneur Lieutenant, you can believe that no harsh measures were ever used against her. Her prison was a pleasant one, as you can tell from her good health. As for beating and discipline, you know that correction and improvement are necessary everywhere, in a convent just like anywhere else, and she was never disciplined without good cause. She should not speak to you about this but should accuse herself, because she disciplined herself more than anyone else did.[323] But I think you

---

322. Plural in manuscript B: "miserable women" (*les malheurées*).

323. See above, note 67.

are bringing up this matter more for your own amusement than to gather information about her, because I cannot believe she would stoop so low." [247]

He replied, "Lady Vicaress, are you calling me a liar? I will prove it to you. Lady Blaisine, come forward and speak for yourself."

Then the poor wretch stepped forward and said without a greeting, "Mother Vicaress, you are all lying through your teeth,[324] because the Sisters [Bernadine] de Gento, [Guillaume] de la Frasse, and [Marguerite] de Bardenenche beat me so much once that my whole body was bruised."

"Why did they beat you?"

"Because," she said, "I did not[325] want to eat the wafer with them and was spinning with my distaff on the Feast of Corpus Christi."

Mother vicaress said, "It was bad for you to do that on such a solemn occasion."

Her sister replied, "Hah, what frauds you are! The poor girl was already enlightened, and you tortured her."

"Yes," she said, "and they kept me in prison, because I could not[326] stand their wicked and vile way of life. At night the lay brothers slept with them, and they hid it from me and from the poor simple sister."[327]

"Hah, Blaisine," said mother vicaress, "you are not telling the truth."

"But you are lying," she said, "and you would eat the best food and serve me last; you are leading a criminal life and living poorly." [248]

"Indeed, you are telling the truth," said mother vicaress, "because we do live poorly when it comes to eating, and you make us devour even the good bits sorrowfully because of your perdition."

"It is true," she said, "that you often eat poorly, but you also feast often. You always live with ill will and discord among you; I could not stand it, and because I criticized you, you locked me in prison and treated me as if I were crazy."

"What?" said mother vicaress. "How dare you say that? Do we not all eat at a table equally, in silence and in perfect unity, and recite divine service

---

324. Literally, lying through (or by) your throats: *vos aves toutes mentir par vostre gorges*.

325. Negative particle missing in manuscript A; added as a correction in manuscript B.

326. Again, negative particle added as a correction in manuscript B.

327. Probably Jacquemine Lille, whom Jussie calls "the poor, simpleminded sister" (*la povre debille de teste*) several times in her chronicle. Lille's status in the convent is intriguing, since the Rule of Saint Clare specifically forbids women who are unable to understand the full significance of their vows to be admitted into the order ("si enfin elle n'est ni trop vieille ni trop malade ni trop simple d'esprit pour mener notre vie", chap. 2, no. 4). See Vorreux, *Sainte Claire d'Assise*, 109.

together in the church likewise and all sleep without distinction in a dormitory?"

"Yes," she said.

"And so it is not true, as you say, that we are always in discord. That proves the opposite. And if disagreement arose among us because of you, we sought each other's counsel with much humility and we recognized our faults in the chapter room and did penance humbly—is that a wicked life? But it is truly very bad and improper for you, who never did anything about it, to praise what you did not do. But I tell you, in the presence of this good company, that you cannot speak ill of the convent except by lying."

She replied, "You are great hypocrites and deceive the poor people," and she said infinite other dissolute words until the company could not stand them anymore. [249]

Then the lieutenant told her, "Be quiet, Lady Blaisine, and show us this prison."

They came down from the grille, and that whole company entered. That miserable woman took them straight to the room in which a raised bed had been made for her, completely enclosed, like a tiny, warm bedroom, with a door that could be locked with a key and a very pretty iron window with an iron cross, and her chest was inside, and there was a table above her bed. Inside they found a whole loaf of bread that she had brought there on the Feast of Saint Bartholomew,[328] some cheese, some butter, and two kinds of wine in flasks, and her bed was well made and proper with a good feather pillow, just as she had left it, for no sister had been there since.

This surprised them, and they said, "Lady Blaisine, is this your prison? Indeed, as the lady vicaress says, it is pleasant, and I wish I had one like it in my house for the comfort of my body."

Then they went up the steps to find the sisters. Some of them turned and said, "Lady Blaisine, which ones did you ask us to bring out?"

She replied, "I want my dear companion Sister Jeanne de Jussie, Sister Colette Masuere, Sister Françoise Rambo, and Sister Guillaume de la Frasse." [250]

When mother vicaress heard this, she almost fainted. Then she straightened up and said, "Hah, you false cat,[329] it will not be so, and you, Messieurs, do not try to do it, because you will not get them out alive, for we will all die for them."

---

328. August 24, three days earlier, the day Blaisine Varembert left the convent.

329. The term *chatte* in middle French referred to an immoral woman or a prostitute; manuscript B changes the vicaress's insult to "false snake" (*faulce serpentine*).

Then she hurried and shouted, "My children, Sister Jeanne, Sister Colette, Sister Françoise, and Sister Guillaume, be valiant[330] and loyal to God, for that miserable woman has asked these people to take you. We have protected you until now, and we will do all we can to protect you if you are steadfast." A pitiable anguish pierced the souls of the poor, grieving sisters, and God alone could give them counsel and comfort. They burst into tears of anguish, and Our Lord—out of pity, I believe—calmed the heretics' fury, and they did not use violence or force on anyone, only seductive and deceitful words, as on Thursday,[331] and they raised the issue of the dowry again.

In the end, those two hundred écus had to be given to them, according to the decision of four or six arbiters, and each side could choose whomever it wanted. The sisters chose Lord Jean Ballard,[332] an aged and trustworthy man, and Lord Etienne Pecollat,[333] a true Catholic who was the city treasurer. The sisters said they would follow their orders. The apostate and her sister chose Michel Balthasar[334] and Claude Bernard,[335] wicked Lutherans and dishonest, [251] lying men who put all piety at risk of perdition and always spoke great words of destruction and perdition. That apostate[336] led them through the convent and took whatever she wanted; no one said anything to stop her; she was bolder than a common prostitute. She went up to her aunt, a poor aged mother more than eighty years old named Sister Claude Lignotte, and she said to her, "Aunt Lignotte, look at me, see how beautiful I am! Don't you think I am more beautiful than before, and haven't I found the way of truth? Indeed, if you were young, I would have advised you to come with me. But no one would know what to do with you except to cover you with ashes, so go ahead and feast and die as you like."

The poor mother tried to change her mind with gentle words, saying, "Yes, my daughter, you are beautiful, but you were even more beautiful in your nun's habit. Know, my child, that you are in grave danger."

The poor mother gave her some thread and other pretty things she had. She also spoke to Sister Jeronyme de Villarseil; none of the others would speak to her but drew back from her as from a rotting carcass. After much

---

330. Female knights, *chevalliere.*

331. The previous day, August 26, 1535.

332. Syndic in 1525 and 1530 who also held other civic offices; also the author of a known chronicle. See Monter, *Calvin's Geneva,* 10–12.

333. Holder of a variety of civic offices and brother of Jean Pecollat.

334. See above, note 191.

335. See above, note 312.

336. Manuscript B says, "That woman filled with the poison of malice, the miserable apostate" (*Celle envenimee de malice, miserable apostate*).

opposition and affliction, the Lutheran women left. The sisters spent that day in as much sorrow and inestimable fear as can be piteously imagined. [252]

CLAUDINE LEVET PREACHES THE GOSPEL TO THE SISTERS

The following is what happened on Saturday, a pitiable and truly remarkable thing that had never been done to poor nuns.

On Saturday, the Feast of Monseigneur Saint Augustine [August 28], the lieutenant returned with eighteen of the biggest heretics, all prominent people, and the apostate's sister, and she brought with her the apothecary Aymé Levet's[337] wife, who was meddling in preaching and proclaiming the Gospel. The poor sisters all took refuge in the church in their usual manner, seeking help and aid from Our Lord. After the heretics said many dreadful things, they told that devilish-tongued woman, "Lady Claude, do your duty!" [253]

She immediately began to preach, although she did not know how; she insulted the Virgin Mary and the saints[338] in paradise and the state of virginity and complete devotion, and she said other things that out of decency I will not repeat and that I am horrified to recall; she praised the state of matrimony and freedom and claimed that Jesus' apostles had all been married, even Saint John and Saint James and Saint Paul, and she said that Saint Paul himself had said it was a good thing to be married[339] and to be two

---

337. A member of the Councils of Two Hundred and of Sixty and a holder of other civic offices, elected syndic in 1536.

338. Jussie mentions both male and female saints: *sains et sanctes*.

339. "But because of cases of sexual immorality, each man should have his own wife and each woman her own husband" (1 Cor 7:2); "I want you to be free from anxieties. The unmarried man is anxious about the affairs of the Lord, how to please the Lord; but the married man is anxious about the affairs of the world, how to please his wife, and his interests are divided. And the unmarried woman and the virgin are anxious about the affairs of the Lord, so that they may be holy in body and spirit; but the married woman is anxious about the affairs of the world, how to please her husband. I say this for your own benefit, not to put any restraint upon you, but to promote good order and unhindered devotion to the Lord. If anyone thinks that he is not behaving properly toward his fiancée, if his passions are strong, and so it has to be, let him marry as he wishes; it is no sin. Let them marry. But if someone stands firm in his resolve, being under no necessity but having his own desire under control, and has determined in his own mind to keep her as his fiancée, he will do well. So then, he who marries his fiancée does well; and he who refrains from marriage will do better. A wife is bound as long as her husband lives. But if the husband dies, she is free to marry anyone she wishes, only in the Lord. But in my judgment she is more blessed if she remains as she is. And I think that I too have the Spirit of God" (1 Cor 2:25–40).

in one flesh.[340] She perverted the Holy Scripture and completely twisted it and turned sweet honey into bitter venom. The sisters could not stand it but shook their heads and shouted, "Oh, the great liar and the false devil incarnate!"[341]

Mother vicaress said to them, "Messieurs, take this fool away and make her be quiet, because we are all horrified to hear her!"

"Hah, Lady Vicaress, keep your insults to yourself," they said, "for she is a holy creature enlightened by God and her holy sermons and divine teaching bear great fruit and convert poor, unenlightened people; she works very hard to save souls, and she would like for you to be among them."

"What?" said mother vicaress. "Do you call that 'converting'? It is 'perverting', from salvation to perdition. I am amazed at the horrible perversity of her rash speech, [254] and if it were not out of respect for you, I would hit her as hard as I could." And the sisters all spat on her.

This made the heretics laugh, and they lowered their heads, although they tried to act proud. But she and her companion wrinkled their brows hideously in great anger.

"Now see here," said the lieutenant, "you are scorning God's word and us. But we are determined to find out what each of you has in her heart, and we will do with you what we think is right; do not be stubborn, but follow our orders and come with us. If you refuse, I swear we will use force to get you out and you will be sorry."

THE SISTERS ARE EXAMINED ONE BY ONE
AS TO THEIR LIFE AND PLANS

At that, the sisters' anguish was inconsolable. Then the heretics counted to see if all the sisters were there, and they found that one was missing, a poor, simpleminded nun [Jacquemine Lille] who had been locked in the infirmary. Next, they split into two groups; some of them stayed in the church to guard the sisters, and the rest went to sit in the chapter room as witnesses with the two women [Hemme Faulson and Claudine Levet]. Two of them were

---

340. "Therefore a man leaves his father and his mother and clings to his wife, and they become one flesh" (Gn 2:24); "And he said, 'For this reason a man shall leave his father and mother and be joined to his wife, and the two shall become one flesh'" (Mt 19:5); "And the two shall become one flesh. So they are no longer two, but one flesh" (Mk 10:8); "For this reason a man will leave his father and mother and be joined to his wife, and the two will become one flesh" (Eph 5:31).

341. Fromment describes in detail Claudine Levet's own conversion to the Reformation and her efforts to convert others, praising her as a model for Christian women. Fromment, *Les actes et gestes*, 15–21.

ordered to bring in the sisters one by one, and they took mother abbess first, which was a pitiable thing. The poor mother, not knowing what they were going to do with her, cried out for mercy in a piteous voice, [255] "Alas, Messieurs, what more do you want from me? Take my life from me, but do not separate me from my beloved sisters!"

Likewise, mother vicaress, prostrate on her knees, asked for mercy, and said, "Oh, Mother, who will watch your sheep, since the shepherd is the first one attacked? For the love of God, Messieurs, let us follow our mother!"

They all wept and lamented inconsolably. But they would not budge, and they were revolting and blaspheming the blood of God, which did not bode well for us. The sisters burst into bitter tears, thinking that the end had come and they would never see each other again. Mother abbess was taken out with great force, and mother vicaress, who tried to follow her, was pushed back, and the door was closed. No one knew where they were taking her. They took her to the lieutenant, who was sitting in the chapter room like another Caiaphas, and she was examined and interrogated on several topics, which I will not write because it would be too long. But after they had kept her there a long time, they did not send her back to be with the others but took her down to the kitchen. Which made her even more sorrowful because the poor mother thought they were taking her out and she was half dead. She did not know what would happen to her poor daughters, nor did the daughters know what would happen to their good mother.

Afterward, to increase their sorrows, without saying what they had done, they came for mother vicaress, who said to them, [256] "Oh, Messieurs, I beg you in God's honor to tell me what you are going to do to us! If you want to put me in prison, I will not refuse it for my God's sake. If you think you are going to convince me with torture or threats, you are deceived indeed. Be gracious and kill us all together, and do not separate us like this."

This upset them, and they said, "Do you think we are murderers? Or if you are making fun of us, come with us like the other old woman and we will decide what to do!"

This renewed the poor sisters' tears and anguish, and they cried out, "Oh, mother vicaress, are you leaving us? Who will guide us? For the love of God, Messieurs, let us follow our mothers and die together! Oh, how painful this separation is to us!"

They said to each other, "The days of anguish and separation have now come. Oh, good mothers of the convent of Saint Clare, what will you do when you learn of this cruel separation and when you hear your poor sisters are being devoured by ravenous wolves?"

It is impossible to describe the piteous sorrow and lamentations among them and how they bid each other farewell so piteously that some of them could not bear it. [257] Mother vicaress was seized and taken away like mother abbess. However, she begged them to encourage the sisters and asked the sisters to have firm patience and steady constancy. When she was before the lieutenant and saw those women seated as witnesses, she said, "Monseigneur Lieutenant, if you want an answer from me, make those fools leave because I cannot stand to have them in my presence."

This angered them, and the apostate's sister said, "This is unbelievable! What hypocrisy! She is not ashamed to be among you men but she cannot see us women! My sister Blaisine was telling the truth when she said she was an unbelievable woman."

Nonetheless, the lieutenant had them leave, saying he wanted to hear each nun's heart privately however she wished to speak, "And since the lady vicaress wants to speak to us alone, go away."

So they returned to the church to try to pervert someone else, and without ceasing she repeated those damnable first words. Then she went through the church and bent her ear down to each nun, which did her no good, because they all rejected her, calling her a fool, a lunatic, and a liar. "It horrifies us greatly to hear you." And she was very angry.

Among them was a man named Claude Paffe, whose reputation [258] and works showed him to be one of the most badly infected Lutherans. God moved him with pity when he saw the sisters so afflicted, and he went up to them and said, "Why are you so mournful? Do not torture yourselves so much! I promise you that no harm will be done to you and you will not be separated, except for those who wish it. To tell you the truth, your sister is the reason for this, because she says that you young nuns would like to do what she did but do not dare to say it because you are afraid of the old ones. This is why the council has ordered us to do this and to find out the truth, one by one, without the others' knowledge. The city will never allow you to leave before knowing each nun's heart and showing you the path of truth again, because it is a great pity for so many beautiful young girls to waste their youth in idleness when they could bear great fruits in the world."

This calmed the sisters a little because they thought that if we were left to decide for ourselves, it was not yet the end and the separation because everyone showed great determination and constancy. In the meantime, mother vicaress was interrogated and examined like mother abbess, and she was sent down to the kitchen with her. When they saw each other they embraced at the joy of being together again. But the [259] joy was not great because they did not yet know what would happen to them or to their poor daughters, and they commended them to God's protection and asked Him to give them one voice and one perfect and good desire.

In accordance with their plans, they were all presented and examined closely in order, one by one. The examination procedure would be too long to write down. The main thing was that they asked the old ones about their faith in baptism and their beliefs, how they had lived in purity of thought and desire, and whether they forced the young ones to stay there against their will, and how they had treated Blaisine, who had complained a lot. They asked them to show them the convent's treasures and to tell them where they had hidden them and why they did not seek unity with the city that had provided for them for such a long time and what they were planning to do.

To the young ones they offered husbands and marriage, great honor and wealth; they said they would never lack for anything and should not be afraid to declare their wishes secretly and other things that should not be written because they would only be horrible and difficult to read. But Our Lord and the Holy Spirit worked miraculously, and a miracle was seen there, visible and worthy of remembrance and great praise to God, for they were all of a single desire and a single answer and opinion, as if they were all parts of a single heart and a single voice, without any disagreement. The examiners were amazed very much that [260] they all said the same words, even though they did not know what the others had said, and some of the examiners were annoyed and said, "Curse those who sent us here, and by the devil we can leave, for we are not doing any good. It would be easier to soften a goldsmith's anvil than any of these women. They all seem to speak with a single mouth. May God alone curse anyone who comes back here for such a reason." And they walked away with gestures of great disbelief.

When they had all been examined and lectured separately and found themselves together again in the kitchen, they regained a bit of strength and cheer. Those envoys also wanted to speak secretly to the poor simpleminded nun [Jacquemine Lille], but she lodged herself between two windows in the refectory and they could not get her out with fine words or with force. Then she lay on the ground, and when they tried to preach to her, she replied only, "May the devil, may the devil, send you a high quartan fever;[342] leave us in peace. You would do better to nourish my poor mothers, whom you make languish in bitter affliction."

One of them said to her, "Sister Jacquemine, Lord Mullatton has asked the city for you and will give alms to provide for you, and we have promised to bring you to him."

She began to weep bitterly and cried out, "Great devil, bring him the devil, who is just like you, and leave me with my mothers!" [261]

---

342. *fievre quartaine*, a fever said to return every four days.

"We are taking them all and will make them take fine husbands."

"That's a lie," she said, "and you may take the quartan illness[343] as wives." She spoke to them so firmly that she did not seem mad but illuminated by God.

This surprised them even more, and she would never answer any of their questions, which could have caused her harm, but remained silent as if she were mute; since she was piteously lacking in understanding, the sisters were very afraid for her. This is why it seemed that God had sent her His holy mercy. She was like that all day long until the night.

Then the lieutenant said, "Now listen here, fine ladies, you are very blind not to recognize the truth of the Gospel, and you are stubborn to live in your errors. But I ask you, on behalf of messieurs and the city, not to say any more offices, high or low. You will hear no more masses in the city or be secluded here any longer. So decide what you want to do, and find two hundred écus to satisfy Blaisine, and give her her share of all of the convent's property too, for it is the reasonable thing to do."

Mother vicaress replied, "The convent's property does not belong to her and must not be divided but has been given by good people for divine service. Our dear, departed mothers left it to us, and we will leave it to those who [262] will come after us, for divine service. Blaisine did not bring anything, for it is all from good creatures' alms.

The whole day was spent discussing that painful matter, until night fell and they left. It was not a restful night for the poor sisters, for they could hardly say a word to each other since there were so many piteous sobs, tears, and sorrows, as God alone knows.

CONCLUSION OF THE SORROWFUL DEPARTURE
OF THE SISTERS OF SAINT CLARE

The following is what happened on Sunday [August 29], how the sisters were attacked again, and the conclusion of their sorrowful departure.

Early Sunday morning, the lieutenant returned with another large company and with the two arbiters of the miserable woman, who was still asking for two hundred écus and many jewels, adornments, and other things, as it is written, and for a share of all of the convent's property and furnishings. Mother vicaress, who spoke for all the sisters at their earnest request, knelt and begged them to believe the truth, "which will be told you by the two

---

343. *la malle quartaine.*

arbiters whom we have chosen, trustworthy men and good citizens, and we will tell them truly everything we are planning to do." [263]

At that, they went away to talk to the poor perverted woman's miserable sister. The sisters' two arbiters asked them to tell them the truth in good faith and to tell them everything they had received from Blaisine and to be careful not to say anything contradictory, because it was a matter of good faith and loyalty, and they asked to speak to the sisters one by one. But they all answered in a single voice, "For the love of God, Messieurs, believe mother vicaress, because it is the whole truth. We declare all her words to be true."

Then she said to them, "You should know, beloved fathers, that Blaisine's father never gave a single maille to the convent, and his daughter was the poorest girl who ever became a nun; we were asked to give her clothes to her sister, the judge's wife.[344] It is true he founded a fine chapel here as a tomb and decorated it with a chasuble[345] of fine white satin. We do not know how much he spent, and we have made no profit from it."

When those good lords heard that, they went up to their opponents to state their charges. But they sternly defied them, saying that it was not true and that the poor girl's property would have to be returned and that because God had enlightened her [264] and shown her the truth, her rights would be preserved. They went back and talked to each side, discussing the matter for a long time.

When the two loyal arbiters realized that the wicked people would not see reason, and when they heard their decision, in great fear and sorrow they asked the sisters for their intentions. Mother vicaress, inspired by Our Lord, replied, "Lords, you are our fathers and our friends, and I believe that you always advise us for the best. I have decided to ask messieurs the syndics to allow us to depart and to protect us as we go, and we will leave the city, for we can no longer maintain our way of life here or observe divine service and are in very great physical danger; we willingly relinquish all the convent's property."

"Indeed," they said, "you are truly inspired, and that is the best thing we could hear, for even though your departure will certainly be very bitter to us, it would cause us even more grief if they used violence against you, as we hear them planning to do."

"In God's name," said mother vicaress, "call for messieurs, who are here, and tell them our wishes."

---

344. A sister of Blaisine Varembert and Hemme Faulson whose husband was a judge in Gex.
345. An outer robe worn by a priest when celebrating the Mass.

So they called them over and said, "Messieurs, these poor ladies, who do not really owe you any money, are willing to give you all they have and go someplace else."

"What?" said the lieutenant. "Fine ladies, where will you go?" [265]

"Wherever God leads us," said mother vicaress. "We ask you only to escort us safely out of your city and you may have the convent and all the valuable furnishings in the church and elsewhere. It will be visited and appraised by you and by our arbiters, and an inventory will be drawn up and given to you, Monseigneur Lieutenant, to keep and to satisfy Blaisine."

"What?" said the syndic. "Lady Vicaress, speak for yourself and let the others say what is in their hearts, because any others, besides Blaisine, who wish to stay, may have their share and the convent."

Mother vicaress said, "They all want what I want. Answer, sisters!"

In a single voice, they all cried out, "We want nothing but to be away from here so that we can serve God in peace, and we beg you to put us safely out of the city, for we will follow her as our mother wherever she goes, and we think everything she does is perfect."

"Now then, fine ladies," said the syndic, "decide what day you would like to leave, and say how you intend to do it."

"Certainly," said mother vicaress. "We beg you to let it be tomorrow at the break of dawn and to give us only our cloaks and our coats to protect us from the cold and our veils to make our heads white." [266]

"Gladly," said the syndic.

Then Michel Balthasar and Claude Bernard stepped forward and said, "What do you mean? By the wounds of God, they must not leave until Lady Blaisine is satisfied!"

"What?" said mother vicaress. "She and you should be well satisfied, for we are leaving you the convent and all the valuable furnishings and supplies that are in it."

"Yes," they said, "but you have already taken the best things out."

"You made sure that we did not," said mother vicaress, "but we did gather all the supplies we could, and we asked our families to keep them, since we never thought we would leave our seclusion, which you have violently broken."

And upon those words they took all the keys to the convent and inspected every room in it very carefully. When they found the well-furnished sacristy and the well-filled attic and all the other furnishings in the household, they were overjoyed, and they locked all the rooms in the convent securely, except for the dormitory and the infirmary, where the poor sisters took refuge. Mother vicaress knelt down and begged for grace again, asking for cloaks, coats, and veils to meet the sisters' meager needs and asking them to leave us.

"Hah, fine ladies," said the syndic and the lieutenant, "each of you may pack [267] what she wants and put it by the door, and we will get eight carts ready to carry all your things, and we promise to take you safely to the bridge over the Arve outside the city limits."

That terrible affair lasted until after sundown. And even though the poor sisters had not yet eaten, no one offered them anything to eat or drink except a cup of anguish, and when they left, the poor sisters did not know what to do. However, mother vicaress gave them a little something to eat. Then she gave each one leave to pack her cloak, coat, and veil. They spent that whole night in moaning, agony, and labor.

After midnight they all gathered in the infirmary with mother abbess, who was very weak, sick, and old. She blessed them all in piety and tears and said, "My children, be brave and obey mother vicaress, whom I ask and beg to take charge of this sorrowful departure. Those who would like to and are able may take some bodily nourishment with God's blessing and the merit of obedience."

But hardly any of them could eat. Mother vicaress comforted them and said, "Dear mothers and sisters, let us have good hope in God and think only of saving our souls and our utterly naked bodies. I have great trust in His goodness, [268] that He will show us mercy in this time of need and in all our poverty. All of you, line up in order and piety and be ready to leave when those men come, and walk two by two holding hands tightly and staying so close together that no one can separate you. And be perfectly silent and do not speak, no matter what they say to you."

Upon those words they promised to risk their lives to protect each other. The poor simpleminded nun, Jacquemine Lille, who was still in bed, was summoned. She would not leave until they told her that mother abbess was already lost. Then she began to weep so hard that no one could soothe her, which was a great pity.

In the meantime, the sisters' arbiters arrived, very frightened, and they said, "For the love of God, Lady Vicaress, leave quickly and do not bother about anything because it is true that the young men of the city are planning to come find you tonight and to cut off all the old nuns' habits and to do what they wish with the young nuns, and they have sworn not to let them leave the city, at least not the six youngest ones. Our sources are reliable. So do not oppose anything messieurs say, and do not let on that we have spoken to you because your guards are good men and our friends and they were not supposed to tell us."

They left, and then the others arrived with our enemies and the apostate's perverted sister. She went right up to the poor sisters' bundles and said, [269] "Hah, Messieurs, look, look what these hypocrites have gathered and what treasures they have put in here! Indeed, if you let them leave like this, my sister will be defrauded. Loyal arbiters, come look at this!" And they put their hands on it.

"Now," said mother vicaress, "Messieurs, do not take back the leave you have granted us, and hurry to get us out while it is still early in the morning, before there are many people. We are all ready, and as for our goods, we leave everything to you, as you well know. Monseigneur lieutenant will take charge of it."

He agreed willingly. While the notary was writing, the sisters took refuge near the cloister and said a "De profundis"[346] and bid a last farewell to the holy departed mothers, begging them with great sobs to convince God never to allow this good convent to be ruined or disrespectfully violated. It was a pitiable thing to hear the poor sisters' sobbing. When those men came and saw and heard that piteous farewell to the dead, and how well they spoke, they drew back as if they were frightened; they felt a chill, and they waited until the sisters' prayers were finished, which moved their hearts so much that they could not hold back their tears and sobs. [270]

Then mother abbess and mother vicaress came forward to confirm what had been written down. It was decided that after they had given two hundred écus' worth to Blaisine, all the rest would be kept and returned to the sisters. But they did nothing of it, and they never returned a single maille's worth. The poor sisters, trusting their promise to return their few things to them, took only their breviaries under their arms and the lightest clothes they could. When mother vicaress asked for the wagons they had promised her that evening, there were none to be found, for they had no intention of letting them take anything with them.

The good Lord [Etienne] Pecollat whispered quietly in mother vicaress's ear, "For the love of God, Mother, hurry up and leave, because my brother [Jean Pecollat], the supreme captain of the wicked ones, told me it is absolutely certain that there are more than five hundred people who have sworn to bring about your perdition and divide you up tonight and that you will never leave the city. You must trust that in this moment God rules the hearts of these messieurs who will guide you safely out of the city."

He himself spoke loudly and said, [271] "Lords, these poor ladies cannot live with this harassment anymore but beg you to take them away, and since

---

346. "De profundis clamavi ad te, Domine" (Out of the depths I cry to you, O Lord; Ps 130:1).

it must be done, better sooner than later, before it is known in the city and causes trouble and discord."

God made them all agree to this, but even though they did it as secretly as possible, the word spread quickly through the city, and more people gathered in the streets where they were to pass, and in front of the convent, than had ever been seen at one time. They crowded each other, low and high, good and bad, men and women.

When she saw this, mother vicaress knelt before the syndic and said, "Monseigneur, we have determined to leave in silence, without saying a word to anyone. Please give strict orders to all who see us not to speak to us, touch us, or come near us, no matter what their status or position and no matter what their intentions, so that we may avoid all the uproar and trouble that might otherwise arise in the good town."

"Truly, Lady Vicaress, you give very good advice, and we will follow it. Do not be afraid of anything, for we will escort you with all of the city guards, [272] about three hundred armed men with good weapons. And I myself will defend you."

Then he ordered everyone, under penalty of immediate and merciless beheading, not to say a word, good or bad, while the poor ladies departed. The good creatures almost collapsed out of pity and sorrow. Many people left the city secretly at that time for the sake of the holy religion, never to return, saying to themselves, "Alas, the whole city is losing all its goodness and all its light today, and it is not good to stay here!"

The syndic returned and gave them permission to leave. He wanted them to go out through the door by the turning window, which they had broken. But the sisters' hearts could not bear to see the dishonor that had been done at the entrance to the church to all the memorials to God and His mother and all the saints.[347] So mother vicaress said, "Messieurs, let us go out through the convent door!"

They were glad to do so, and when they were all there, the door was opened. Several of the sisters almost fainted with fear. But mother vicaress took heart and said, "Be brave, sisters! Make the sign of the cross and keep Our Lord in your hearts and remember your promises and be faithful!" [273]

Taking her sister, Sister Catherine,[348] who was the sickest one and amazingly weak and who carried a walking stick and was supported on one side by the nurse, Sister Cecile [Thoriere], the vicaress very bravely went out first, followed by mother abbess, who was very feeble because of age, sorrow, and

---

347. Male and female saints: *sains et saintes*.
348. Catherine de Montluel from Châteaufort.

sickness and who had a strong sister supporting her. Then the vicaress took Sister Jeanne de Jussie's hand and gave it to mother portress, Sister Guillaume de Villette, and said, "Here, Sister Guillaume! I put your niece into your hands. The mother abbess and I have taken good care of her up until now. Do what you can to keep her safe!"

At those words, the poor mother took Sister Jeanne's arm firmly and said, "Mother Vicaress, you may believe that I will take as good care of her as of myself, and I will not abandon her for death or for life!"

Sister Colette [Masuere] was given to Sister Françoise [Rambo], the strongest of the company; Sister Guillaume de la Frasse was given to her good aunt, Sister Jeannette;[349] and so they went, two by two, hand in hand, their faces fully covered and in proper order and composure and silence, which was very good, because they never would have been able to leave otherwise, with the great crowd and commotion. It was a pitiable [274] thing to see and hear their moans and sobs, although they tried to hide them.

An admirable thing occurred, wonderful and worthy of great remembrance for divine praise and so that we may be even more certain of the goodness and mercy of God, who never abandons those who serve Him with true hearts and who trust in His goodness. At that moment the wicked people who had most desired the sisters' perdition were so changed, enlightened, and moved by pity that they became their loyal guides and protected them from other heretical enemies, giving the poor sisters what they received from no other living creature, not from family or friends, for they had no one but God to comfort them, except a poor lay brother named Brother Nicolas des Arnox, who was still so sick he could hardly stand. However, he did find the strength to keep the sisters company and to watch what was happening to them because it was a very pitiable thing to see them alone among the enemies of God and of the religion and among those who had previously done everything they could to bring about their perdition. When the syndic saw that several of them could not walk, he called for some strong men to help support them, and at their sides were the syndic, the lieutenant, Balthasar, and Pecollet, who watched closely over the sisters to see that no harm was done to them; Pecollet alone among the whole company was secretly a good Christian. [275] In front of them and at their sides were at least three hundred archers, well armed to protect the syndics, which was a good thing. For when the wicked Genevans, who had already decided the night before to pillage and violate the sisters, gathered, there were soon at least five hundred of them, and they blocked the Serrière de Saint Antoine,[350] on

---

349. Jeanne Ponsette from Sallanches.

350. A narrow street leading to the faubourg Saint Antoine.

the sisters' path, thinking they would pull the young sisters aside and hold them back, and they stood in front of them. One of them came close to the poor simple nun—and mother vicaress was at her side to protect her so that she would not be misled one way or another—and he whispered in her ear, "Sister Jacquemine, come with me! I will treat you like my sister."

Mother vicaress replied, "Hah! Wicked guard, you are lying!" She shouted, "Monseigneur Syndic, look how poorly you are obeyed! Get these boys out of the road!"

At those words everyone froze, and when the syndic saw that band of wicked troublemakers, God made him very angry, and in a furious and horrible voice he swore on the blood of God, "If any man moves, he will have his head cut off mercilessly on the spot!" [276]

He said to the archers, "Good comrades, be brave, and do your duty if necessary."

And God caused them to be terrified; they bared their teeth in malice and retreated and watched the sisters from a distance. The sisters continued on their way trembling with fear, there is no doubt. When they reached the bridge over the Arve, which marked the city limits, everyone stopped. Some people, in mockery, shouted at them just like they shouted at Our Lord, "Where are all the great nobles to meet them and the tents and canopies to protect them from the rain?"

The others, in ridicule, pretended to weep, and said, "Alas, Geneva, who will protect you? You are losing your light!"

The others shouted, "Farewell, mice! They have left their nest and will scatter in the fields like poor, lost creatures."

But the good people wept bitterly, in great sobs, and even the syndic, when it came time to leave them, was moved with such pity that he sobbed loudly and shed bitter tears, and his whole company led the sisters in order to the bridge and told them good-bye, and he said, "Farewell, fine ladies! Your departure truly grieves me."

And he said to himself like another Caiaphas:[351] [277] "Hah, Geneva, you are losing all your goodness and light!"

When they were all on the bridge, he clapped his hands and said, "It is finished. Now there is no other remedy, and we will speak of it no more."

The sisters were all alone on the bridge and did not know where to go because no one from the city dared to cross it, since it led to the land

---

351. "But one of them, Caiaphas, who was high priest that year, said to them, 'You know nothing at all! You do not understand that it is better for you to have one man die for the people than to have the whole nation destroyed.' He did not say this on his own, but being high priest that year he prophesied that Jesus was about to die for the nation" (Jn 11:49–51).

of Monseigneur of Savoy and they were afraid men were waiting to attack them. However, when they saw that the poor aged and ill nuns could go no further, they gave permission to six or eight[352] city sentinels to escort them off the bridge, which they did willingly, as much out of pity as to see what would happen to them and who would guide them on from there.

Sister Colette had a sister, a good Catholic at the time, who asked permission to keep her poor sister company, pretending she was following her to try to bring her back. But she did her best to encourage her. When they had crossed the bridge, although they did not yet find anyone to comfort them, it was a great relief to be out of the city limits and in monseigneur's lands. Then mother vicaress asked their escorts to return to safety in the city, thanking them for their good service and claiming there would soon be a great company of men to escort them and that they had heard they were not faraway, which made them too afraid to go any further. [278]

Near the bridge there lived a man named Burdet, a very honorable man, and he came out to greet the sisters and brought them into the safety of his home and offered to let them rest there and wait until Our Lord sent them aid. But, alas, their enemies were so close that they did not feel safe, so they thanked him humbly and asked him to show them the way to Saint-Julien [en Genevois]. But the good man swore that they would not leave until they had a little something to eat to soothe their poor, afflicted hearts. He gave each of them a nice round loaf of white bread and some good, aged cheese, and a cup of the best wine he could find, and he said, "Eat, and ask for anything else you want! It will not be kept from you. I have never given alms so willingly, and I promise you that I felt an indescribable comfort when I saw you coming, and it seemed to me that God and the Holy Virgin Mary were present here." It was a great comfort and relief to the poor sisters.

And that is the true manner of the poor nuns' pitiable departure from their convent and from the town. It was on the same Monday as the Feast of Saint Felix and Saint Audactus, August 29,[353] 1535, at five o'clock in the morning. [279]

THE SISTERS' JOURNEY TO THE CASTLE OF LA PERRIÈRE

The following is how they were guided and how Our Lord helped them and the honor that was shown them everywhere they passed.

---

352. Manuscript B says "six or seven" (*six ou sept*).
353. It was actually August 30, the Feast of Saint Felix and Saint Audactus.

While they were lodged at that place, Our Lord sent word of their departure to a good father who was dedicated to serving them, Friar Thomas Garnier, a good and pious monk, and he came to visit the villages nearby to see what was happening to the sisters. He soon found them at that house. They were overjoyed, and he was too, and he gave great thanks to God when he discovered they had all escaped without any physical harm, which no one could believe.

The poor lay brother [Nicolas des Arnox] had worked hard to pay for a wagon to carry the poor aged and ill nuns who were weakening on the journey. They were overjoyed, and they set forth to try to put greater distance between themselves and their enemies. Mother vicaress said, "Since God has given us help and guidance, let us hurry to go [280] further. Because it is not safe or respectable for us to stay in this inn, even though the host is an honorable man and has shown us great mercy, which we must not forget."

And thanking him, they left and set out for Saint-Julien. As they left they saw more than two hundred men, all armed, wicked Lutherans, watching to see what they would do. It was said that they were planning to rob the sisters, which frightened them. But it may piteously be believed that Our Lord protected the sisters and did not allow the Lutherans to go any further. The young sisters were put in the very front, and the aged and poor sick ones in the wagon, and they went as quickly as they could, accompanied only by the good father[354] and a young soldier, the son of the apothecary, Lord Aymé de la Rive, who took a poor, sick nun by the arm, and a good woman of the village, named Louise Deshermitte, and the wagoner. The lay brother went ahead to announce their coming in Saint-Julien.

It was a piteous thing to see that holy company in such a piteous state, so afflicted and overcome by sorrow and trial that several of them collapsed and fainted on the way, and since it was rainy and the path was muddy [281] they could not get up, and they were all on foot, except four poor sick ones who were in the wagon.

There were six poor aged nuns, who had been in the convent for more than fifty years[355]—and two of them more than sixty-six years[356]—without ever having seen anything in the world. They faltered at each blow and could not bear the strong wind. When they saw the animals in the fields, they thought the cows were bears and the sheep were ravenous wolves. No one

354. Presumably Thomas Garnier, mentioned above.

355. Claude Lingotte (the aunt of Blaisine Varembert), Louise Rambo (the abbess), Angele Rubie, Bernardine de Gento, Jeannette Ponsette, and Jeronyme de Villarseil.

356. Claude Lingotte, Louise Rambo, and Angele Rubie had been in the convent the longest.

who met them on the way could say a word to them, they were so overcome by compassion. And even though mother vicaress had given them all good shoes to keep them from hurting their feet, most of them did not know how to travel by foot, but carried them attached to their belts. In that state they traveled until almost nightfall, from five o'clock in the morning, when they had left Geneva, until they reached Saint-Julien, which was only a very short distance away.

Monseigneur the duke's herald, Lord Jean Faulcon,[357] and monseigneur his brother [Claude Faulcon], who had a castle, had been informed of their coming by the lay brother, and they had quickly assembled the clergy and all the parish, which [282] was a fine company because they were celebrating the feast and the occasion of Monseigneur Saint Felix,[358] and many people came up to the sisters carrying the cross and banners and ringing bells in great piety, as at a procession. The lord herald and his brother[359] prepared their house for them, and they came up to speak to them on behalf of their parish and bowed to them, with their wives, honorable ladies, and other noble gentlewomen and their servants, leading fine horses that were handsomely arrayed so that the women who wished could ride them. They sent the lay brother back quickly and told the sisters to wait for the parish, which wanted to show them honor and reverence in accordance with monseigneur the duke's intentions. For he had given orders to all of the districts and parishes in his lands that, if they happened to leave Geneva, the sisters should be revered and received in complete piety, as if it were His Excellency[360] himself, as at a procession. But when the parishioners saw the sisters in such a state, they almost fainted out of pity, and there were so many cries of pity the clerics could no longer raise their tearful voices.

All the poor sisters, as if they had seen a new light, threw themselves to the ground and knelt, with their hands stretched out toward heaven, and they worshiped the holy cross and gave thanks to Our Lord, who had brought them back among good Christians. It was a long time before anyone could say a word to anyone else. [283] The herald, an honorable lord, took the mother abbess, and his brother took mother vicaress. Then lords and ladies on each side escorted the sisters, supporting them under their arms and following the procession, to the house of the Lords Faulcon. They

357. Jean Faulcon had a castle in Ternier.

358. The Feast of Saint Felix and Saint Audactus, August 30.

359. Manuscript A says only "the lord herald" followed by possessive plural adjectives; manuscript B adds "and his brother."

360. That is, the Duke of Savoy.

received them with great honor and reverence and gave them lodging and had them sleep that night in the room they had made exclusively for His Excellency Monseigneur. They made a great fire for the sisters' comfort, and they treated them well, giving them food and drink and all necessities.

Then the two lords came alone into the room with the two ladies, their wives. They asked how they had left and if God had had the grace to allow them all to leave without bodily injury, for which they gave many thanks to God, because people had thought it was impossible, considering how ill disposed the heretics were toward them.

Afterward, they asked them what they were planning to do. "Lords," said mother vicaress, "we plan to go to La Perrière, to the house of Monseigneur the Baron of Viry,[361] my cousin. I trust very much in [284] his goodness, and I think he will lend us the castle, which is a good fortress, for a short time, and divine service can be observed in the chapel, which is very fine. In the meantime, we will let monseigneur the duke know about our misfortune so that he may have us escorted to his monastery in Annecy, which he offered to us previously."

"That is very well advised," said the herald. "Write your letters here, and tell monseigneur all your intentions. Also write how we offered you this house and all our goods for His Excellency and how according to his wishes and commandments this parish and his whole district of Ternier received you in complete honor and piety and treated you honorably until you were out of this district. When your letters are finished, I will dispatch a post early in the morning to carry them to monseigneur in the Piedmont."

And so it was done. Sister Jeanne de Jussie wrote all night long without sleeping, even though she was very sick with a fever and had just recovered from a deathly illness; in the letters she told the whole story of their sorrowful departure and how divine goodness had miraculously spared them all from any harm to their bodies or souls and that only the one lost girl, Dominique Varembert's daughter, had remained and that she had been easily deceived. The whole thing was also written in great detail to madame the duchess, Beatrice of Portugal, who had great [285] love for and devotion to the convent. When the letters were finished they were examined by the lords, who found them fine and well written, and when they read them they shed many tears of pity and devotion.

On the next day, which was the last day of August, the Lords Faulcon had six wagons prepared very respectably and with good guides. All the

---

361. Michel de Viry. For information on Michel de Viry, see Revilliod's 1853 edition of Jussie's chronicle, xvii–xviii.

clergy and people of other estates throughout the district of Ternier were ordered to accompany those poor ladies as if in a procession and to help them in any other way they could. They were taken honorably to the church to hear Mass. Then they were obliged to dine at the Faulcons' house again. They prepared two measures of wheat for them to take for later to protect them from difficulty and other goods.

Then they were put on the wagons and accompanied very honorably by all kinds of people, in a fine procession and in piety, until they reached the next parish, which greeted them. Thus they went from parish to parish, until they reached the Castle of La Perrière. The good Lord Baron of Viry greeted them there with great piety and in tears. As he helped his cousin, mother vicaress, down first, she said to him, "My cousin, I have the presumption to place these poor, sorrowful nuns into your hands so that they may have better rest and safety." [286]

Then the good baron took the keys to the castle and gave them to her and said, "Madame, my cousin, you were here before I was. I give you the house and all my property, and I do not want anyone to enter without your permission. Do not be afraid or fear anything because the castle is well furnished with good weapons and my men and I will keep close watch."

He sent all his men away and told them to seek lodging in the city. He himself slept very little on a bit of hay in a barn, and he kept close watch. It was a good thing he did because as soon as the Genevans heard how everyone was honoring those poor sisters and how happy the sisters were to be away from the Genevans' infection, they regretted having chased them away. They plotted to go out at night with weapons and bring them back. The baron was told of it, and he kept such close watch that he justly defeated several spies he found around the castle at night, although he said nothing about it to the sisters.

It was proclaimed throughout his barony of Viry that all people should do what they could to provide for the handmaidens and servants of Our Lord, who were in refuge there and destitute of all property. When it was announced, all kinds of people came and the sisters were visited by the nobles of the region. [287]

THE SISTERS RESUME THE CLOISTERED LIFE

The sisters decided among themselves to observe the rule of their order as best they could. Mother vicaress sent the portresses to the door to receive alms and to satisfy the people. They decided to recite the Divine Office in the chapel, which was very fine and dedicated, all the canonical hours. They decided to avoid secular people unless they were important people ordered by the prelates. They did their best to follow the rule and were so serene that no one saw them with their faces uncovered except out of obedience to the abbess at their parents' and friends' requests.

During the day they stayed together in one room, and at night they slept in groups of six in several rooms, for there were thirty-six excellent rooms in that castle with fireplaces and fine folding beds, all furnished with fine curtains and cords of white and red satin and with very good mattresses and fine covers, because that castle had been completely renovated by the lord's father, mother vicaress's uncle.[362] He had made special rooms and halls for all the world's princes, all well furnished. It was beautiful and wonderfully sumptuous. But, alas, the German-speaking heretics burned it out of spite very soon afterward.[363] [288]

The sisters went on in that manner, consoling each other as best they could, helped by Our Lord's grace and mercy and monseigneur's good will,[364] and they were still afraid. The father confessor and his associates had been taken to the other side of the castle, and they said Mass every day in front of the sisters. The tertiaries stayed on the other side, and the sisters prepared the food as they did in their convent.

THE SISTERS ARE TAKEN TO ANNECY

The next Thursday [September 2], monseigneur the judge from Gex, the noble François Barrat, received letters and orders from monseigneur the duke, telling him that he knew of the poor nuns' banishment and giving orders for them to be escorted and taken honorably, as if it were His Excellency[365] in person, to Annecy, to his Monastery of the Holy Cross,[366] which he was giving to them for [289] refuge and to restore them to their proper path so that they could observe the Divine Office. He also wrote to the president of Annecy [Angellin de Pontverre] and the whole city and requested that they greet them with piety and honor, just as they would greet him. The judge immediately sent his brother, monseigneur the secretary, a wise and discreet man, with a letter containing his orders, and he came in great haste to find the sisters. When he said why he had come, he was let in, and he

---

362. Aymé, Baron of Viry.
363. The Bernese seized the area around Saint Julien and Viry in February 1536.
364. Manuscript B eliminates the reference to Monseigneur.
365. That is, the Duke of Savoy.
366. The former Augustinian Monastery of the Holy Cross was empty at the time.

greeted the sisters, who were all present. Then out of compassion he began to weep in such anguish that he could not say why he had come or what his orders were, but instead placed his letters in mother abbess's hands. But he wept so sorrowfully that no one could read the letters silently or aloud. The father confessor was called in to read them. But when he heard what they were about, he was as speechless as the others, and they were in that state for a long time, unable to say a word. Finally the secretary gathered up the strength to open the letters and he read them out loud, including monseigneur's orders to take the sisters to Annecy.

At that news, which they received gladly, the sisters decided among themselves that it would be safer and more respectable to be in a monastery than a castle. They wrote a letter to monseigneur the judge saying they would be very pleased [290] to be escorted by him and that, if he were willing to take them there, they would obey him. When the response was written, the secretary left to hurry back, even though it was very late.

Early Friday morning [September 3], the lord judge arrived with his brother and with the lord of the Castle of Gaillard, Lord [Claude] Serventis. When they were before the sisters, he again stated his orders and read his letters patent from monseigneur, which contained the pitiable matter of their departure, and the bitter tears began again. Then after a short time they were consoled and decided to leave the next morning. So all their belongings and a sturdy wagon to carry the sisters were prepared.[367] The good peasants in the district and barony of Monseigneur of Viry were ordered to give them wagons and good drivers to convey them comfortably, and the whole district and the clergy were told to accompany them piously, as in a procession, which was done in piety and pitiable reverence, as follows.

As they had admirably decided, the judge and his company arrived on Saturday morning [September 4]. They gave the sisters breakfast so they could bear [291] the agony of the journey better. In the meantime, the good baron himself attended to and prepared the wagons and gave his men orders. He had his finest horse outfitted and wore his most sumptuous attire, and he and the whole company were well armed beneath their robes; when everything was ready, they went into the chapel and the good lord opened a chest containing a fine piece of the flesh of the true, precious body of Monseigneur Saint Romanus,[368] which was fine, fresh, and sweet-smelling. The good father Friar Antoine Garin gave it to the sisters to kiss, and he blessed the whole company.

---

367. Manuscript B eliminates this reference to a wagon.

368. Fifth-century hermit and abbot who founded several monasteries in the French Jura.

I, who write this, was there with a high fever, and by the merits of God's glorious knight, whose holy relics they kissed, I was healed all at once, and as a memorial to the event, I left in the chapel the stick I had been using to support myself.

He had put them[369] on the altar while they were at the castle, and as it is written above, he had given all the keys to mother vicaress, his cousin, and he himself had guided them and taken them to visit the whole fine castle. As a diversion he had shown them the cell containing his library, which was amazingly rich, filled with all the books and stories one could ask for. The whole *City of God*[370] was there, written on fine parchment, amply illuminated in gold and blue, which had cost a great deal to have written, and he had given it to them for their [292] consolation while they were there. Then he had shown them the secret cell containing his treasury, which was very fine. All the deeds to his lands and barony and the nobility and progeny of his noble ancestors were there, all in good order and appearance, and his other rich and secret possessions. During the short time they were there, he did all he could to honor and comfort them. I beg all of you in the future to remember and commend him.

When the sisters went out and bowed before the holy cross and all the clerics and people who were waiting for them and bid them farewell, many tears were shed. The good people cried out, "Alas, farewell, holy ladies! The poor land is losing its light. Who will comfort us from now on? For no creature, no matter how sorrowful, has ever spoken to them without being comforted, and God has always protected us because of their holy merits." They said other piteous words of grief.

When they had climbed into the wagons, which the good baron himself had covered with fine red and white[371] blankets, the procession began in good order. Then the wagons came, in order, each led by four honorable men, and there were eight wagons. On each side [293] the handsomely attired lords walked grandly, Lord Serventis and his convoy and monseigneur the judge from Gex with his company.

When they had walked like that for a good part of the way, the baron received news of some pressing business that he had to attend to that day, so he was obliged to bid them farewell amid much weeping and sobbing.

---

369. Referent unclear; perhaps the holy relics.

370. Defense of Christianity written in the fifth century by Augustine (lived 354–430; Bishop of Hippo 396–430). A new translation of the text has appeared recently: *The City of God against the Pagans*, trans. Robert W. Dyson (Cambridge: Cambridge University Press, 1998).

371. The colors of the House of Savoy.

Mother vicaress thanked him for all of them and asked him to tell the procession and all the good people to turn around, since the rainy weather was making it so hard for them, "and we have good and noble company." At that, they returned to their parish.

The sisters remained under the protection of those good drivers and traveled until they approached the Abbey of Bonlieu.[372] The good ladies of the convent came up to them in a fine procession and in piety, and they took them in gladly; the sisters got down from the wagons to stay there because it was late at night. They bid their good drivers from Viry farewell and told them to leave, which upset them, because they intended to take them all the way to Annecy. But monseigneur the judge had ordered them to take them only to the next district, because he thought Monseigneur [Alexandre] of Sallenôve would treat them just as the good [294] baron had. But he acted differently, because he was insulted that the sisters had not come to his castle. And because he was displeased, he sent his son, Monseigneur of Saint Denis, with a flask of wine and a dish of grapes for his two aunts, mother vicaress and her sister, with the message that the castle was amply supplied with food that they could eat there but that he would not send it out to them. He would not help them in any other way.

The sisters spent that night in the abbey in a very poorly furnished room, and they rested their heads against each other. On Sunday [September 5] they heard Mass and the ladies' matins piously. Then they were given dinner, and monseigneur the judge paid for it, which was a great expense, because there were about fifty people and more than thirty animals, both cows and horses.

After dinner, all the ladies came to pay their respects and to keep them company until their departure, and it was about eleven o'clock before they could find any wagons. Even so, the people who were forced to come by the prince's orders were crude and ill mannered, and their wagons were in very bad condition. Nonetheless, because of their desire to be in a peaceful place away from secular people as soon as possible, the sisters went with them willingly, and even though it was raining and they had nothing to protect them and the wagons were covered with nothing but thin sheets that the abbess had lent them, they left Bonlieu and set out for [295] Annecy. But they had such misfortune that it was soon very late and completely dark.

In all the villages and parishes through which they passed, they were

372. The Cistercian Abbey of Bonlieu near Sallenôves in Upper Savoy was founded in 1160 by the house of Viry-Sallenôve and transferred to Annecy in 1640.

welcomed with processions, with bells ringing and all the roads filled with people who ran in front of and behind them to get a look at them.

When they reached La Balme [de Sillingy], a small locality near Annecy, it was almost sunset. They were greeted there with great honor and reverence. The lords and ladies[373] offered to let them spend the night there. But monseigneur the judge did not want them to stay, for he said he had told messieurs of Annecy that they would arrive that day and he did not want to fail. This upset the lords and ladies who had offered to give the sisters lodging, and they forced the wagons to stop and made the sisters drink. They gave each of them some good bread and aged cheese and good white and red wine, and they did it so willingly that it was a pleasure to watch them serve. I am writing it down so that it will be remembered.

Afterward, they quickly set out for Annecy, but when they reached Cran, the river [Fier] was high and very loud. The cows and horses would not go over the bridge. They were delayed for a long time because they had to force them to go over one at a time and several of them had to be carried over. Then the men [296] had to pull all the wagons over the bridge. So they found themselves in the dark of night. Messieurs of Annecy sent lights and men to hurry them along and said that the city had been waiting all day for them.

THE SISTERS' ARRIVAL IN ANNECY

The road from Annecy to Cran was full of people, without a break, carrying lights, torches, and lanterns, and all the bells rang out melodiously. The men all came from the city to greet them, and the burgher ladies and other women lined the streets, with lots of light; torches were lit in all the windows of every house, and the whole city looked like it was on fire. Everyone was upset that it was so late and that they could not see and revere the sisters as they wished and that the sisters could not respond to their greetings and welcome. But they all knelt, their hands folded and extended toward the heavens, and not without tears. The drivers went from side to side in the wagon and thanked the good people.

In that manner they went straight to the home of monseigneur the high president, the noble Angellin de Pontverre, Lord of Chavaroche, who was waiting for them in front of [297] his house with many nobles. He first greeted them by expressing his anger toward monseigneur the judge, saying

---

373. Manuscript A adds the enigmatic *de darma*. Manuscript B copies this phrase, and Jussie's 1611 editor omits it. *Le levain du calvinisme* (1611), 212.

that they had taken too long and that it was not a proper hour to bring such ladies into a prince's city. Then he called out, "Sister Pernette de Châteaufort, my mistress, where are you? I was subject to you in the past. From now on you will rely on my mercy!" As he said that, he lifted her down and embraced her tenderly, weeping, for he loved her as a friend, and he said she was the cause of all his happiness. For when he had been a young page of Monseigneur de Châteaufort, she had taught him and had reprimanded him for his indiscretions, which he knew very well. He had married her cousin, the daughter of Monseigneur of Saint Andrieu, the noble Gabrielle de Viry, who was there to greet them.

Then they helped the reverend mother abbess down, and then the rest, one at a time, and they welcomed and comforted them. The judge helped them down on one side, and he placed each one in the lord's hand and said, "Monseigneur, I give to you as many as I took charge of, which is twenty-three. I commend them to you, and as for me, by handing them over to you, I have fulfilled the charge and commission I received from monseigneur to the best of my ability, and I have exposed myself to great danger; I believe piteously that God preserved and protected us by their good merits, for my company and I truly thought we would be attacked before we arrived here. Indeed, [298] we found several spies from Geneva in front of and behind us. But we scolded a few of them so severely that the others went away."

He was telling the truth, for the Genevans had sent some petty criminals to do their dirty work and spy on them. When they were threatened with beating, they confessed their evil deeds. But they met three wicked armed guards. One of them stayed cleverly to the side and aimed his harquebus at the judge. But the secretary, who was the judge's brother, noticed and said to him, "Hah, Monseigneur, step forward quickly!" As he said that, he raised his pike and the others raised their harquebuses. And that criminal ran away like a flash.

After that discussion, the sisters were led into the house of monseigneur the president. But several of them were so sick because of the strong wind and the exertion that they were carried straight to bed. They were heartily welcomed there, and they found a great fire to warm them and much food prepared for their supper. As soon as [299] they were all gathered in a room, at mother vicaress's request, the president sent the multitude of people away from them and then he seated them privately and served them honorably all sorts of expensive food, no meat, and plentiful white and red wine of several kinds, and they slept very well on good mattresses. But it was so late that they could hardly eat or drink, they were so sick and weary. However, they had the consolation of being in a safe place. They spent the night there.

THE NUNS OF SAINT CLARE ARE PUT IN THE
MONASTERY OF THE HOLY CROSS

The following is the end of their trials and sorrows, and how they were put honorably in the monastery.

On Monday morning [September 6], the president sent bread, wine, cheese, and other good things to the sisters' room for breakfast for those who wished it and for the poor sick ones. The good observant fathers who lived in Annecy came to see and welcome them. Then, to satisfy the city that wished to pay its respects and see them at its leisure, monseigneur the president led the fine [300] company to the Franciscan monastery to hear Mass. The sisters did not allow the men to lead them there, but lined up two by two, hand in hand, with their faces well covered so that although the people leaned down to get a look at them, they could only see their eyes. There were so many people that they formed a wall on each side. Monseigneur the president went ahead of the sisters with all his judicial supporters, clearing the way, to the monastery and to a fine chapel that was honorably prepared and where the monks were ready to say the Mass.

The illustrious and excellent prince monseigneur the viscount, François of Luxembourg,[374] was waiting there for the sisters, and messeigneurs his most noble children, Monseigneur Charles[375] and Monseigneur Sebastien[376] and Mademoiselle Philippe,[377] and his whole noble entourage and the high nobility and gentlemen of the land. After they had heard the Holy Mass piously together, they humbly paid their respects to each other. The good prince blessed them, and [301] all the nobles, benevolently. All the ladies and burgher women gathered to welcome them when they left the chapel, and countless numbers of all kinds of people were on both sides.

The sisters were asked if they wanted to return to monseigneur the president's house to wait for the convent to be set up, since it was very poorly furnished. But the mothers replied, "Since God has allowed us to find a place for divine service, we beg you to take us there without delay, for we desire only to be separated from the world."

---

374. François of Luxembourg, Viscount of Martigues and Marquis of Baugey; the son of François of Luxembourg and Louise of Savoy.

375. Charles of Luxembourg, later married to Claude de Foix.

376. Sébastien of Luxembourg, Marquis of Baugey, Viscount of Martigues, and Duke of Pentheure, later married to Marie de Beaucaire.

377. According to seventeenth-century genealogists Scévole and Louis de Saincte-Marthe, François of Luxembourg had three daughters: Madeleine, Marie, and Françoise. *Histoire généalogique de la Maison de France*, (Paris: N. Buon, 1628), 2: 809.

This inspired them very much, and they told everyone to line up and accompany them. The good fathers processed ahead of them singing "In Exitu Israel,"[378] etc. Messeigneurs the children followed them. Monseigneur the viscount escorted the reverend mother abbess first and supported her on his arm, monseigneur the president escorted mother vicaress, and then all, one after another, were escorted by two gentlemen, and all the people followed them. They entered the monastery in that order and went straight to the church, where they prostrated themselves in the middle of the choir and, with a fine voice, recited the "Salve regina" aloud and other words of praise, giving thanks to God, who had allowed them to reach this safe place. [302]

Monseigneur the viscount and his nobles retreated, as did the crowd of people, following his orders, saying that they would leave them alone to eat their meal, for which monseigneur the president had sent them bread, wine, and many kinds of good foods, all prepared in his house. He gave them at least thirty drinking glasses to start to set up their household. That day they were still served by secular people.

After dinner, the good prince and all the nobles returned and humbly asked the sisters to go to vespers at the Dominican monastery and to put holy water on madame the viscountess, his mother [Louise of Savoy, daughter of Janus of Savoy], and Madame de Martigues, his wife, the most excellent noble Charlotte [de Brosse] of Brittany who had died in childbirth less than a year ago. The sisters asked to be excused, saying that since God had been gracious enough to give them refuge in such a good convent, they should never leave it again. But monseigneur the judge and the president advised them do that good prince's act of piety, "because you are not here by your own right, but only because of the prince's wishes."

They were taken out and led to the Dominican monastery, and they heard the monks' vespers.[379] After vespers they were taken to the noble princesses' tombs. [303] There they said a "De profundis" in unison and other prayers, which consoled the good prince. The monks, displeased by their coming, did not pay much attention to them, which scandalized everyone.

The good prince took them to Notre Dame de Liesse,[380] and they were welcomed there by the lord canons and taken up to the image of Our Lady. The sisters said a "Salve" there in a fine voice. At that same instant a child who had been stillborn two days earlier miraculously made a great sign of

---

378. "When Israel went out from Egypt" (Ps 114:1).

379. In the monastery church of Saint-Maurice.

380. A church and well-known pilgrimage site in Annecy.

life and received a fitting baptism, and many people were present and all the bells were rung for that miracle.

Then they were taken to Monseigneur the Count Philippe of Savoy's tomb[381] and they said a "De profundis" and prayers for the dead piously. In complete piety they returned to the convent and monastery that monseigneur had given to them as a refuge. They never left it again. However, they found it unfit for their needs because there were six doors without locks. And even though there was an iron grille, there was not yet a door or curtain in front of it and there were no steps or landing outside it. [304]

In the church there were large windows without any glass or doors. Instead of a dormitory there were twenty-eight small, separate bedrooms without furnishings or any other necessary objects, except that each of them had a bed frame; the kitchen was paved with very sharp and jagged stones,[382] and there was no turning window to talk as they were accustomed; the place to make their garden was subject to the city and had three open gates by which anyone could enter; the church and the whole convent were still profane and not yet sanctified, which greatly surprised them. They spent that night and that whole winter in great poverty and in very harsh conditions. They slept two to a bed on a bit of straw, without blankets, and they had neither cloaks nor coats to comfort them.

On Tuesday, the eve [September 7] of the Feast of the Birth of Our Lady, the great general pardons began in Annecy, and there were countless people in all the land. All the nobles came to the convent to see the sisters, and on the Feast of Our Lady [September 8] too. Because the sisters were not yet secluded, everyone came there, causing such disorder that it was impossible to turn around. The sisters stayed together in the refectory, in pious order as best they could. Everyone [305] wept pitiably and showed them honor and reverence. On that eve of the Feast of Our Lady they began to observe vespers in the choir of the church, and then they said matins in a bedroom because no flame would remain lit in the church since there were no doors or windows. The Divine Office has been said in the convent day and night ever since then,[383] until today, in all piety and reverence.

The good prince, monseigneur the viscount, knowing that the poor sisters were very tired and despondent, treated them all with as much humanity and consideration as he could, and he came every day for three weeks with messieurs his children and all the nobles; he had people sing and bring the

---

381. He had died on September 19, 1533, in Marseilles.

382. A particular hardship for the Poor Clares, who generally went barefoot.

383. This sentence stops here in manuscript B.

organ from Liesse and all sorts of diversions in all piety. He brought and showed them all the jewelry, gems, and adornments that belonged to him and to madame, his departed wife. On Sunday he brought food and good wine and he had the sisters eat with him; he treated them very well and gave them everything they needed. He still gives much alms every year, and we are very grateful to him.

He also bought them fifteen florins' worth of white and black thread and needles so they could pass the time doing needlework, and he showed them more kindness than it is possible to write. The lord president did the same. [306]

THE LAST NEWS OF THE FATE OF THE
DUCAL HOUSE OF SAVOY

In a few days, the sisters received letters patent from monseigneur the duke and madame the duchess, his noble wife, by which they consoled them with holy words of caution and patience and ceded to them the monastery with its garden, orchard, and tower, and they ordered Monsieur the Master Butet[384] to bring them furnishings to use and two hundred florins, a hundred in food and a hundred in silver, for their comfort, and monseigneur told them, moreover, that he would always keep them in his protection and remember them, and madame likewise, which they always did mercifully.

But, alas, Our Lord soon sent pitiable sorrow to them, for his good land of Savoy, because of the Genevans, was seized by some German-speaking Lutheran heretics and forced into that damnable heresy. The duchy was seized and made subject to King Francis, the duke's own nephew. The good duke and the noble duchess were banished like poor people and exiled from their land. They took refuge in Annecy. When Our Lord saw their benevolent patience and great suffering, just as to another Saint Job,[385] he added more extreme sorrow and called back to his blessed side their daughter, a fine, beautiful [307] and wise maiden named Madame Catherine Charlotte,[386] who was their delight, and on the next Christmas Day, he

---

384. Jussie may perhaps be referring to Burdet, above, who fed the nuns just after they crossed the bridge into the territory of the Duke of Savoy. Jussie's 1611 editor changes manuscript A's *monseigneur le maistre buttet* to *Monsieur le Maistre de Butet.*

385. "While he was still speaking, another came and said, 'Your sons and daughters were eating and drinking wine in their eldest brother's house, and suddenly a great wind came across the desert, struck the four corners of the house, and it fell on the young people, and they are dead; I alone have escaped to tell you" (Job 1:18–19).

386. She died in Milan in 1536, at the age of seven, and was buried in the cathedral in Turin.

called back to his side their eldest son, monseigneur the prince, Louis,[387] who was twelve or thirteen years old and who was the handsomest prince in the world and who was developing handsomely in great virtue, which no one can describe, since he was in Spain in the emperor's household.

After those grievous woes, the noble duchess was seized by a mortal illness and gave birth to a fine son who did not live long and was not named. A few days later, the good lady also died,[388] full of virtue and great merit and in the prime of her life and the most fine and pious lady ever seen in the land, who loved the order of Madame Saint Clare very much and gave them very many alms and kindnesses, especially those of us from Geneva, and she did us much good. When she was in Geneva, she came to the convent in disguise with a dozen of her ladies and stayed there out of piety from morning until the stars came out, and she dined at the sisters' table and ate their coarse bread and said the whole canonical office like the sisters, every day.

It was at that time[389] that a good and aged mother named Sister Jacque de Vy[390] died. [308] The good lady[391] wanted to attend the funeral, and she came to the convent in the morning and listened to the whole service and looked at the body and kissed its feet in great piety and humility, and she had her confessor preach a fine sermon, and she had Monseigneur the Bishop of Portugal[392] do the burial service. Monseigneur the duke also came in person, with several high bishops, counts, barons, and other nobles. The good lady often entered secretly and privately that day, to protect herself from all vanity and say her office more piously. It would take too long to describe her humility and virtues and the goods and support she gave the convent, as did the good duke.

To get back to the subject, the good duke was tested by Our Lord so much that in a short time he lost his land, his wife, and his children, and he was left alone with a single son, who was raised so virtuously that he is now in the Emperor Charles' household and reputed to be one of the most handsome, wise, and virtuous princes in the world, and his name is Philibert

---

387. The crown prince of Savoy died in Madrid on December 25, 1536, at the age of thirteen, and was buried in Granada.

388. Beatrice of Portugal died on January 8, 1538.

389. That is, while the duchess was in Geneva.

390. Jacque de Vy from Orbe, who died on January 14, 1524, was the fourth abbess of the Convent of Saint Clare and preceded Louise Rambo.

391. That is, the duchess.

392. Probably the child cardinal Alfonso of Portugal (1509–40), brother of the Duchess Beatrice. He was made a cardinal by Pope Leo X on July 1, 1517, at the age of eight, and he became Prince Bishop of Lisbon on February 20, 1523.

Emmanuel.[393] May God let him prosper and be all joy and consolation to monseigneur, who gave us more comfort and [309] consolation than it is possible to write. Even when he was deprived of his land and found himself in so much sorrow, he did not cease to console us and all creatures who turned to him. You will find elsewhere a record of the good things he did here[394] and of how he nourished and sustained us and of our other benefactors, whom I will name so that we may better remember them.

393. Emmanuel-Philibert of Savoy met the Emperor Charles V in Genoa in 1541 and remained in his inner circle until 1546, at which point he dedicated himself to military campaigns. He became Duke of Savoy after his father's death in 1553. He regained his lands in the Treaty of Cateau-Cambresis in 1559. In this treaty, he also negotiated a marriage to Marguerite, the youngest daughter of Francis I, thus securing a reconciliation between Savoy and France.

394. The sentence—and chronicle—ends here in manuscript B, perhaps because there is no indication that Jussie wrote the intended text to which she refers here. Ganter, however, suggests that manuscript A is missing the last two pages, which would have detailed the duke's gifts to the convent and have named other benefactors. Ganter, *Les Clarisses*, 214.

SERIES EDITORS'
BIBLIOGRAPHY

PRIMARY SOURCES

Alberti, Leon Battista. *The Family in Renaissance Florence*. Translated by Renée Neu Watkins. Columbia, S.C.: University of South Carolina Press, 1969.

Arenal, Electa, and Stacey Schlau, eds. *Untold Sisters: Hispanic Nuns in Their Own Works*. Translated by Amanda Powell. Albuquerque, N.M.: University of New Mexico Press, 1989.

Astell, Mary. *The First English Feminist: Reflections on Marriage and Other Writings*. Edited and with an introduction by Bridget Hill. New York: St. Martin's Press, 1986.

Atherton, Margaret, ed. *Women Philosophers of the Early Modern Period*. Indianapolis, Ind.: Hackett Publishing, 1994. Aughterson, Kate, ed. *Renaissance Woman: Constructions of Femininity in England: A Source Book*. London and New York: Routledge, 1995.

Barbaro, Francesco. *On Wifely Duties*. Translated by Benjamin Kohl. In *The Earthly Republic*, edited by Benjamin Kohl and R. G. Witt, 179–228. Philadelphia: University of Pennsylvania Press, 1978

Behn, Aphra. *The Works of Aphra Behn*. 7 vols. Edited by Janet Todd. Columbus, Ohio: Ohio State University Press, 1992–96.

Boccaccio, Giovanni. *Famous Women*. Edited and translated by Virginia Brown. The I Tatti Renaissance Library. Cambridge, Mass.: Harvard University Press, 2001.

———. *Corbaccio or the Labyrinth of Love*. Transated by Anthony K. Cassell. 2d rev. ed. Binghamton, N.Y.: Medieval and Renaissance Texts and Studies, 1993.

Booy, David, ed. *Autobiographical Writings by Early Quaker Women*. Aldershot and Brookfield, UK: Ashgate Publishing, 2004.

Brown, Sylvia. *Women's Writing in Stuart England: The Mother's Legacies of Dorothy Leigh, Elizabeth Joscelin and Elizabeth Richardson*. Thrupp, Stroud, Gloceter: Sutton, 1999.

Bruni, Leonardo. "On the Study of Literature (1405) to Lady Battista Malatesta of Moltefeltro." In *The Humanism of Leonardo Bruni: Selected Texts*, translated and with an introduction by Gordon Griffiths, James Hankins, and David Thompson, 240–51. Binghamton, N.Y.: Medieval and Renaissance Studies and Texts, 1987.

Castiglione, Baldassare. *The Book of the Courtier*. Translated by George Bull. New York: Penguin, 1967.

———. *The Book of the Courtier*. Edited by Daniel Javitch. New York: W. W. Norton, 2002.

Clarke, Danielle, ed. *Isabella Whitney, Mary Sidney and Aemilia Lanyer: Renaissance Women Poets.* New York: Penguin Books, 2000.

Crawford, Patricia, and Laura Gowing, eds. *Women's Worlds in Seventeenth-Century England: A Source Book.* London and New York: Routledge, 2000.

"Custome Is an Idiot": Jacobean Pamphlet Literature on Women. Edited by Susan Gushee O'Malley. Afterword by Ann Rosalind Jones. Chicago and Urbana: University of Illinois Press, 2004.

Daybell, James, ed. *Early Modern Women's Letter Writing, 1450–1700.* Houndmills, England, New York: Palgrave, 2001.

Elizabeth I: Collected Works. Edited by Leah S. Marcus, Janel Mueller, and Mary Beth Rose. Chicago: University of Chicago Press, 2000.

Elyot, Thomas. *Defence of Good Women: The Feminist Controversy of the Renaissance.* Edited by Diane Bornstein. Facsimile Reproductions. New York: Delmar, 1980.

Erasmus, Desiderius. *Erasmus on Women.* Edited by Erika Rummel. Toronto: University of Toronto Press, 1996.

Female and Male Voices in Early Modern England: An Anthology of Renaissance Writing. Edited by Betty S. Travitsky and Anne Lake Prescott. New York: Columbia University Press, 2000.

Ferguson, Moira, ed. *First Feminists: British Women Writers 1578–1799.* Bloomington, Ind.: Indiana University Press, 1985.

Galilei, Maria Celeste. *Sister Maria Celeste's Letters to her father, Galileo.* Edited and translated by Rinaldina Russell. Lincoln, Neb., and New York: Writers Club Press of Universe.com, 2000.

———. *To Father: The Letters of Sister Maria Celeste to Galileo, 1623–1633.* Translated by Dava Sobel. London: Fourth Estate, 2001.

Gethner, Perry, ed. *The Lunatic Lover and Other Plays by French Women of the 17th and 18th Centuries.* Portsmouth, N.H.: Heinemann, 1994.

Glückel of Hameln. *The Memoirs of Glückel of Hameln.* Translated by Marvin Lowenthal. New Introduction by Robert Rosen. New York: Schocken Books, 1977.

Harline, Craig, ed. *The Burdens of Sister Margaret: Inside a Seventeenth-Century Convent.* New Haven: Yale University Press, abr. ed., 2000.

Henderson, Katherine Usher, and Barbara F. McManus, eds. *Half Humankind: Contexts and Texts of the Controversy about Women in England, 1540–1640.* Urbana, Ill: University of Illinois Press, 1985.

Hoby, Margaret. *The Private Life of an Elizabethan Lady: The Diary of Lady Margaret Hoby 1599–1605.* Phoenix Mill, England: Sutton Publishing, 1998.

Humanist Educational Treatises. Edited and translated by Craig W. Kallendorf. The I Tatti Renaissance Library. Cambridge, Mass.: Harvard University Press, 2002.

Hunter, Lynette, ed. *The Letters of Dorothy Moore, 1612–64.* Aldershot and Brookfield, UK: Ashgate Publishing, 2004.

Joscelin, Elizabeth. *The Mothers Legacy to Her Unborn Childe.* Edited by Jean leDrew Metcalfe. Toronto: University of Toronto Press, 2000.

Kaminsky, Amy Katz, ed. *Water Lilies, Flores del agua: An Anthology of Spanish Women Writers from the Fifteenth through the Nineteenth Century.* Minneapolis: University of Minnesota Press, 1996.

Kempe, Margery. *The Book of Margery Kempe.* Translated and edited by Lynn Staley. A Norton Critical Edition. New York: W.W. Norton, 2001.

King, Margaret L., and Albert Rabil, Jr., eds. *Her Immaculate Hand: Selected Works by and about the Women Humanists of Quattrocento Italy*. Binghamton, N.Y.: Medieval and Renaissance Texts and Studies, 1983; second revised paperback edition, 1991.

Klein, Joan Larsen, ed. *Daughters, Wives, and Widows: Writings by Men about Women and Marriage in England, 1500–1640*. Urbana, Ill.: University of Illinois Press, 1992.

Knox, John. *The Political Writings of John Knox: The First Blast of the Trumpet against the Monstrous Regiment of Women and Other Selected Works*. Edited by Marvin A. Breslow. Washington: Folger Shakespeare Library, 1985.

Kors, Alan C., and Edward Peters, eds. *Witchcraft in Europe, 400–1700: A Documentary History*. Philadelphia: University of Pennsylvania Press, 2000.

Krämer, Heinrich, and Jacob Sprenger. *Malleus Maleficarum* (ca. 1487). Translated by Montague Summers. London: Pushkin Press, 1928; reprint New York: Dover, 1971.

Larsen, Anne R., and Colette H. Winn, eds. *Writings by Pre-Revolutionary French Women: From Marie de France to Elizabeth Vigée-Le Brun*. New York and London: Garland Publishing, 2000.

de Lorris, William, and Jean de Meun. *The Romance of the Rose*. Translated by Charles Dahlbert. Princeton: Princeton University Press, 1971; reprint University Press of New England, 1983.

Marguerite d'Angoulême, Queen of Navarre. *The Heptameron*. Translated by P. A. Chilton. New York: Viking Penguin, 1984.

Mary of Agreda. *The Divine Life of the Most Holy Virgin*. Abridgment of *The Mystical City of God*. Abridged by by Fr. Bonaventure Amedeo de Caesarea, M.C. Translated from the French by Abbé Joseph A. Boullan. Rockford, Ill.: Tan Books, 1997.

Mullan, David George. *Women's Life Writing in Early Modern Scotland: Writing the Evangelical Self, c. 1670—c. 1730*. Aldershot and Brookfield, UK: Ashgate Publishing, 2003.

Myers, Kathleen A., and Amanda Powell, eds. *A Wild Country out in the Garden: The Spiritual Journals of a Colonial Mexican Nun*. Bloomington, Ind.: Indiana University Press, 1999.

de Pizan, Christine. *The Book of the City of Ladies*. Translated by Earl Jeffrey Richards. Foreward by Marina Warner. New York: Persea Books, 1982.

———. *The Treasure of the City of Ladies*. Translated by Sarah Lawson. New York: Viking Penguin, 1985.

———. *The Treasure of the City of Ladies*. Translated and with an introduction by Charity Cannon Willard. Edited and with an introduction by Madeleine P. Cosman. New York: Persea Books, 1989.

Russell, Rinaldina, ed. *Sister Maria Celeste's Letters to Her Father, Galileo*. San Jose and New York: Writers Club Press, 2000.

Teresa of Avila, Saint. *The Life of Saint Teresa of Avila by Herself*. Translated by J. M. Cohen. New York: Viking Penguin, 1957.

Travitsky, Betty, ed. *The Paradise of Women: Writings by Englishwomen of the Renaissance*. Westport, Conn.: Greenwood Press, 1981.

Weyer, Johann. *Witches, Devils, and Doctors in the Renaissance: Johann Weyer, De praestigiis daemonum*. Edited by George Mora with Benjamin G. Kohl, Erik Midelfort, and Helen Bacon. Translated by John Shea. Binghamton, N.Y.: Medieval and Renaissance Texts and Studies, 1991.

Wilson, Katharina M., ed. *Medieval Women Writers*. Athens, Ga.: University of Georgia Press, 1984.

————, ed. *Women Writers of the Renaissance and Reformation*. Athens, Ga.: University of Georgia Press, 1987.

Wilson, Katharina M., and Frank J. Warnke, eds. *Women Writers of the Seventeenth Century*. Athens, Ga.: University of Georgia Press, 1989.

Wollstonecraft, Mary. *A Vindication of the Rights of Men and a Vindication of the Rights of Women*. Edited by Sylvana Tomaselli. Cambridge: Cambridge University Press, 1995.

————. *The Vindications of the Rights of Men, The Rights of Women*. Edited by D. L. Macdonald and Kathleen Scherf. Peterborough, Ontario, Canada: Broadview Press, 1997.

Women Critics 1660–1820: An Anthology. Edited by the Folger Collective on Early Women Critics. Bloomington, Ind.: Indiana University Press, 1995.

Women Writers in English 1350–1850. 15 volumes published through 1999 (projected 30-volume series suspended). Oxford: Oxford University Press, 1993–1999.

Wroth, Lady Mary. *The Countess of Montgomery's Urania*. 2 parts. Edited by Josephine A. Roberts. Tempe, Ariz.: MRTS, 1995, 1999.

————. *Lady Mary Wroth's "Love's Victory": The Penshurst Manuscript*. Edited by Michael G. Brennan. London: The Roxburghe Club, 1988.

————. *The Poems of Lady Mary Wroth*. Edited by Josephine A. Roberts. Baton Rouge, La: Louisiana State University Press, 1983.

de Zayas Maria. *The Disenchantments of Love*. Translated by H. Patsy Boyer. Albany, N.Y.: State University of New York Press, 1997.

————. *The Enchantments of Love: Amorous and Exemplary Novels*. Translated by H. Patsy Boyer. Berkeley: University of California Press, 1990.

SECONDARY SOURCES

Abate, Corinne S., ed. *Privacy, Domesticity, and Women in Early Modern England*. Aldershot and Brookfield, IK: Ashgate Publishing, 2003.

Ahlgren, Gillian. *Teresa of Avila and the Politics of Sanctity*. Ithaca, N.Y.: Cornell University Press, 1996.

Akkerman, Tjitske, and Siep Sturman, eds. *Feminist Thought in European History, 1400–2000*. London and New York: Routledge, 1997.

Allen, Sister Prudence, R.S.M. *The Concept of Woman: The Aristotelian Revolution, 750 B.C.—A.D. 1250*. Grand Rapids, Mich.: William B. Eerdmans Publishing Company, 1997.

————. *The Concept of Woman: Volume II: The Early Humanist Reformation, 1250–1500*. Grand Rapids, Mich.: William B. Eerdmans Publishing Company, 2002.

Amussen, Susan D., and Adele Seeff, eds. *Attending to Early Modern Women*. Newark: University of Delaware Press, 1998.

Andreadis, Harriette. *Sappho in Early Modern England: Female Same-Sex Literary Erotics 1550–1714*. Chicago: University of Chicago Press, 2001.

Armon, Shifra. *Picking Wedlock: Women and the Courtship Novel in Spain*. New York: Rowman and Littlefield Publishers, 2002.

Backer, Anne Liot Backer. *Precious Women*. New York: Basic Books, 1974.

Ballaster, Ros. *Seductive Forms*. New York: Oxford University Press, 1992.

Barash, Carol. *English Women's Poetry, 1649–1714: Politics, Community, and Linguistic Authority*. New York and Oxford: Oxford University Press, 1996.

Battigelli, Anna. *Margaret Cavendish and the Exiles of the Mind*. Lexington, Ky.: University of Kentucky Press, 1998.

Beasley, Faith. *Revising Memory: Women's Fiction and Memoirs in Seventeenth-Century France*. New Brunswick, N.J.: Rutgers University Press, 1990.

Becker, Lucinda M. *Death and the Early Modern Englishwoman*. Aldershot and Brookfield, UK: Ashgate Publishing, 2003.

Beilin, Elaine V. *Redeeming Eve: Women Writers of the English Renaissance*. Princeton: Princeton University Press, 1987.

Benson, Pamela Joseph. *The Invention of Renaissance Woman: The Challenge of Female Independence in the Literature and Thought of Italy and England*. University Park, Penn.: Pennsylvania State University Press, 1992.

Benson, Pamela Joseph, and Victoria Kirkham, eds. *Strong Voices, Weak History? Medieval and Renaissance Women in Their Literary Canons: England, France, Italy*. Ann Arbor: University of Michigan Press, 2003.

Berry, Helen. *Gender, Society and Print Culture in Late-Stuart England*. Aldershot and Brookfield, UK: Ashgate Publishing, 2003.

Bicks, Caroline. *Midwiving Subjects in Shakespeare's England*. Aldershot and Brookfield, UK: Ashgate Publishing, 2003.

Bilinkoff, Jodi. *The Avila of Saint Teresa: Religious Reform in a Sixteenth-Century City*. Ithaca, N.Y.: Cornell University Press, 1989.

Bissell, R. Ward. *Artemisia Gentileschi and the Authority of Art*. University Park, Penn.: Pennsylvania State University Press, 2000.

Blain, Virginia, Isobel Grundy, and Patricia Clements, eds. *The Feminist Companion to Literature in English: Women Writers from the Middle Ages to the Present*. New Haven: Yale University Press, 1990.

Bloch, R. Howard. *Medieval Misogyny and the Invention of Western Romantic Love*. Chicago: University of Chicago Press, 1991.

Bogucka, Maria. *Women in Early Modern Polish Society, against the European Background*. Aldershot and Brookfield, UK: Ashgate Publishing, 2004.

Bornstein, Daniel, and Roberto Rusconi, eds. *Women and Religion in Medieval and Renaissance Italy*. Translated by Margery J. Schneider. Chicago: University of Chicago Press, 1996.

Brant, Clare, and Diane Purkiss, eds. *Women, Texts and Histories, 1575–1760*. London and New York: Routledge, 1992.

Briggs, Robin. *Witches and Neighbours: The Social and Cultural Context of European Witchcraft*. New York: HarperCollins, 1995; Viking Penguin, 1996.

Brink, Jean R., ed. *Female Scholars: A Tradition of Learned Women before 1800*. Montréal: Eden Press Women's Publications, 1980.

Brink, Jean R., Allison Coudert, and Maryanne Cline Horowitz. *The Politics of Gender in Early Modern Europe*. Sixteenth Century Essays and Studies. Volume 12. Kirksville, Mo.: Sixteenth Century Journal Publishers, 1989.

Broude, Norma, and Mary D. Garrard, eds. *The Expanding Discourse: Feminism and Art History*. New York: HarperCollins, 1992.

Brown, Judith C. *Immodest Acts: The Life of a Lesbian Nun in Renaissance Italy*. New York: Oxford University Press, 1986.

Brown, Judith C., and Robert C. Davis, eds. *Gender and Society in Renaisance Italy*. London: Addison Wesley Longman, 1998.

Burke, Victoria E. Burke, ed. *Early Modern Women's Manuscript Writing*. Aldershot and Brookfield, UK: Ashgate Publishing, 2004.

Bynum, Carolyn Walker. *Fragmentation and Redemption: Essays on Gender and the Human Body in Medieval Religion*. New York: Zone Books, 1992.

————. *Holy Feast and Holy Fast: The Religious Significance of Food to Medieval Women*. Berkeley: University of California Press, 1987.

Cambridge Guide to Women's Writing in English. Edited by Lorna Sage. Cambridge: Cambridge University Press, 1999.

Cavallo, Sandra, and Lyndan Warner. *Widowhood in Medieval and Early Modern Europe*. New York: Longman, 1999.

Cavanagh, Sheila T. *Cherished Torment: The Emotional Geography of Lady Mary Wroth's "Urania"*. Pittsburgh: Duquesne University Press, 2001.

Cerasano, S. P., and Marion Wynne-Davies, eds. *Readings in Renaissance Women's Drama: Criticism, History, and Performance 1594–1998*. London and New York: Routledge, 1998.

Cervigni, Dino S., ed. *Women Mystic Writers*. *Annali d'Italianistica* 13 (1995) (entire issue).

Cervigni, Dino S., and Rebecca West, eds. *Women's Voices in Italian Literature*. *Annali d'Italianistica* 7 (1989) (entire issue).

Charlton, Kenneth. *Women, Religion and Education in Early Modern England*. London and New York: Routledge, 1999.

Chojnacka, Monica. *Working Women in Early Modern Venice*. Baltimore: Johns Hopkins University Press, 2001.

Chojnacki, Stanley. *Women and Men in Renaissance Venice: Twelve Essays on Patrician Society*. Baltimore: Johns Hopkins University Press, 2000.

Cholakian, Patricia Francis. *Rape and Writing in the Heptameron* of Marguerite de Navarre . Carbondale and Edwardsville, Ill.: Southern Illinois University Press, 1991.

————. *Women and the Politics of Self-Representation in Seventeenth-Century France*. Newark: University of Delaware Press, 2000.

Christine de Pizan: A Casebook. Edited by Barbara K. Altmann and Deborah L. McGrady. New York: Routledge, 2003.

Clogan, Paul Maruice, ed. *Medievali et Humanistica: Literacy and the Lay Reader*. Lanham, Md.: Rowman and Littlefield, 2000.

Clubb, Louise George. *Italian Drama in Shakespeare's Time*. New Haven: Yale University Press, 1989.

Clucas, Stephen, ed. *A Princely Brave Woman: Essays on Margaret Cavendish, Duchess of Newcastle*. Aldershot and Brookfield, UK: Ashgate Publishing, 2003.

Conley, John J., S.J. *The Suspicion of Virtue: Women Philosophers in Neoclassical France*. Ithaca, N.Y.: Cornell University Press, 2002.

Crabb, Ann. *The Strozzi of Florence: Widowhood and Family Solidarity in the Renaissance*. Ann Arbor: University of Michigan Press, 2000.

Crowston, Clare Haru. *Fabricating Women: The Seamstresses of Old Regime France, 1675–1791*. Durham, N.C.: Duke University Press, 2001.

Cruz, Anne J., and Mary Elizabeth Perry, eds. *Culture and Control in Counter-Reformation Spain*. Minneapolis: University of Minnesota Press, 1992.

Datta, Satya. *Women and Men in Early Modern Venice*. Aldershot and Brookfield, UK: Ashgate Publishing, 2003.

Davis, Natalie Zemon. *Society and Culture in Early Modern France*. Stanford: Stanford University Press, 1975. Especially chapters 3 and 5.

————. *Women on the Margins: Three Seventeenth-Century Lives*. Cambridge, Mass.: Harvard University Press, 1995.

DeJean, Joan. *Ancients against Moderns: Culture Wars and the Making of a Fin de Siècle*. Chicago: University of Chicago Press, 1997.

————. *Fictions of Sappho, 1546–1937*. Chicago: University of Chicago Press, 1989.

————. *The Reinvention of Obscenity: Sex, Lies, and Tabloids in Early Modern France*. Chicago: University of Chicago Press, 2002.

————. *Tender Geographies: Women and the Origins of the Novel in France*. New York: Columbia University Press, 1991.

————. *The Reinvention of Obscenity: Sex, Lies, and Tabloids in Early Modern France*. Chicago: University of Chicago Press, 2002.

Dictionary of Russian Women Writers. Edited by Marina Ledkovsky, Charlotte Rosenthal, and Mary Zirin. Westport, Conn.: Greenwood Press, 1994.

Dixon, Laurinda S. *Perilous Chastity: Women and Illness in Pre-Enlightenment Art and Medicine*. Ithaca, N.Y.: Cornell University Press, 1995.

Dolan, Frances, E. *Whores of Babylon: Catholicism, Gender and Seventeenth-Century Print Culture*. Ithaca, N.Y.: Cornell University Press, 1999.

Donovan, Josephine. *Women and the Rise of the Novel, 1405–1726*. New York: St. Martin's Press, 1999.

Encyclopedia of Continental Women Writers. 2 vols. Edited by Katharina Wilson. New York: Garland, 1991.

De Erauso, Catalina. *Lieutenant Nun: Memoir of a Basque Transvestite in the New World*. Translated by Michele Ttepto & Gabriel Stepto. Foreward by Marjorie Garber. Boston: Beacon Press, 1995.

Erdmann, Axel. *My Gracious Silence: Women in the Mirror of Sixteenth-Century Printing in Western Europe*. Luzern: Gilhofer and Rauschberg, 1999.

Erickson, Amy Louise. *Women and Property in Early Modern England*. London and New York: Routledge, 1993.

Ezell, Margaret J. M. *The Patriarch's Wife: Literary Evidence and the History of the Family*. Chapel Hill, N.C.: University of North Carolina Press, 1987.

————. *Social Authorship and the Advent of Print*. Baltimore: Johns Hopkins University Press, 1999.

————. *Writing Women's Literary History*. Baltimore: Johns Hopkins University Press, 1993.

Farrell, Michèle Longino. *Performing Motherhood: The Sévigné Correspondence*. Hanover, N.H., and London: University Press of New England, 1991.

The Feminist Companion to Literature in English: Women Writers from the Middle Ages to the Present. Edited by Virginia Blain, Isobel Grundy, and Patricia Clements. New Haven, Conn.: Yale University Press, 1990.

The Feminist Encyclopedia of German Literature. Edited by Friederike Eigler and Susanne Kord. Westport, Conn.: Greenwood Press, 1997.

Feminist Encyclopedia of Italian Literature. Edited by Rinaldina Russell. Westport, Conn.: Greenwood Press, 1997.

Ferguson, Margaret W. *Dido's Daughters: Literacy, Gender, and Empire in Early Modern England and France.* Chicago: University of Chicago Press, 2003.

Ferguson, Margaret W., Maureen Quilligan, and Nancy J. Vickers, eds. *Rewriting the Renaissance: The Discourses of Sexual Difference in Early Modern Europe.* Chicago: University of Chicago Press, 1987.

Ferraro, Joanne M. *Marriage Wars in Late Renaissance Venice.* Oxford: Oxford University Press, 2001.

Fletcher, Anthony. *Gender, Sex and Subordination in England 1500–1800.* New Haven: Yale University Press, 1995.

French Women Writers: A Bio-Bibliographical Source Book. Edited by Eva Martin Sartori and Dorothy Wynne Zimmerman. Westport, Conn.: Greenwood Press, 1991.

Frye, Susan, and Karen Robertson, eds. *Maids and Mistresses, Cousins and Queens: Women's Alliances in Early Modern England.* Oxford: Oxford University Press, 1999.

Gallagher, Catherine. *Nobody's Story: The Vanishing Acts of Women Writers in the Marketplace, 1670–1820.* Berkeley: University of California Press, 1994.

Garrard, Mary D. *Artemisia Gentileschi: The Image of the Female Hero in Italian Baroque Art.* Princeton: Princeton University Press, 1989.

Gelbart, Nina Rattner. *The King's Midwife: A History and Mystery of Madame du Coudray.* Berkeley: University of California Press, 1998.

Glenn, Cheryl. *Rhetoric Retold: Regendering the Tradition from Antiquity through the Renaissance.* Carbondale and Edwardsville, Ill.: Southern Illinois University Press, 1997.

Goffen, Rona. *Titian's Women.* New Haven: Yale University Press, 1997.

Goldberg, Jonathan. *Desiring Women Writing: English Renaissance Examples.* Stanford: Stanford University Press, 1997.

Goldsmith, Elizabeth C. *Exclusive Conversations: The Art of Interaction in Seventeenth-Century France.* Philadelphia: University of Pennsylvania Press, 1988.

———, ed. *Writing the Female Voice.* Boston: Northeastern University Press, 1989.

Goldsmith, Elizabeth C., and Dena Goodman, eds. *Going Public: Women and Publishing in Early Modern France.* Ithaca, N.Y.: Cornell University Press, 1995.

Grafton, Anthony, and Lisa Jardine. *From Humanism to the Humanities: Education and the Liberal Arts in Fifteenth-and Sixteenth-Century Europe.* London: Duckworth, 1986.

Grassby, Richard. *Kinship and Capitalism: Marriage, Family, and Business in the English-Speaking World, 1580–1740.* Cambridge: Cambridge University Press, 2001.

Greer, Margaret Rich. *Maria de Zayas Tells Baroque Tales of Love and the Cruelty of Men.* University Park, Penn.: Pennsylvania State University Press, 2000.

Gutierrez, Nancy A. *"Shall She Famish Then?" Female Food Refusal in Early Modern England.* Aldershot and Brookfield, UK: Ashgate Publishing, 2003.

Habermann, Ina. *Staging Slander and Gender in Early Modern England.* Aldershot and Brookfield, UK: Ashgate Publishing, 2003.

Hackett, Helen. *Women and Romance Fiction in the English Renaissance.* Cambridge: Cambridge University Press, 2000.

Hall, Kim F. *Things of Darkness: Economies of Race and Gender in Early Modern England.* Ithaca, N.Y.: Cornell University Press, 1995.

Hampton, Timothy. *Literature and the Nation in the Sixteenth Century: Inventing Renaissance France.* Ithaca, N.Y.: Cornell University Press, 2001.

Hannay, Margaret, ed. *Silent but for the Word.* Kent, Ohio: Kent State University Press, 1985.

Hardwick, Julie. *The Practice of Patriarchy: Gender and the Politics of Household Authority in Early Modern France.* University Park, Penn.: Pennsylvania State University Press, 1998.

Harris, Barbara J. *English Aristocratic Women, 1450–1550: Marriage and Family, Property and Careers.* New York: Oxford University Press, 2002.

Harth, Erica. *Ideology and Culture in Seventeenth-Century France.* Ithaca, N.Y.: Cornell University Press, 1983.

———. *Cartesian Women: Versions and Subversions of Rational Discourse in the Old Regime.* Ithaca, N.Y.: Cornell University Press, 1992.

Harvey, Elizabeth D. *Ventriloquized Voices: Feminist Theory and English Renaissance Texts.* London and New York: Routledge, 1992.

Haselkorn, Anne M., and Betty Travitsky, eds. *The Renaissance Englishwoman in Print: Counterbalancing the Canon.* Amherst, Mass.: University of Massachusetts Press, 1990.

Hendricks, Margo, and Patricia Parker, eds. *Women, "Race," and Writing in the Early Modern Period.* London and New York: Routledge, 1994.

Herlihy, David. "Did Women Have a Renaissance? A Reconsideration." *Medievalia et Humanistica* NS 13 (1985): 1–22.

Hill, Bridget. *The Republican Virago: The Life and Times of Catharine Macaulay, Historian.* New York: Oxford University Press, 1992.

Hills, Helen, ed. *Architecture and the Politics of Gender in Early Modern Europe.* Aldershot and Brookfield, UK: Ashgate Publishing, 2003.

A History of Central European Women's Writing. Edited by Celia Hawkesworth. New York: Palgrave Press, 2001.

A History of Women in the West.

Volume 1: *From Ancient Goddesses to Christian Saints.* Edited by Pauline Schmitt Pantel. Cambridge, Mass.: Harvard University Press, 1992.

Volume 2: *Silences of the Middle Ages.* Edited by Christiane Klapisch-Zuber. Cambridge, Mass.: Harvard University Press, 1992.

Volume 3: *Renaissance and Enlightenment Paradoxes.* Edited by Natalie Zemon Davis and Arlette Farge. Cambridge, Mass.: Harvard University Press, 1993.

A History of Women Philosophers. Edited by Mary Ellen Waithe. 3 vols. Dordrecht: Martinus Nijhoff, 1987.

A History of Women's Writing in France. Edited by Sonya Stephens. Cambridge: Cambridge University Press, 2000.

A History of Women's Writing in Germany, Austria and Switzerland. Edited by Jo Catling. Cambridge: Cambridge University Press, 2000.

A History of Women's Writing in Italy. Edited byLetizia Panizza and Sharon Wood. Cambridge: University Press, 2000.

A History of Women's Writing in Russia. Edited by Alele Marie Barker and Jehanne M. Gheith. Cambridge: Cambridge University Press, 2002.

Hobby, Elaine. *Virtue of Necessity: English Women's Writing 1646–1688.* London: Virago Press, 1988.

Horowitz, Maryanne Cline. "Aristotle and Women." *Journal of the History of Biology* 9 (1976): 183–213.

Howell, Martha. *The Marriage Exchange: Property, Social Place, and Gender in Cities of the Low Countries, 1300–1550.* Chicago: University of Chicago Press, 1998.

Hufton, Olwen H. *The Prospect before Her: A History of Women in Western Europe, 1:1500–1800.* New York: HarperCollins, 1996.

Hull, Suzanne W. *Chaste, Silent, and Obedient: English Books for Women, 1475–1640.* San Marino, Calif.: The Huntington Library, 1982.

Hunt, Lynn, ed. *The Invention of Pornography: Obscenity and the Origins of Modernity, 1500–1800.* New York: Zone Books, 1996.

Hutner, Heidi, ed. *Rereading Aphra Behn: History, Theory, and Criticism.* Charlottesville, Va.: University Press of Virginia, 1993.

Hutson, Lorna, ed. *Feminism and Renaissance Studies.* New York: Oxford University Press, 1999.

Italian Women Writers: A Bio-Bibliographical Sourcebook. Edited by Rinaldina Russell. Westport, Conn.: Greenwood Press, 1994.

Jaffe, Irma B., with Gernando Colombardo. *Shining Eyes, Cruel Fortune: The Lives and Loves of Italian Renaissance Women Poets.* New York: Fordham University Press, 2002.

James, Susan E. *Kateryn Parr: The Making of a Queen.* Aldershot and Brookfield, UK: Ashgate Publishing, 1999.

Jankowski, Theodora A. *Women in Power in the Early Modern Drama.* Urbana, Ill.: University of Illinois Press, 1992.

Jansen, Katherine Ludwig. *The Making of the Magdalen: Preaching and Popular Devotion in the Later Middle Ages.* Princeton: Princeton University Press, 2000.

Jed, Stephanie H. *Chaste Thinking: The Rape of Lucretia and the Birth of Humanism.* Bloomington, Ind.: Indiana University Press, 1989.

Jones, Ann Rosalind, and Peter Stallybrass. *Renaissance Clothing and the Materials of Memory.* Cambridge, UK: Cambridge University Press, 2000.

Jordan, Constance. *Renaissance Feminism: Literary Texts and Political Models.* Ithaca, N.Y.: Cornell University Press, 1990.

Kagan, Richard L. *Lucrecia's Dreams: Politics and Prophecy in Sixteenth-Century Spain.* Berkeley: University of California Press, 1990.

Kehler, Dorothea, and Laurel Amtower, eds. *The Single Woman in Medieval and Early Modern England: Her Life and Representation.* Tempe, Ariz.: MRTS, 2002.

Kelly, Joan. "Did Women Have a Renaissance?" In Joan Kelly *Women, History, and Theory.* Chicago: University of Chicago Press, 1984. Also in Renate Bridenthal, Claudia Koonz, and Susan M. Stuard, eds., *Becoming Visible: Women in European History.* 3d ed.. Boston: Houghton Mifflin, 1998.

———. "Early Feminist Theory and the *Querelle des Femmes.*" In *Women, History, and Theory.*

Kelso, Ruth. *Doctrine for the Lady of the Renaissance.* Foreword by Katharine M. Rogers. Urbana, Ill.: University of Illinois Press, 1956, 1978.

Kendrick, Robert L. *Celestial Sirens: Nuns and their Music in Early Modern Milan.* New York: Oxford University Press, 1996.

Kermode, Jenny, and Garthine Walker, eds. *Women, Crime and the Courts in Early Modern England.* Chapel Hill, N.C.: University of North Carolina Press, 1994.

King, Catherine E. *Renaissance Women Patrons: Wives and Widows in Italy, c. 1300–1550.* New York and Manchester: Manchester University Press (distributed in the U.S. by St. Martin's Press), 1998.

King, Margaret L. *Women of the Renaissance.* Foreword by Catharine R. Stimpson. Chicago: University of Chicago Press, 1991.

Krontiris, Tina. *Oppositional Voices: Women as Writers and Translators of Literature in the English Renaissance*. London and New York: Routledge, 1992.

Kuehn, Thomas. *Law, Family, and Women: Toward a Legal Anthropology of Renaissance Italy*. Chicago: University of Chicago Press, 1991.

Kunze, Bonnelyn Young. *Margaret Fell and the Rise of Quakerism*. Stanford: Stanford University Press, 1994.

Labalme, Patricia A., ed. *Beyond Their Sex: Learned Women of the European Past*. New York: New York University Press, 1980.

Lalande, Roxanne Decker, ed. *A Labor of Love: Critical Reflections on the Writings of Marie-Catherine Desjardina (Mme de Villedieu)*. Madison, N.J.: Fairleigh Dickinson University Press, 2000.

Lamb, Mary Ellen. *Gender and Authorship in the Sidney Circle*. Madison: University of Wisconsin Press, 1990.

Laqueur, Thomas. *Making Sex: Body and Gender from the Greeks to Freud*. Cambridge, Mass.: Harvard University Press, 1990.

Larsen, Anne R., and Colette H. Winn, eds. *Renaissance Women Writers: French Texts/ American Contexts*. Detroit: Wayne State University Press, 1994.

Laven, Mary. *Virgins of Venus: Enclosed Lives and Broken Vows in the Renaissance Convent*. London: Viking, 2002.

Lerner, Gerda. *The Creation of Patriarchy and Creation of Feminist Consciousness, 1000–1870*. 2 vols. New York: Oxford University Press, 1986, 1994.

Levin, Carole, and Jeanie Watson, eds. *Ambiguous Realities: Women in the Middle Ages and Renaissance*. Detroit: Wayne State University Press, 1987.

Levin, Carole, Jo Eldridge Carney, and Debra Barrett-Graves. *Elizabeth I: Always Her Own Free Woman*. Aldershot and Brookfield, UK: Ashgate Publishing, 2003.

Levin, Carole, et al. *Extraordinary Women of the Medieval and Renaissance World: A Biographical Dictionary*. Westport, Conn.: Greenwood Press, 2000.

Levy, Allison, ed. *Widowhood and Visual Culture in Early Modern Europe*. Aldershot and Brookfield, UK: Ashgate Publishing, 2003.

Lewalsky, Barbara Kiefer. *Writing Women in Jacobean England*. Cambridge, Mass.: Harvard University Press, 1993.

Lewis, Jayne Elizabeth. *Mary Queen of Scots: Romance and Nation*. London: Routledge, 1998.

Lindenauer, Leslie J. *Piety and Power: Gender and Religious Culture in the American Colonies, 1630–1700*. London and New York: Routledge, 2002.

Lindsey, Karen. *Divorced Beheaded Survived: A Feminist Reinterpretation of the Wives of Henry VIII*. Reading, Mass.: Addison-Wesley Publishing, 1995.

Lochrie, Karma. *Margery Kempe and Translations of the Flesh*. Philadelphia: University of Pennsylvania Press, 1992.

Longino Farrell, Michèle. *Performing Motherhood: The Sévigné Correspondence*. Hanover, N.H.: University Press of New England, 1991.

Lougee, Carolyn C. *Le Paradis des Femmes: Women, Salons, and Social Stratification in Seventeenth-Century France*. Princeton: Princeton University Press, 1976.

Love, Harold. *The Culture and Commerce of Texts: Scribal Publication in Seventeenth-Century England*. Amherst, Mass.: University of Massachusetts Press, 1993.

Lowe, K. J. P. *Nuns' Chronicles and Convent Culture in Renaissance and Counter-Reformation Italy*. Cambridge: Cambridge University Press, 2003.

MacCarthy, Bridget G. *The Female Pen: Women Writers and Novelists 1621–1818*. Preface by Janet Todd. New York: New York University Press, 1994. (Originally published by Cork University Press, 1946–47).

Maclean, Ian. *Woman Triumphant: Feminism in French Literature, 1610–1652*. Oxford: Clarendon Press, 1977.

————. *The Renaissance Notion of Woman: A Study of the Fortunes of Scholasticism and Medical Science in European Intellectual Life*. Cambridge: Cambridge University Press, 1980.

MacNeil, Anne. *Music and Women of the Commedia dell'Arte in the Late Sixteenth Century*. New York: Oxford University Press, 2003.

Maggi, Armando. *Uttering the Word: The Mystical Performances of Maria Maddalena de' Pazzi, a Renaissance Visionary*. Albany: State University of New York Press, 1998.

Marshall, Sherrin. *Women in Reformation and Counter-Reformation Europe: Public and Private Worlds*. Bloomington, Ind.: Indiana University Press, 1989.

Masten, Jeffrey. *Textual Intercourse: Collaboration, Authorship, and Sexualities in Renaissance Drama*. Cambridge: Cambridge University Press, 1997.

Matter, E. Ann, and John Coakley, eds. *Creative Women in Medieval and Early Modern Italy*. Philadelphia: University of Pennsylvania Press, 1994.

McGrath, Lynette. *Subjectivity and Women's Poetry in Early Modern England*. Burlington, Vt.: Ashgate, 2002.

McLeod, Glenda. *Virtue and Venom: Catalogs of Women from Antiquity to the Renaissance*. Ann Arbor: University of Michigan Press, 1991.

Medwick, Cathleen. *Teresa of Avila: The Progress of a Soul*. New York: Alfred A. Knopf, 2000.

Meek, Christine, ed. *Women in Renaissance and Early Modern Europe*. Dublin-Portland: Four Courts Press, 2000.

Mendelson, Sara and Patricia Crawford. *Women in Early Modern England, 1550–1720*. Oxford: Clarendon Press, 1998.

Merchant, Carolyn. *The Death of Nature: Women, Ecology and the Scientific Revolution*. New York: HarperCollins, 1980.

Merrim, Stephanie. *Early Modern Women's Writing and Sor Juana Inés de la Cruz*. Nashville, Tenn.: Vanderbilt University Press, 1999.

Messbarger, Rebecca. *The Century of Women: The Representations of Women in Eighteenth-Century Italian Public Discourse*. Toronto: University of Toronto Press, 2002.

Miller, Nancy K. *The Heroine's Text: Readings in the French and English Novel, 1722–1782*. New York: Columbia University Press, 1980.

Miller, Naomi J. *Changing the Subject: Mary Wroth and Figurations of Gender in Early Modern England*. Lexington, Ky.: University Press of Kentucky, 1996.

Miller, Naomi J., and Gary Waller, eds. *Reading Mary Wroth: Representing Alternatives in Early Modern England*. Knoxville, Tenn.: University of Tennessee Press, 1991.

Monson, Craig A., ed. *The Crannied Wall: Women, Religion, and the Arts in Early Modern Europe*. Ann Arbor: University of Michigan Press, 1992.

Moore, Cornelia Niekus. *The Maiden's Mirror: Reading Material for German Girls in the Sixteenth and Seventeenth Centuries*. Wiesbaden: Otto Harrassowitz, 1987.

Moore, Mary B. *Desiring Voices: Women Sonneteers and Petrarchism*. Carbondale, Ill.: Southern Illinois University Press, 2000.

Mujica, Bárbara. *Women Writers of Early Modern Spain*. New Haven, Conn.: Yale University Press, 2004.

Musacchio, Jacqueline Marie. *The Art and Ritual of Childbirth in Renaissance Italy.* New Haven: Yale University Press, 1999.

Newman, Barbara. *God and the Goddesses: Vision, Poetry, and Belief in the Middle Ages.* Philadelphia: University of Pennsylvania Press, 2003.

Newman, Karen. *Fashioning Femininity and English Renaissance Drama.* Chicago and London: University of Chicago Press, 1991.

O'Donnell, Mary Ann. *Aphra Behn: An Annotated Bibliography of Primary and Secondary Sources.* 2d ed. Aldershot and Brookfield, UK: Ashgate Publishing, 2004.

Okin, Susan Moller. *Women in Western Political Thought.* Princeton: Princeton University Press, 1979.

Ozment, Steven. *The Bürgermeister's Daughter: Scandal in a Sixteenth-Century German Town.* New York: St. Martin's Press, 1995.

———. *Flesh and Spirit: Private Life in Early Modern Germany.* New York: Penguin Putnam, 1999.

———. *When Fathers Ruled: Family Life in Reformation Europe.* Cambridge, Mass.: Harvard University Press, 1983.

Pacheco, Anita, ed. *Early [English] Women Writers: 1600–1720.* New York and London: Longman, 1998.

Pagels, Elaine. *Adam, Eve, and the Serpent.* New York: Harper Collins, 1988.

Panizza, Letizia, ed. *Women in Italian Renaissance Culture and Society.* Oxford: European Humanities Research Centre, 2000.

Parker, Patricia. *Literary Fat Ladies: Rhetoric, Gender and Property.* London and New York: Methuen, 1987.

Pernoud, Regine, and Marie-Veronique Clin. *Joan of Arc: Her Story.* Revised and translated by Jeremy DuQuesnay Adams. New York: St. Martin's Press, 1998 (French original, 1986).

Perry, Mary Elizabeth. *Crime and Society in Early Modern Seville.* Hanover, N.H.: University Press of New England, 1980.

———. *Gender and Disorder in Early Modern Seville.* Princeton: Princeton University Press, 1990.

Petroff, Elizabeth Alvilda, ed. *Medieval Women's Visionary Literature.* New York: Oxford University Press, 1986.

Perry, Ruth. *The Celebrated Mary Astell: An Early English Feminist.* Chicago: University of Chicago Press, 1986.

Rabil, Albert. *Laura Cereta: Quattrocento Humanist.* Binghamton, N.Y.: MRTS, 1981.

Ranft, Patricia. *Women in Western Intellectual Culture, 600–1500.* New York: Palgrave, 2002.

Rapley, Elizabeth. *A Social History of the Cloister: Daily Life in the Teaching Monasteries of the Old Regime.* Montreal: McGill-Queen's University Press, 2001.

Raven, James, Helen Small and Naomi Tadmor, eds. *The Practice and Representation of Reading in England.* Cambridge: University Press, 1996.

Reardon, Colleen. *Holy Concord within Sacred Walls: Nuns and Music in Siena, 1575–1700.* Oxford: Oxford University Press, 2001.

Reiss, Sheryl E., and David G. Wilkins, ed. *Beyond Isabella: Secular Women Patrons of Art in Renaissance Italy.* Kirksville, Mo.: Truman State University Press, 2001.

Rheubottom, David. *Age, Marriage, and Politics in Fifteenth-Century Ragusa.* Oxford: Oxford University Press, 2000.

Richardson, Brian. *Printing, Writers and Readers in Renaissance Italy.* Cambridge: University Press, 1999.

Riddle, John M. *Contraception and Abortion from the Ancient World to the Renaissance.* Cambridge, Mass.: Harvard University Press, 1992.

————. *Eve's Herbs: A History of Contraception and Abortion in the West.* Cambridge, Mass.: Harvard University Press, 1997.

Roper, Lyndal. *The Holy Household: Women and Morals in Reformation Augsburg.* New York: Oxford University Press, 1989.

Rose, Mary Beth. *The Expense of Spirit: Love and Sexuality in English Renaissance Drama.* Ithaca, N.Y.: Cornell University Press, 1988.

————. *Gender and Heroism in Early Modern English Literature.* Chicago: University of Chicago Press, 2002.

————, ed. *Women in the Middle Ages and the Renaissance: Literary and Historical Perspectives.* Syracuse: Syracuse University Press, 1986.

Rosenthal, Margaret F. *The Honest Courtesan: Veronica Franco, Citizen and Writer in Sixteenth-Century Venice.* Foreword by Catharine R. Stimpson. Chicago: University of Chicago Press, 1992.

Rublack, Ulinka, ed. *Gender in Early Modern German History.* Cambridge: Cambridge University Press, 2002.

Sackville-West, Vita. *Daughter of France: The Life of La Grande Mademoiselle.* Garden City, N.Y.: Doubleday, 1959.

Sánchez, Magdalena S. *The Empress, the Queen, and the Nun: Women and Power at the Court of Philip III of Spain.* Baltimore: Johns Hopkins University Press, 1998.

Scaraffia, Lucetta, and Gabriella Zarri. *Women and Faith: Catholic Religious Life in Italy from Late Antiquity to the Present.* Cambridge, Mass.: Harvard University Press, 1999.

Schiebinger, Londa. *The Mind Has No Sex?: Women in the Origins of Modern Science.* Cambridge, Mass.: Harvard University Press, 1991.

————. *Nature's Body: Gender in the Making of Modern Science.* Boston: Beacon Press, 1993.

Schofield, Mary Anne, and Cecilia Macheski, eds. *Fetter'd or Free? British Women Novelists, 1670–1815.* Athens, Ohio: Ohio University Press, 1986.

Schutte, Anne Jacobson. *Aspiring Saints: Pretense of Holiness, Inquisition, and Gender in the Republic of Venice, 1618–1750.* Baltimore: Johns Hopkins University Press, 2001.

Schutte, Anne Jacobson, Thomas Kuehn, and Silvana Seidel Menchi, eds. *Time, Space, and Women's Lives in Early Modern Europe.* Kirksville, Mo.: Truman State University Press, 2001.

Seifert, Lewis C. *Fairy Tales, Sexuality and Gender in France 1690–1715: Nostalgic Utopias.* Cambridge, UK: Cambridge University Press, 1996.

Shannon, Laurie. *Sovereign Amity: Figures of Friendship in Shakespearean Contexts.* Chicago: University of Chicago Press, 2002.

Shemek, Deanna. *Ladies Errant: Wayward Women and Social Order in Early Modern Italy.* Durham, N.C.: Duke University Press, 1998.

Smith, Hilda L. *Reason's Disciples: Seventeenth-Century English Feminists.* Urbana, Ill.: University of Illinois Press, 1982.

————. *Women Writers and the Early Modern British Political Tradition.* Cambridge: Cambridge University Press, 1998.

Sobel, Dava. *Galileo's Daughter: A Historical Memoir of Science, Faith, and Love.* New York: Penguin Books, 2000.

Sommerville, Margaret R. *Sex and Subjection: Attitudes to Women in Early-Modern Society.* London: Arnold, 1995.

Soufas, Teresa Scott. *Dramas of Distinction: A Study of Plays by Golden Age Women.* Lexington, Ky.: The University Press of Kentucky, 1997.

Spencer, Jane. *The Rise of the Woman Novelist: From Aphra Behn to Jane Austen.* Oxford: Basil Blackwell, 1986.

Spender, Dale. *Mothers of the Novel: 100 Good Women Writers Before Jane Austen.* London & New York: Routledge, 1986.

Sperling, Jutta Gisela. *Convents and the Body Politic in Late Renaissance Venice.* Foreword by Catharine R. Stimpson. Chicago: University of Chicago Press, 1999.

Steinbrügge, Lieselotte. *The Moral Sex: Woman's Nature in the French Enlightenment.* Translated by Pamela E. Selwyn. New York: Oxford University Press, 1995.

Stephenson, Barbara. *The Power and Patronage of Marguerite de Navarre.* Aldershot and Brookfield, UK: Ashgate Publishing, 2004.

Stocker, Margarita. *Judith, Sexual Warrior: Women and Power in Western Culture.* New Haven: Yale University Press, 1998.

Stretton, Timothy. *Women Waging Law in Elizabethan England.* Cambridge: Cambridge University Press, 1998.

Stuard, Susan M. "The Dominion of Gender: Women's Fortunes in the High Middle Ages." In *Becoming Visible: Women in European History,* edited by Renate Bridenthal, Claudia Koonz, and Susan M. Stuard. 3d ed. Boston: Houghton Mifflin, 1998.

Summit, Jennifer. *Lost Property: The Woman Writer and English Literary History, 1380–1589.* Chicago: University of Chicago Press, 2000.

Surtz, Ronald E. *The Guitar of God: Gender, Power, and Authority in the Visionary World of Mother Juana de la Cruz (1481–1534).* Philadelphia: University of Pennsylvania Press, 1991.

———. *Writing Women in Late Medieval and Early Modern Spain: The Mothers of Saint Teresa of Avila.* Philadelphia: University of Pennsylvania Press, 1995.

Suzuki, Mihoko. *Subordinate Subjects: Gender, the Political Nation, and Literary Form in England, 1588–1688.* Aldershot and Brookfield, UK: Ashgate Publishing, 2003.

Teague, Frances. *Bathsua Makin, Woman of Learning.* Lewisburg, Penn.: Bucknell University Press, 1999.

Thomas, Anabel. *Art and Piety in the Female Religious Communities of Renaissance Italy: Iconography, Space, and the Religious Woman's Perspective.* New York: Cambridge University Press, 2003.

Tinagli, Paola. *Women in Italian Renaissance Art: Gender, Representation, Identity.* Manchester: Manchester University Press, 1997.

Todd, Janet. *The Secret Life of Aphra Behn.* London, New York, and Sydney: Pandora, 2000.

———. *The Sign of Angelica: Women, Writing and Fiction, 1660–1800.* New York: Columbia University Press, 1989.

Tomas, Natalie R. *The Medici Women: Gender and Power in Renaissance Florence.* Aldershot and Brookfield, UK: Ashgate Publishing, 2004.

Traub, Valerie. *The Renaissance of Lesbianism in Early Modern England.* Cambridge: Cambridge University Press, 2002.

Valenze, Deborah. *The First Industrial Woman.* New York: Oxford University Press, 1995.

Van Dijk, Susan, Lia van Gemert, and Sheila Ottway, eds. *Writing the History of Women's Writing: Toward an International Approach*. Proceedings of the Colloquium, Amsterdam, 9–11 September. Amsterdam: Royal Netherlands Academy of Arts and Sciences, 2001.

Vickery, Amanda. *The Gentleman's Daughter: Women's Lives in Georgian England*. New Haven: Yale University Press, 1998.

Vollendorf, Lisa, ed. *Recovering Spain's Feminist Tradition*. New York: Modern Language Association, 2001.

Walker, Claire. *Gender and Politics in Early Modern Europe: English Convents in France and the Low Countries*. New York: Palgrave, 2003.

Wall, Wendy. *The Imprint of Gender: Authorship and Publication in the English Renaissance*. Ithaca, N.Y.: Cornell University Press, 1993.

Walsh, William T. *St. Teresa of Avila: A Biography*. Rockford, Ill.: TAN Books and Publications, 1987.

Warner, Marina. *Alone of All Her Sex: The Myth and Cult of the Virgin Mary*. New York: Knopf, 1976.

Warnicke, Retha M. *The Marrying of Anne of Cleves: Royal Protocol in Tudor England*. Cambridge: Cambridge University Press, 2000.

Watt, Diane. *Secretaries of God: Women Prophets in Late Medieval and Early Modern England*. Cambridge, UK: D. S. Brewer, 1997.

Weaver, Elissa. *Convent Theatre in Early Modern Italy*. New York: Cambridge University Press, 2002.

Weber, Alison. *Teresa of Avila and the Rhetoric of Femininity*. Princeton: Princeton University Press, 1990.

Welles, Marcia L. *Persephone's Girdle: Narratives of Rape in Seventeenth-Century Spanish Literature*. Nashville, Tenn.: Vanderbilt University Press, 2000.

Whitehead, Barbara J., ed. *Women's Education in Early Modern Europe: A History, 1500–1800*. New York and London: Garland Publishing, 1999.

Wiesner, Merry E. *Working Women in Renaissance Germany*. New Brunswick, N.J.: Rutgers University Press, 1986.

Wiesner-Hanks, Merry E. *Christianity and Sexuality in the Early Modern World: Regulating Desire, Reforming Practice*. New York: Routledge, 2000.

———. *Gender, Church, and State in Early Modern Germany: Essays*. New York: Longman, 1998.

———. *Gender in History*. Malden, Mass.: Blackwell, 2001.

———. *Women and Gender in Early Modern Europe*. Cambridge, UK: Cambridge University Press, 1993.

———. *Working Women in Renaissance Germany*. New Brunswick, N.J.: Rutgers University Press, 1986.

Willard, Charity Cannon. *Christine de Pizan: Her Life and Works*. New York: Persea Books, 1984.

Winn, Colette, and Donna Kuizenga, eds. *Women Writers in Pre-Revolutionary France*. New York: Garland Publishing, 1997.

Woodbridge, Linda. *Women and the English Renaissance: Literature and the Nature of Womankind, 1540–1620*. Urbana, Ill.: University of Illinois Press, 1984.

Woodford, Charlotte. *Nuns as Historians in Early Modern Germany*. Oxford: Clarendon Press, 2002.

Woods, Susanne. *Lanyer: A Renaissance Woman Poet.* New York: Oxford University Press, 1999.

Woods, Susanne, and Margaret P. Hannay, eds. *Teaching Tudor and Stuart Women Writers.* New York: Modern Language Assocation, 2000.

INDEX